T0083526

Karolinum Press

MODERN CZECH CLASSICS

Martin Machovec
Writing Underground

Reflections on Samizdat Literature
in Totalitarian Czechoslovakia

KAROLINUM PRESS 2019

KAROLINUM PRESS
Karolinum Press is a publishing department of Charles University
Ovocný trh 560/5, 116 36 Prague 1
Czech Republic
www.karolinum.cz

Text © 2019 by Martin Machovec
Translation © 2017 by Kip Bauersfeld, 2008 by Melvyn Clarke,
2017 by Vanda Krutsky, 2015 by Markéta Pokorná, 2017 by Marek Tomin,
2007, 2010 and 2018 by Gerald Turner
Cover photo © 1974 by Ivo Pospíšil

Designed by Zdeněk Ziegler
Set and printed in the Czech Republic by Karolinum Press
Proofreading by Peter Kirk Jensen
First English edition

Cataloguing-in-Publication Data is available from the National Library
of the Czech Republic

ISBN 978-80-246-4125-6
ISBN 978-80-246-4151-5 (pdf)
ISBN 978-80-246-4291-8 (mobi)
ISBN 978-80-246-4292-5 (epub)

CONTENTS

1. THE GROUP OF WRITERS AROUND THE PŮLNOC SERIES (1949-1955): A SPECIFIC EXAMPLE OF UNDERGROUND CULTURAL ACTIVITIES

Nowadays there is quite an extensive literature, comprising literary history, essays and memoirs[1] on the activities of the underground group of poets and prose writers who brought out their works in one

1) BONDY, Egon, "Kořeny českého literárního undergroundu v letech 1949-1953" [The Roots of the Czech Literary Underground, 1949-1953], *Haňťa Press* 2, no. 8 (1990); in MACHOVEC, Martin (ed.), *Pohledy zevnitř. Česká undergroundová kultura ve svědectvích, dokumentech a interpretacích*, Praha: FF UK, 2008; In English in MACHOVEC, Martin (ed.), *Views from the Inside. Czech Underground Literature and Culture (1948-1989)*, Praha: FF UK, 2006; 2nd edition, Praha: Karolinum Press, 2018; BONDY, Egon, *Prvních deset let* [The First Ten Years], Praha: Maťa, 2002; BOUDNÍK, Vladimír, *Z literární pozůstalosti* [From the Literary Papers], Praha: Pražská imaginace, 1993; HRABAL, Bohumil, "Co je poezie?" [What is Poetry?], "Made in Czechoslovakia", "Blitzkrieg", in *Jarmilka. Sebrané spisy Bohumila Hrabala 3* [Collected Works of Bohumil Hrabal 3, Jarmilka], Praha: Pražská imaginace, 1992; JELÍNEK, Oldřich, "Jak to všechno začalo..." [How it All Began], *Haňťa Press* 5, no. 14 (1993); MACHOVEC, Martin, "Pokus o nástin geneze a vývoje básnického díla Egona Bondyho" [Attempted Outline of the Birth and Development of Egon Bondy's Poetic Work], *Vokno*, no. 21 (1990); MACHOVEC, Martin, "Šestnáct autorů českého literárního podzemí (1948-1989)" [Sixteen Authors from the Czech Literary Underground], *Literární archiv PNP*, no. 25 (1991); MACHOVEC, Martin, "Několik poznámek k podzemní ediční řadě Půlnoc" [Several Notes on the Underground Midnight Series], *Kritický sborník* 13, no. 3 (1993); MACHOVEC, Martin, "Vídeňská bohemistika o Půlnoci (Česká podzemní literatura 1948-1953)" [A Viennese Student of Czech Literature on Půlnoc (Czech Underground Literature 1948-1953)], *Kritický sborník* 18, no. 2-3 (1999); MACHOVEC, Martin, "Náčrt života a díla Egona Bondyho" [Outline of Life and Work of Egon Bondy], in *Bouda Bondy. Projekt Bouda IV.* [Czech National Theatre Summer Stage], Praha: Národní divadlo, 2007; MAINX, Oskar, *Poezie jako mýtus, svědectví a hra. Kapitoly z básnické poetiky Egona Bondyho* [Poetry as Myth, Testimony and Game. Chapters from the Poetics of Egon Bondy], Ostrava (Czech Republic): Protimluv, 2007; PILAŘ, Martin, *Underground*. Brno (Czech Republic): Host, 1999; TROUP, Zdeněk, "Poezie totality" [Poetry of Totality], *Rozeta* 1, no. 1 (1991); TYPLT, Jaromír F., "Dvě svědectví o Židovských jménech" [Two Testimonies of Jewish Names], *Host* 13, no. 3 (1997); TYPLT, Jaromír F., "Absolutní realismus a Totální hrobař" [Absolute Realism and the Totalitarian Gravedigger], *Host* 22, no. 1 (2006); VODSEĎÁLEK, Ivo - MAZAL, Tomáš, "S Ivo Vodseďálkem o letech radostného budování 49-53" [With Ivo Vodseďálek on the Years of Happy Building up Socialism 49-53], *Vokno*, no. 18 (1990); VODSEĎÁLEK, Ivo, *Felixír života* [Felixir of Life],

of the first ever Czech samizdat series (discounting underground works under the Protectorate) in the Půlnoc [Midnight] series and as separate associated texts, in individual volumes sorted by names, which were dated 1951-1955, but which were mostly written between 1949 and 1953. As the actual literary work that was brought out in the Půlnoc series has been preserved more or less in its entirety and was then mostly published[2] as early as in the first half of the 1990s, the situation is now fairly clear.

Brno (Czech Republic): Host, 2000; ZAND, Gertraude, *Totaler Realismus und Peinliche Poesie. Tschechische Untergrund-Literatur 1948-1953*, Wien: Peter Lang, 1998; ZANDO-VÁ, Gertraude, "Básník – svědek – aktivista: Poetický program a vydavatelský projekt Egona Bondyho v čase stalinismu" [Poet, Witness, Activist: The Poetic Programme and Publishing Project of Egon Bondy under Stalinism], *Česká literatura* 46, no. 6 (1998); KUŽEL, Petr (ed.), *Myšlení a tvorba Egona Bondyho* [Egon Bondy's Thoughts and Literary Activity], Praha: Filosofia, 2018; PŘIBÁŇ, Michal (ed.), *Český literární samizdat 1949-1989. Edice – časopisy – sborníky* [Czech Literary Samizdat 1949-1989. Series of Editions - Magazines - Anthologies], Praha: Academia – Ústav pro českou literaturu AV ČR, 2018 [on Půlnoc series see pp. 208-210; on Boudník's Explosionalismus series see pp. 183-185].

2) This primarily involves the first two volumes of the nine-volume work of BONDY, Egon, *Básnické dílo Egona Bondyho I.-IX.* [The Poetic Work of Egon Bondy I-IX], Praha: Pražská imaginace, 1990–1993; or, more recently, the first volume of Bondy's *Básnické spisy I.-III.* [Collected Poetic Works I-III], Praha: Argo, 2014-2016; see also the first two volumes of the five-volume *Dílo Ivo Vodseďálka – 1. Zuření* [Fury], 1992; *2. Snění* [Dreaming], Praha: Pražská imaginace, 1992; see also Vodseďálek's one volume *Dílo* [Works], Praha: Argo, 2019; see also a volume of texts by KREJCAROVÁ, Jana, *Clarissa a jiné texty* [Clarissa and Other Texts], Praha: Concordia, 1990; see also KREJCAROVÁ-ČERNÁ, Jana, *Tohle je skutečnost (Básně, prózy, dopisy)* [This is reality (poems, prose, letters)], Praha: Torst, 2016; see also a selection from the samizdat volume by SVOBODA, Pavel, "Poesie i prósy" [Poetry and Prose], *Haňťa Press* 7, no. 17 (1995); see also an excerpt from a text by BORN, Adolf – JELÍNEK, Oldřich, "Urajt", *Haňťa Press* 7, no. 17 (1995); see also SVOBODA, Pavel – MACHOVEC, Martin, "Zapomenutý spolutvůrce 'trapné poetiky'" [A Forgotten Co-Creator of 'Embarrasing Poetics'], *Revolver Revue*, no. 93 (2013); Bondy's complete translations of Morgenstern from 1951 were published in a single volume: MORGENSTERN, Christian – BONDY, Egon, *Galgenlieder / Šibeniční písně* [Gallows Songs], Praha: Labyrint, 2000; 2nd edition, *Šibeniční písně*, Praha: Labyrint, 2010; Bondy's experimental "novel" *2000* (written in 1949-1950) was published in *Revolver Revue*, no. 45 (2001); another part of it is found in Bondy's memoirs *Prvních deset let* – see Footnote 1; a problem is presented by Karel Žák's literary work, which might well have been "passed down orally" by

Within the broad range of unofficial cultural activities which were originally given the avant-garde label and which existed at least in trace form after 1948 (hence leaving aside those writers who emigrated, fell entirely silent, were imprisoned or, of course, those who after "victorious February" attempted to comply or join the mainstream in one way or another, pride of place is taken by Teige and Effenberger's surrealist group, which carried on its pre-1948 activities almost entirely in isolation. Its most prominent talents were clearly Mikuláš Medek and Karel Hynek. Activities also continued in Zbyněk Havlíček's the "Spořilov" group and among some members of Skupina 42 [Group 42], particularly Jan Hanč, Jindřich Chalupecký, and Jiří Kolář. Entirely isolated from the other posthumous children of the Czech avant-garde was the Záběhlice surrealist group known as the Libeň psychics (librarian Zdeněk Buřil, 1924–1994, varnisher Jiří Šmoranc, 1924–2003, radio mechanic Vladimír Vávra, 1924–2005, and bookbinder Stanislav Vávra, *1933), whose 1950s work was as a whole considered lost or destroyed, so that it only very gradually penetrated the Czech literary context after 1989.[3] However, as

other Půlnoc participants, but which never actually appeared in the series. A couple of fragments from this work from between 1947 and 1955 were collected in 1979 by Ivo Vodseďálek in the samizdat volume *Hra prstíčků mých neklidných* [Game of my Restless Little Fingers], from which again only a couple of small samples were presented a/ in *Haňťa Press* 3, no. 9 (1991), b/ in *Voknoviny* 1, no. 2 (2014); a curious second samizdat edition of Vodseďálek's *Trapná poesie* [Embarrassing Poetry], 1952, richly illustrated by Adolf Born and Oldřich Jelínek in a single samizdat copy, has never been published by regular printing presses.

3) With regard to the Záběhlice (or Libeň) group see the memoir article by VÁVRA, Stanislav: "Záběhlická skupina surrealistů – Libenští psychici" [The Záběhlice Surrealist Group – Libeň Psychics], *Jarmark umění*, no. 2 (April 1991); see also *Haňťa Press* 3, no. 10 and 11 (1991); see also extracts from original work by S. Vávra and J. Šmoranc in *Haňťa Press* 3–5, no. 14 – no. 17 (1993–1995); also an interview: VÁVRA, Stanislav – TYPLT, Jaromír F., "Ukázat pramen a podat pohár" [To Show a Spring and to Offer a Goblet], *Iniciály* 2, no. 17/18 (1991); the fictionalized memoirs of S. Vávra present a testimony that is rather late and highly stylized (VÁVRA, Stanislav, *Zvířený prach* [Swirling Dust], Praha: MČ Praha 8, 2004); see also the three following volumes of texts by the "Libeň Psychics": VÁVRA, Vladimír, *Muž v jiných končinách světa* [A Man in Other Corners of the Earth], Praha: Pražská imaginace, 1992; VÁVRA, Stanislav, *Snovidění* [Dreamseeing], Praha: Pražská imaginace 1992; ŠMORANC, Jiří, *Děti periferie* [Children of the Periphery], Praha: Pražská imaginace, 1996.

early as 1948 the former avant-gardists became aware of Vladimír Boudník, with his first "explosionalist" manifesto on 14th August 1948. Bohumil Hrabal (and evidently Hrabal's "neo-poetist" associate Karel Marysko, 1915–1988, who made a living as a performing concert musician) apparently got to know Jiří Kolář back in 1946, although awareness of Hrabal's breakthrough 1950 texts that were so highly rated decades later[4] only got through to this very limited "public" some time later, perhaps around the mid-1950s. Skupina Ra [The Ra Group] entirely ceased its activities. Of those mentioned above, Teige and Hynek died shortly afterwards and none of those remaining were able to obtain vocation relating in any way to literature at least from 1949 until the mid-1950s. Most of them were engaged in working-class occupations. Kolář, who from 1948 to 1951 eked out a living at the Dílo co-operative and then at the Propaganda Section of the SNKLHU [State Literature, Music and Art Publishers], was imprisoned from 1952 to 1953, and did not go back to work when he was released. Other "maladjusted individuals" in similar straitened circumstances during the first half of the 1950s included Josef Škvorecký, Vratislav Effenberger, Vladimír Vokolek, Ladislav Dvořák, and Jan Zábrana, while repudiated Czech literary grandmasters such as Vladimír Holan, Jakub Deml, Bohuslav Reynek and a large number of other authors were totally isolated with no hope of publication. Subsistence issues of a similar kind also affected all the members of the group whose work was brought together in the Půlnoc samizdat series.

The initiators, creators and most prolific authors of the series, Ivo Vodseďálek (1931–2017) and in particular Egon Bondy, actual name Zbyněk Fišer (1930–2007), were in a certain sense the "renegades" from Teige's and Effenberger's surrealist group. Bondy made his sam-

It was not until after the death of Vladimír Vávra in 2005 that his younger brother Stanislav Vávra managed to reconstruct from his surviving manuscripts an anthology of texts by the "Libeň Psychics" lost in the 1950s. This anthology was published under the title *Libeňští psychici. Sborník básnických a prozaických textů z let 1945-1959* [Libeň Psychics. Collected Poetic and Prose Works from 1945–1959], Praha: Concordia, 2009.
4) HRABAL, Bohumil, *Bambino di Praga - Barvotisky - Krásná Poldi* [Bambino di Praga – Color Prints – Beautiful Poldi], Praha: Československý spisovatel, 1990; see also *Sebrané spisy Bohumila Hrabala*, vol. 2 - *Židovský svícen* [Jewish Candleholder], also vol. 3 - *Jarmilka*, Praha: Pražská imaginace, 1991 and 1992.

izdat debut, for the first time with his Jewish pseudonym, in what was still an entirely surrealist anthology *Židovská jména* [Jewish Names], which came out in early 1949 with Vratislav Effenberger, Karel Hynek, Oldřich Wenzl, Jan Zuska, Zdeněk Wagner, Jana Krejcarová and others[5] all represented under other Jewish pseudonyms. To a large extent, in spite of their manifesto for a radical schism with the poetics of surrealism, as documented particularly in the programme collections *Ich und es: totální realismus* [Ich und es: Total Realism][6] (Egon Bondy, samizdat 1951)[7] and *Trapná poesie*[8] [Embarrassing Poetry] (I. Vodseďálek, samizdat 1951). It is also possible to include their work from the early 1950s, like that of Hrabal at the same time and much of Skupina 42 (Kolář, Blatný and Kainar) among the work of those who repeatedly insisted on matching themselves with the surrealist legacy. In the case of Bondy and Vodseďálek, there remained the poetics of the *objet trouvé*, the idea of dreams being equal to life (and of course life being equal to dreams!), admiration for the poetics of horror and the *roman noir*, the requirement for "purety", "nakedness", the linkage of the unlinkable, the drasticity of testimony aiming to épater le bourgeois [shock the bourgeois], the stylization of "childish naiveté", the inability to hierarchize values, and in particular dogmatic "leftishness", faith in the socialist revolution (albeit of a Trotskyist anti-Stalinist kind) and resistance to "religious obscurantism". Some of these traits are more evident in Bondy, others in Vodseďálek, and still others in Krejcarová, but all of them can be pointed out in the Půlnoc series texts as a whole. What was radical, however, was the retreat from metaphor and imagery in poetic language, the drastic "purification" and "de-aestheticization". Key works from the Půlnoc series, some of which were to be of crucial importance to the aesthetic orientation of the 1970s artistic

5) MACHOVEC, Martin (ed.), *Židovská jména* [Jewish Names], Praha: NLN, 1995; see also MACHOVEC, Martin, "Židovská jména rediviva. Významný objev pro dějiny samizdatu" [The Jewish Names Revived. An Important Finding for the History of Samizdat], *A2* 3, no. 51-52 (2007).
6) For this and other cited texts from the 1950s see BONDY, Egon, *Básnické spisy I.-III.* (see Footnote 2).
7) Dtto.
8) For this and other cited texts from the 1950s see VODSEĎÁLEK, Ivo, *Dílo Ivo Vodseďálka I., II.* (see Footnote 1).

underground include Bondy's poem *Jeskyně divů aneb Prager Leben (Pražský život)* [Cave of Wonders or Prager Leben; Prague Life] (1951), the poetics of which are notably similar to those of Hrabal's *Bambino di Praga*, which was written around the same time, even though Bondy and Hrabal did not know of each other at that time and met first only by the end of 1951. In other respects, it hints at Bondy's future development as an implacable critic, a regular firebrand and a dogmatic "wielder of the truth". Also of importance is the collection *Für Bondys unbekannte Geliebte aneb Nepřeberné bohatství* [For Bondy's Unknown Love or Inexhaustible Wealth] (1951), which to some extent restores the direct connection to the poetics used by surrealists at that time (e.g., applying Dalí's paranoid-critical method and Hynek's "graphic poetry" principle), as well as *Velká kniha* [Great Book] (1952), which was to be highly popular in the *underground*, particularly with its groundbreaking section *Ožralá Praha* [Hammered Prague], its barbaric-style antipoetisms, its nursery rhyme pseudo-primitivisms and of course its "naive realist" testimonies of the absurdities of the era, which form a striking counterpoint, e.g., to Kolář's contemporary "eye-witness" poetics. The long poem *Zbytky eposu* [Remnants of an Epic] (1955), is outstanding for several of its highly de-tabooing passages, which show inadvertent parallels between Bondy's early poetical works and several elements in those of writers of American Beat generation, as well as being a splendid display of surrealist poetics linking the unlinkable and ultimately testimony of Bondy's return to some sources of Czech literary modernism (Erben, Mácha, and Havlíček Borovský).

In his Půlnoc texts, Ivo Vodseďálek is far more consistent in adhering to the poetics of "embarrassment", disrupting the traditional punchline and of course the imagery of the poetical text (e.g., in the collection *Cesta na Rivieru* [Trip to the Riviera], 1951, *Smrt vtipu* [Death of the Joke], 1951, *Pilot a oráč* [Pilot and Ploughman], 1951, *Americké básně* [American Poems], 1953) poetics, which in a reevaluation of the surrealist *objet trouvé* and in contrast to Bondy's poetic work anticipates all the pathos-free poetics of American pop-art and hyperrealism. He also, on the other hand, revives the beauty of surrealist spectrality and chimerality in novel contexts (in the collection *Krajina a mravnost* [Landscape and Morality], 1953, the prose work *Kalvarie* [Calvary], 1954), while generally in a number of his texts he uncovers the appeal of "Soviet mythology" (e.g., in the collection *Kvetoucí Ukrajina* [Blooming Ukraine], 1950, 1953), while admitting to his defencelessness in the face of the myth accepted by the masses and the futility of any resistance, which he nevertheless does offer, even though he is aware of the absurdity of such conduct, thus again presciently anticipating the ideas of some of his underground successors. (However, Vodseďálek's work was unknown to the underground circle surrounding the Plastic People.)

In hindsight, it is quite tempting to see this grouping as a more or less monolithic school of poetry, if not actually as some kind of latent resistance cell, even though circumstances around the late forties and early fifties, i.e., the political reality of the times and the personal situations of the majority of members of that group, who were mostly around twenty years of age, largely rules out anything of that nature. Zand[9] calls them a "poetic circle" in an attempt to indicate the low degree of homogeneity within the group. The fact is that both initiators of the Půlnoc series – Bondy and Vodseďálek – were classmates at the Ječná Street grammar school in Prague, and they were brought together mainly by their interest in modern art in general and surrealism in particular, as well as ultimately to attempt a joint debut, which unfortunately took place during the period immediately following February 1948. These two artists, whose early works (i.e., at least until 1952) still bore many of the signs of juvenilia (e.g., experimenting and seeking out new forms, attempting a wide variety of genres, much "finding oneself" as it were, and almost desperate attempts to come up with something novel, independent and non-epigonic), had the good fortune to find a couple of congenial writers and artists among their contemporaries (poet and collagist Pavel Svoboda, 1930–2014, Jana Krejcarová-Fischlová-Černá-Ladmanová, 1928–1981, sculptor and poet Karel Žák, 1929–2015, and later book graphic artist and photographer Jaromír Valoušek, 1928–1993, in the early 1950s chemistry student and for a short time Vodseďálek's wife Dana "Dagmara" Prchlíková, 1931–2006, at that time the "suprasexdadaists" Adolf

9) ZANDOVÁ, Gertraude, *Totální realismus a trapná poezie. Česká neoficiální literatura 1948-1953* [Total Realism and Embarrassing Poetry. Unofficial Czech Literature 1948-1953], Brno (Czech Republic): Host, 2002; ZANDOVÁ, Gertraude, "Básník – svědek – aktivista" (see Footnote 1).

Born, 1930-2016, and Oldřich Jelínek, *1930, later psychologist Miloš Černý, 1931-2018, poet Emil Hokeš, 1931-2000 and perhaps a couple of others), who showed appreciation for their creative ambitions and who at least to some extent responded to them by showing them their own works. Another who was close to this group, or at least to some of its members, during the first half of the 1950s (typically, not all the aforementioned personally knew all those named below!) was a quite unknown secondary graphic art school graduate, Vladimír Boudník (1924-1968)[10] whom Zbyněk Fišer got to know as early as in 1948, as well as Mikuláš Medek (1926-1974), Emila Medková (1928-1985), Jaroslav Dočekal (1926-1975), Karel Hynek (1925-1953), Zbyněk Sekal (1923-1998) and Jan "Hanes" Reegen (1922-1952)[11] to name at least those whose familiarity with underground publishing

10) Regarding his work, see BOUDNÍK, Vladimír, *Z literární pozůstalosti* (see Footnote 1); BOUDNÍK, Vladimír, *Z korespondence* [From The Correspondence] *I (1949-1956)*, *Z korespondence II (1957-1968)*, Praha: Pražská imaginace, 1994; MERHAUT, Vladislav, *Zápisky o Vladimíru Boudníkovi* [Notes on Vladimír Boudník], Praha: Edice Revolver Revue, 1997.

11) The literary work of Mikuláš Medek, in which connections can be found with the Půlnoc writers, was published in the volume: MEDEK, Mikuláš, *Texty* [Texts], Praha: Torst, 1995; of great value with regard to Medek and Boudník's relationship to Bondy and his circle is the correspondence between Medek and Boudník: HARTMANN, Antonín - MRÁZ, Bohumír (eds.), "Boudník a Medek, korespondence" [Boudník and Medek, Correspondence], *Umění/Art* 45, no. 3/4 (1997); see also HARTMANN, Antonín - MRÁZ, Bohumír (eds.), "Boudník a Medek, dodatek ke korespondenci a další 'texty pro Mikuláše Medka'" [Boudník and Medek, Additions to Correspondence and Other Texts for Mikuláš Medek], *Umění/Art* 45, no. 5 (1997); the work of the artist and writer Jaroslav Dočekal has not yet been successfully collected in its entirety, nor has it been appropriately examined. For samples of his work see: DOČEKAL, Jaroslav, "Smršťovače - hořké dávky. Z dopisů Jaroslavu Rotbauerovi" [Shrinkers - Bitter Doses. From Letters to Jaroslav Rotbauer], *Revolver Revue*, no. 29 (1995); see also *Dopisy Jaroslava Dočekala Vladimíru Boudníkovi I.-II.* [Letters of Jaroslav Dočekal to Vladimír Boudník I-II], Praha: Jan Placák - Ztichlá klika, 2017; HYNEK, Karel, *S vyloučením veřejnosti* [With the Exclusion of the Public], Praha: Torst, 1998. Regarding Jan Reegen see the samizdat volume: REEGEN, Jan, *Listy příteli. Dopisy Vladimíru Boudníkovi (1949-1952)* [Letters to a Friend. Letters to Vladimír Boudník 1949-1952], published by Václav Kadlec as the 56th publication is his samizdat *Pražská imaginace series* in 1989 (Stream 4, vol. 8). Bondy provides a testimony of his friendship with Reegen in his memoirs: BONDY, Egon, *Prvních deset let* (see Footnote 1).

activities at Půlnoc can be verified in some way.[12] (The Medeks and Hynek formed a connection for some time at least between Bondy's and Vodseďálek's circle and Effernberger's surrealist group, to whom it seems otherwise Bondy had a rather ambivalent relationship). The late avant-gardist JUDr. Bohumil Hrabal (1914–1997), who was quite isolated in the late 1940s and early 1950s, did not get to know Bondy until the end of 1951 (according to the latter's information), although the dating and content of Boudník's short story *Noc* [Night] – 10th October 1951 – indicate that they actually got to know each other somewhat earlier. Bondy recalls that (probably as early as 1951, but quite likely in 1952, evidently from 1951 or 1952) he met not only Boudník at Hrabal's, but also Karel Marysko.[13]

Surprisingly, however, the authors of the "Midnight Circle" did not have any demonstrable contacts with some of the other prominent artists and writers who at least for some time and in some respects "went underground", and who were in frequent contact during the 1950s with Hrabal and particularly with Jan Zábrana or Jiří Kolář (whose work they knew at least to some extent according to various testimonies), and Kolář's artistic and human double Josef Hiršal, who stated himself that he got to know Bondy's translations of Morgenstern at Hrabal's maybe in 1952, but perhaps as late as 1955, i.e., at a time when contacts between Bondy and Hrabal were again very limited.[14] Out of all the Půlnoc authors, Jana Krejcarová was the one who always led the most sociable life, and she evidently

12) In his memoirs *Prvních deset let* (see above) for the 1949–1955 period Bondy also refers to contacts with e.g. Alexej Kusák, Miroslav Lamač, Jaroslav Puchmertl, František Jůzek, Blanka Sochorová, Josef Lehoučka, Konstantin Sochor, František Drtikol, psychiatrist Václav Pinkava (Jan Křesadlo), or Andrej Bělocvětov. At Charles University, Faculty of Arts, where Ivo Vodseďálek studied aesthetics part-time, he got to know Milan Kundera, and even though he maintained occasional contact with him throughout the 1950s, he allegedly never told him about his literary ambitions.
13) The conspicuous similarity between some of Karel Marysko's poetic work and some of Egon Bondy's is pointed out in a study by MACHOVEC, Martin, "Literární dílo Karla Maryska" [The Literary Work of Karel Marysko], *Revolver Revue*, no. 34 (1997); Egon Bondy confirmed that he had met Marysko at Hrabal's home in Libeň in a personal conversation with the author.
14) HIRŠAL in MORGENSTERN, Christian, *Bim bam bum*, Praha: Český spisovatel, 1971, also in MORGENSTERN, Christian, *Morgenstern v Čechách. 21 proslulých básní ve 179 českých překladech 36 autorů* [Morgenstern in Bohemia. 21 Famous Poems in

had the most contacts with people outside the isolated circles of post-avantgardists, even though she evidently gained a reputation as the rather extravagant, albeit charmingly eloquent and forthright daughter of Milena Jesenská and Jaromír Krejcar, not as an underground writer, which is indirectly indicated by her alleged apprehension and indignation following the samizdat "publication" without her consent of her prose work *Clarissa* in 1951.[15] A more remote awareness of the Půlnoc authors' activities can be attributed to several more quite prominent writers who found themselves to be in more or less similar straitened circumstances in the early 1950s, e.g., Oldřich Wenzl, Zbyněk Havlíček, Ludvík Kundera (as testified for example, by correspondence between Kundera and Zdeněk Wagner[16]), Vratislav Effenberger, Jaroslav Rotbauer[17], Jan Bouše, and Libor Fára. Until their premature deaths, Záviš Kalandra and Karel Teige were also allegedly in contact with Bondy at least, although hard evidence is thin on the ground, and for the most part we can only rely on the memories and indirect testimonies.[18] Clearly, as

179 Czech translations of 36 authors], Praha: Vida vida, 1996; see also HIRŠAL, Josef – GRÖGEROVÁ, Bohumila, *Let let* [Flight of Years], Praha: Rozmluvy, 1993.

15) VODSEĎÁLEK in KREJCAROVÁ, *Clarissa a jiné texty* (see Footnote 2).

16) Extracts from the correspondence of Zdeněk Wagner (1923–1991), a former participant in the *Židovská jména* anthology who became a veterinarian, were printed in TYPLT, Jaromír, F. – WAGNER, Zdeněk, "Fascinantně divý muž Zdeněk Wagner" [The Fascinatingly Wild Man Zdeněk Wagner], *Host* 16, no. 5 (2000); an extract from a letter dated 3rd January 1949, entitled "Slovo o pluku Fišerově" [A Word on Fišer's Regiment], testifies to the fact that at that time Fišer (E. Bondy) made a considerable impression upon Wagner (even if evidently a somewhat ambiguous one); though what is also rather conspicuous is that Wagner does not make the slightest mention of the *Židovská jména* project, which was to come to a head just as this letter was being written. Wagner's complete work (including quoted correspondence) was published in book form: WAGNER, Zdeněk, *Virgule* [Rod], Praha: Cherm, 2007.

17) EFFENBERGER, Vratislav, *Moderní kultura v socialistické revoluci* [Modern Culture in a Socialist Revolution] (manuscript from 1965, whose existence is testified in TYPLT, Jaromír F., "Dvě svědectví o Židovských jménech" (see Footnote 1); concerning Jaroslav Rotbauer, see also DOČEKAL, Jaroslav, "Smršťovače – hořké dávky" (Footnote 11).

18) See BONDY, Egon, *Prvních deset let* (Footnote 1); [HERDA, Milan], *Protokolární výpověď o trockistech* [Protocol testimony on Trotskyists], Czech Interior Ministry Archive, file shelf No. 305-738-1 –"Trotskyist surrealists. Testimonies to the police

soon as the Půlnoc series was established, i.e., late 1950/early 1951, its creators kept their activities hidden for obvious reasons, even from some of their former friends from whom they had in any case gradually become artistically estranged one way or another.

Since the Půlnoc series was primarily the offspring of its two initiators, then again in retrospect it is possible to gain the somewhat erroneous impression that its primary contents were mainly meant to be Bondy's and Vodseďálek's "totally realistic", "embarrassing", "anti-poetic", "de-tabooing", "neo-Dadaist", often specifically political, or "witness" reactions to some surrealist practices, which as has become evident with the passage of time, already had its precedent in the somewhat similar reactions of some members of Group 42 and the Ra Group (in any case Bondy undoubtedly found an affinity with Hrabal and Boudník due to this similarity). What is more likely is that this (partly illustrated) typescript series was originally meant to serve more as a platform for **creative dialogue** with parallel unofficial artistic trends, and even more probably as a platform for attempts to continue this dialogue even under the extraordinary and absurd conditions of the day. Evidence of these efforts is confirmed by the "guest" appearances made by Hrabal, Boudník, Born and Jelínek. In 1950, it was still undoubtedly unclear where the artistic paths of these two – Bondy and Vodseďálek – were taking them and which of the other Půlnoc authors would produce works of lasting value that might compete with them one way or another, and in particular, in which political and social circumstances the work of all those involved might develop further. Back in 1950, everything was bogged down by doubts and uncertainties that were surely much greater than those which twenty years later dogged Bondy and Vodseďálek's "underground" successors, who were thrust into a situation that was otherwise quite similar. The fact that the creators of the series saw the early 1950s as some kind of stopgap situation whose duration could only be guessed at is confirmed by

and Gestapo on Trotskyists. Trotskyist leaflets", its part was published in a section in *Jarmark umění (Bulletin Společnosti Karla Teiga)*, no. 11/12 (1996); [HERDA, Milan], "Protokolární výpověď M. H." [M. H. Protocol testimony], in ALAN, Josef (ed), *Alternativní kultura. Příběh české společnosti 1945–1989* [Alternative Culture. The Story of Czech Society 1945–1989], Praha: NLN, 2001, p. 523.

Vodseďálek's statement[19] that the usual Půlnoc edition, represented generally by four typed copies (1 + 3), was primarily intended to **conserve** the texts that had been written, i.e., to preserve them until they could be published, which of course was ultimately to be four decades later, and the question arises whether just an intimation of this fact would not have entirely undermined the creativity of writers who were around twenty years of age. The similarities between the early 1950s and the early 1970s were considerable for debuting artists and writers, e.g., the loss of the option to publish freely and the imposition of political repression; however, the early 1970s had its precedent in the early 1950s, so then it was possible to look back and seek examples.

Hence, while **in retrospect** it is evident (from an art history or literary history standpoint) that the most prominent "core" authors in the "Půlnoc circle" were Bondy and Vodseďálek, while Hrabal and Boudník remained on its "periphery", this did not yet necessarily appear to be the case around the early 1950s. There is no doubt that much was expected from Jana Krejcarová, whose literary work has only come down to us in fragments, though the reputation of her output is enhanced by the legend of her life.[20]

What might the **objective** of the Půlnoc series creators have been? Probably first and foremost to continue to address other non-conformists and modernists (hence in 1950 this could only take place "underground") and to enter into debate with them. They un-

19) VODSEĎÁLEK, Ivo – MAZAL, Tomáš, "S Ivo Vodseďálkem o letech radostného budování 49–53" (Footnote 1).

20) This is borne out not only by the Austrian documentary film by director Nadja Seelich made in 1992, *Sie sass im Glashaus und warf mit Steinen*, on Krejcarová's life, but also by a monograph which Krejcarová (Černá) herself wrote on her own mother: ČERNÁ, Jana, *Adresát Milena Jesenská* [Addressee Milena Jesenská], Praha: Divoké víno, 1969 (1st edition); Praha: Concordia, 1991 (2nd edition); Praha: Torst, 2014 (3rd edition). There are also numerous testimonies stating that the poet also used this text to project her own twists and turns in life onto her mother's fate, e.g. VODSEĎÁLEK, Ivo, *Felixír života* (Footnote 1); see also BONDY, Egon, *Prvních deset let* (Footnote 1); see also MILITZ, Anna, *Ani víru, ani ctnosti člověk nepotřebuje ke své spáse: příběh Jany Černé* [Neither Religion, nor Virtue are Necessary for One's Salvation: the Story of Jana Černá], Olomouc (Czech Republic): Burian a Tichák, 2015.

doubtedly wished to create a fitting and a true reflection of the times in which they lived, and not to succumb to the enormous pressure of mass psychosis and the general mythologization of reality, but rather to unmask the imposed myths with particular mockery, and thus somehow to actually "disarm" them. They also wanted to maintain the continuity of modern art and modern literature (to be specific, at the time this meant the continuity of artistic work, which was still understood as avant-garde, i.e., inventive, pioneering, and innovative). They might have also wanted a confrontation in which they could stand up for their particular articulated artistic credo and their own distinctive standpoint, but these efforts only succeeded to a limited degree: echoes of Bondy's work (but almost to no extent that of Vodseďálek) can be found in some works by Hrabal, to some extent Boudník, as well as to a limited extent for example in Medek, Hynek, and Marysko. Only Bondy's poetic work, and of course his later prose and philosophical work, exercised a profound influence on the younger generations of underground authors some twenty years later, even though this was all rather spontaneous and had little to do with the Půlnoc authors' original aspirations. Hence Bondy's and Vodseďálek's attempt of some kind in the early 1950s to make their texts at least part of a substitute literary scene can be said for the most part to have been unsuccessful, as such a "practice" only emerged to a very limited extent even within the Půlnoc series itself; today it is clear that some of their publication activities between 1950 and 1955 were primarily rather **individual matters** of a "piratical" nature which the other Půlnoc authors did not necessarily know about (as was already the case for the compilation of the *Židovská jména* collection around 1948/1949; not all of these authors were informed about being involved in this "business"). Hence fear of prosecution clearly played a greater role here than the organizers cared to admit.

In the given circumstances, they could rule out any idea of accomplishing Bondy's subsequent objective, as testified by Vodseďálek[21], of making the Půlnoc authors into an artistic group which (doubtless on the model of the various surrealist groups!) would be highly homogeneous and would strive (as in the case, at least for

21) See VODSEĎÁLEK, Ivo, *Felixír života* (op. cit.).

some time, of André Breton's group) not only to achieve a "revolutionary change in human consciousness", but also for a material "revolutionary change throughout the world". However, it is also evident that the mere declaration and articulation of such an immodest ambition could have been conceived by Bondy in the early 1950s as an inspiring and stimulating necessity. In any case, a number of other "immodest" aims and ambitions showed up in his subsequent life and work.

The **reactions at the time of the Půlnoc authors' artistic fellow travellers** were, generally speaking, insofar as they can be followed at all, rather restrained.[22] We might well include those of Boudník, who indeed maintained an aesthetic distance from Bondy and Vodseďálek – more in the graphic arts than in literature – but less with regard to "world view": his explosionism did not in the least lag behind Bondy's maximalist postulates in its radicalism and his artistic work and lifestyle were viewed even by those artistically close to him with some distrust if not disdain. The most prominent fellow-traveller of the Půlnoc authors was undoubtedly Bohumil Hrabal, who was also the only one to always have a full understanding of, and high appreciation for, Bondy's work. However, he was certainly not one of them, as his age, education and life experience alone inspired respect and kept him at a certain distance. It is doubtless little exaggeration to conclude that artists like Medek, Fára, Havlíček, Wenzl, Effenberger (and ultimately, Born and Jelínek too, who were still Applied Arts College students in the early 1950s) were above all apprehensive about Bondy's political explicitness and so rather sought to distance themselves from the Půlnoc "core". This might also have been caused by nothing more than a simple distaste for Bondy's and Krejcarová's (not to mention Boudník's) extravagant, eccentric behaviour and minimum social adjustment, which could appear quite dangerous in the early 1950s.[23] Bondy's ostentatious

---

22) HAVLÍČEK, Zbyněk – PRUSÍKOVÁ, Eva, *Dopisy Evě / Dopisy Zbyňkovi* [Letters to Eva / Letters to Zbyněk], Praha: Torst, 2003, pp. 45, 152–153; see also MEDEK, Mikuláš, *Texty* (Footnote 7); DOČEKAL, Jaroslav, "Smršťovače – hořké dávky" (Footnote 11), also EFFENBERGER, Vratislav in TYPLT, Jaromír F., "Dvě svědectví o Židovských jménech" (Footnote 17).

23) [HERDA, Milan], Protokolární výpověď M. H., 2001 (Footnote 18).

leftish and "revolutionary" tendencies[24] could also have been off-putting, while for many Bondy and Vodseďálek's "desertion" of "high" art was incomprehensible. The question remains whether the primary objections and aversions involved in their disassociation with them were of a purely personal nature (and this applies not just to Bondy, but above all to Krejcarová, whose "spontaneous animalism" simply frightened many of her contemporaries and friends, as a number of testimonies bear witness), or mainly aesthetic, artistic or relating to their world-view. Here, we are compelled to remain in the realm of speculation, as we cannot ascertain to what extent the later testimonies of the participants are influenced by their view of that period through the prism of later events. In any case, the Půlnoc group had fallen apart by 1955 anyway[25] and communications between its former participants were irregular and occasional in the following years, as they all went their separate ways.

It is no exaggeration to say that the Půlnoc series and the literary works published in it have become a tale, a pseudo-fiction and a legend, which was occasionally perpetuated, no doubt deliberately and consciously, by Bohumil Hrabal in his works published during the 1960s, but whose original creator was undoubtedly Egon Bondy: let us recall his cycle *Legendy* [Legends] from the collection *Für Bondys unbekannte Geliebte*[26]. Several contemporaries testify to his numerous statements from the 1960s in "as the poet Bondy spake" mode. (Bondy's "split" into "I" and "he", which is well-represented as an autostylization throughout his lifelong work, was repossessed

---

24) For example, the graphic artist Vladimír Šmerda, who associated with the young Zbyněk Fišer 1947–1948 recalls how at that time Z. F. repeatedly assured a number of friends that after the victorious socialist revolution they would "hang them in their own interest": whether he was serious, half-serious or only joking it was clear that such arguments were not necessarily to everybody's taste (from a personal conversation between the author and V. Š. in spring 2000).

25) BONDY, Egon, *Prvních deset let* (Footnote 1); VODSEĎÁLEK, Ivo – MAZAL, Tomáš, "S Ivo Vodseďálkem o letech radostného budování 49–53" (Footnote 1).

26) BONDY, Egon, *Básnické dílo Egona Bondyho II* [The Poetic Work by Egon Bondy II], Praha: Pražská imaginace, 1992; BONDY, Egon, *Básnické spisy I* [Collected Poetic Works I], Praha: Argo, 2014.

in masterly fashion by Hrabal in his *Něžný barbar*, 1973[27], which is actually a kind of legend of a legend.)

As regards **the State Security's (StB) familiarity** with Bondy's and Vodseďálek's activities, the only material that is so far publicly available at the Interior Ministry archive (now ABS) relates mostly to the 1948–1949 period, i.e., **before** the Půlnoc series was launched. There is an undated testimony from Milan Herda, imprisoned in the 1950s, evidently from the period between 1952 and 1954[28], which indicates two things: although the testifier attempted to rather trivialize the artistic (and indeed the political) activities of Bondy (always called Fišer in the report), Vodseďálek and Krejcarová (Fischlová), to portray them as grandiose mystifications, or as ordinary economic crime (especially in comparison with the "seriousness" of the activities of Karel Teige, to whom the entire testimony relates), although he provides facts which could definitely have been of some use to State Security. (For example, he mentions the plan – fulfilled later, in 1950, – to smuggle Czech glass to Vienna.) Hence it can be assumed that if the State Security had wanted, they could have monitored the Půlnoc organizers activities from an early stage.[29]

Public reactions to the activities of one of the first and most original underground artistic groupings were general practically zero until the late 1960s: the Půlnoc works from the 1950s were not published and the activities of the initiators were only a "legend".

27) See HRABAL, Bohumil, "Něžný barbar", in *Obrazy v hlubině času. Sebrané spisy Bohumila Hrabala 6* [Collected Works of Bohumil Hrabal 6, Images in the Depth of Time], Praha: Pražská imaginace, 1992; the book was to come out in the English translation by Stacey Knecht in 2017 under a title *The Tender Barbarian* by Archipelago Books – see their website https://archipelagobooks.org/book/the-tender-barbarian/, visited 26th Jan 2017, but has not got to print by 2019.

28) [HERDA, Milan], Protokolární výpověď o trockistech (Footnote 18). Another part of this testimony, this time dealing directly with the Fišer-Bondy circle and friends, was printed in the Documentation section in ALAN, Josef, *Alternativní kultura* op. cit, pp. 523–527. See also BONDY, Egon, *Prvních deset let* (Footnote 1).

29) Research over the last few years has confirmed that throughout the 1950s State Security monitored the activities of people connected to Půlnoc, not just because of their literary work, but also due to their political, i.e. anti-Soviet attitudes, which were considered "Trotskyist". See the "Surrealists" file No. 11135 from the Czech Security Services Archive (Archiv bezpečnostních složek, ABS, Prague).

(One exception is Boudník's **artistic** work, but that is only rather indirectly related to the Půlnoc authors' **literary** activities, running in parallel to them.)

So again, it is only a slight exaggeration to say that if **Bondy's** poetic work had not been discovered in the late 1960s by director Radim Vašinka,[30] literary critic Jan Lopatka, and in the early 1970s art historian Ivan Martin Jirous, the Půlnoc underground would only have lived on as Bondyian and Hrabalian legend until 1989, if not to this day. It is only the fact that the early 1970s underground artists enthusiastically seized upon Bondy's poetry and began to put it to music and so to spread it among a public that was of a very different character, education, and social origin that allows the underground Půlnoc circle to be understood in retrospect as a kind of prelude to the greatly differentiated underground activities of the 1970s and 1980s. Without this capitalization, the Půlnoc circle would have remained a mere episode in the history of the Czech unofficial cultural scene, as was unfortunately the case with so many small groups and individuals, e.g., the "Libeň psychics" and the various regional activities. The public (albeit narrow and limited) only started to be aware of the importance of the Půlnoc authors' artistic and literary activities, in fact only those of Egon Bondy and perhaps also of Jana Krejcarová, in the late sixties and the early seventies. It was only many years later as the importance of the role played by this little group in the creation of the later Czech underground movement became evident.

The circle around the Půlnoc series can in any case be considered to be one of the most prominent examples of **underground artistic activities** in the 1950s. The main reason is that the group did not carry on its previous **public** activities underground, as in the case of the great majority of other unofficial activities performed by individual artists who after February 1948 were merely trying to **continue** illegally, i.e., underground, what they had been able to do legally up until that time, but now actually "making their debut" in the underground. Hence for the public it was now "dead",

---

30) VAŠINKA, Radim, "Vydolováno z nepaměti I–V" [Retrieved from Time out of Mind I–V], *Divadelní noviny* 10, no. 5-9 (2001); VAŠINKA, Radim, "Bondy a Orfeus" [Bondy and Orpheus], in *Bouda Bondy, projekt Bouda IV,* Praha: National Theatre, 2007.

"inexistent" and indeed "underground" in the true sense. Moreover, the Půlnoc initiators made their underground debut with artistic works that were for the most part so innovative that it would be difficult to find anything similar even in published literature before February 1948 (hence they were not weighed down by any concerns at all regarding censorship or the "acceptability of the work", which any **publishing** author would have had to deal with to a greater or lesser extent). These were works which often very specifically, drastically, veristically, and realistically portrayed the times in which they were written, i.e., the Stalinist pandemonium of the early 1950s in Czechoslovakia: *ergo* **they could not have been written in any other way but in the underground**, and in a form which only a couple of decades later started to be called **samizdat**, thus – paradoxically – following the example of the Soviet Union.

2001, 2008
Translated by Melvyn Clarke

2. UNDERGROUND AND "UNDER-THE-GROUND"

*The standpoints of the underground community
in Czech society in the 1970s and 1980s and the specific values
of the underground culture*[1]

The terms "underground" and "under-the-ground"[2] have not been clearly defined in Czech culture so far. Traditionally, "underground" comprises the community which emerged in the early 1970s around the rock band The Plastic People of the Universe. This community, which later became part of Czech dissent and to a great extent merged with the community around Charter 77, was composed of poets, musicians, artists, as well as philosophers, essayists, and samizdat publishers of various focus and political orientation.

Let's start with a few quotes linked to the question of what is and what is not "underground" in Czech, or also even world culture, and what misunderstandings may arise and prevail with regard to this term, with all its historical, literary and, in the broad sense, cultural connotations.

The first comes from Ivan M. Jirous's memoir *Pravdivý příběh Plastic People* [The True Story of the Plastic People]. There is a rather humorous passage in which the author remembers how, in the early 70s, he tried to explain to the less bright members of the Plastic People the difference between "psychedelic" and "underground" music:

> I explained to them that psychedelic music is a matter of an artistic genre or style whereas underground is a spiritual attitude. As an example I named Lennon and The Beatles, who was underground, although

---

1) The study was first written in English, then translated into Czech and published abridged, then translated back into English and published again. See the details in Author's Note.
2) In Czech: "underground" and "podzemí"; "podzemí" being the literal translation of the English word, carrying the same secondary meaning, referring to "unofficial cultural sphere", "counter-culture", "anti-establishment movements" etc., however, with a broader meaning, i.e. culture and art not necessarily inspired by Anglo-American "underground culture", but by some domestic predecessors as well.

The Beatles cannot be considered an underground band. Ştevich[3] simplified this into the rule 'no fires, that's the underground', which we later often quoted in our group.[4]

The catchphrase "no fires, that's the underground" (unlike psychedelic rock shows where such effects were essential) was later used by Milan Hlavsa and Jan Pelc as a title of the publication of their interview about the fate of the Plastic People and the establishment and development of the Czech underground as such.[5]

The next quote is a statement which was made in a debate following another English lecture by the author at a textology conference at the University of Seattle in October 1997.[6] After the author suggested a certain parallel between the early stage of the Czech underground culture, represented in the early 1950s primarily by Egon Bondy and other authors around the samizdat Edice Půlnoc [Midnight Series], and the beginnings of the literature of the Beat Generation, in particular with respect to poems by Allen Ginsberg from the same period, prof. David Greetham (City University of New York Graduate Center) made an authoritative comment saying *Ginsberg was no underground*, which had such a disarming effect on the lecturer that any potential polemics rather faded away.

The misunderstandings concerning what is and what is not underground primarily stem from the ambiguous meaning of the term, naturally with respect to its figurative, metaphorical meaning. In the Anglo-American cultural sphere, the term "underground" will mostly refer to unofficial cultural events, or to publishing of texts

---

3) Jiří Přemysl Ştevich was a guitar player in The Plastic People band at the turn of the 1960s–1970s.
4) JIROUS, Ivan Martin, "Pravdivý příběh Plastic People", in JIROUS, Ivan Martin, *Magorův zápisník* (ed. Michael Špirit), Praha: Torst, 1997, pp. 255–256.
5) See HLAVSA, Milan – PELC, Jan, *Bez ohňů je underground* [No Fires, That's the Underground], Praha: BSF, 1992; 2nd edition: Praha: Maťa – BSF, 2001; 3rd edition: Praha: Maťa – BSF, 2016.
6) See MACHOVEC, Martin, "Czech Underground Literature, 1969–1989. A Challenge to Textual Studies", in MODIANO, R. – SEARLE, L. F. – SCHILLINGSBURG, P. (eds.), *Voice, Text, Hypertext: Emerging Practices in Textual Studies*, Seattle – London: Walter Chapin Simpson Center for the Humanities – The University of Washington Press, 2003, pp. 345–357.

using one's own means, without any institutional backing, i.e., something quite similar to the samizdat in the former Soviet Bloc. In the field of popular music it originally (i.e., most likely already at the turn of the 50s and 60s) applied to deliberately non-commercial trends as an opposition to the requirements of show business, against the entertaining pop music that was popular with the consumerist society. And it is also very well known that in the latter meaning of the word, this Anglicism made its way into the Czech culture in the late 1960s where it was confronted with its Czech equivalent, "podzemí" which may be translated as "under-the-ground" to point out the difference: the term "underground" does not have an identical meaning to the Czech word "podzemí" since it does not directly refer to any particular "counter-cultural" sphere of the Anglo-American culture. And this very non-identity of the meaning logically implies numerous misunderstandings, not only in English-Czech translations but also in attempted interpretations. For instance, how do you explain in English that the university professors Jan Patočka and Václav Černý, after they had been forbidden to work in their respective university departments in the early 1970s, were still able to work "unofficially", in a "hidden" way, that is, in fact "under-the-ground" (though, probably not really illegally), but definitely did not belong to the "underground"? Professor Černý's sharp criticisms[7] of the Czech cultural "underground" (or, better to say of what he himself understood under the name, as it is quite clear from his texts that he knew very little about what this term really referred to; however, this is rather irrelevant in the given context) show that he was well aware of the difference between the words "podzemí" and "underground" in the Czech language. Let's admit that the criticisms raised by Václav Černý, forgetting for the time being that his concept was faulty, were also partly true. If the intolerance of the totalitarian regimes chased

7) See the study ČERNÝ, Václav, "Nad verši Věry Jirousové a o kulturním stanovisku našeho undergroundu" [On Věra Jirousová's Poetry; also on the Cultural Standpoint of our Underground], in ČERNÝ, Václav, *Tvorba a osobnost*, Praha: Odeon, 1992, pp. 900-908; ČERNÝ, Václav, "O všem možném, dokonce i o 'hippies' a 'novém románu'" [Miscellanea, even on "Hippies" and "The Nouveau Roman"], in ČERNÝ, Václav, *Tvorba a osobnost II*, Praha: Odeon, 1993, pp. 553-562 (eds. of both volumes: Jaroslav Kabíček and Jan Šulc); and ČERNÝ, Václav, *O povaze naší kultury* [On the Nature of Our Culture], Brno (Czechoslovakia): Atlantis, 1991, mainly pp. 61-62.

intellectuals, scholars, leading minds away "**under the ground**", that did not mean they had to share aesthetic, ideological and value preferences with the audience of the **underground**, which indeed originally drew on the values of the cultural revolution initiated by the rock music sphere in the 1960s; a revolution which also radically transformed the entire lifestyle of those who were young in the 1960s. Naturally, this cultural revolution first started in the West, but soon it also arrived behind the Iron Curtain – to the great displeasure of the Soviet *Kulturträgers*. So at the beginning of the 1960s, a majority of the young people in the West (including also the absurd "Soviet Bloc", which became the "East" only in the wake of the bipolar political arrangement of the world then, although a major part of it has always belonged to the "West" in terms of culture) went through a radical reassessment of values – while this decidedly was not only due to the negation of values which had been "dominant" by then. It is common knowledge, it was the representatives of the anti-commercial "underground rock" who were most radical in this reassessment.

But where were the dismissed Czech university professors and where were the admirers of the music played by bands like The Velvet Underground, The Fugs, The Mothers of Invention, or Captain Beefheart's Magic Band!?

And still, the cultural community of the Czech intellectuals forced to go "under the ground" and the Czech rockers living "underground" had a lot in common. The Czech underground oriented itself mainly to the revolt of American rock, the hippy movement, including the relatively popular communitarian way of life,[8] but in a broader perspective also to protest songs, the liberalism of the representatives of the rebellions at US universities in the 1960s, to the Afro-American culture and also the poetics of the Beat Generation. The cultural community of the Czech underground was also much inspired by, for instance, so-called *poètes maudits*, both French and Czech, existentialists like Boris Vian, anarchists, decadents and various intellectual solitary figures and "outcasts": the cultural genealogy of the Czech underground should also include František Gellner, Arthur Breisky, Jakub Deml, Ladislav Klíma and even Karel

---

8) See the anthology STÁREK, František Čuňas – KOSTÚR, Jiří (eds.), *Baráky. Souostroví svobody* [Shanties. The Archipelagos of Freedom], Praha: Pulchra, 2010.

Hynek Mácha, later also Bohumil Hrabal and his "tender barbarians" of the early 1950s.

And it is also well known that this curious cultural hybrid, which the Czech underground culture of the 1970s and 1980s surely was, was shaped based on a certain affiliation or even co-existence of a number of intellectuals and artists with the rock "primitives". In this respect, the role of Ivan Martin Jirous is absolutely unique. At the same time, though, the cultural values of the Czech underground of the 1970s were also largely affected by Jiří Němec, Egon Bondy, and last but not least, Václav Havel – the last maybe "only" by being able to mediate these values to people from other unofficial groupings, by being able to rouse interest in them and in this way providing the underground poets, musicians and artists with a certain amount of feedback.

On the other hand, it must be said that the rocker rebels did indeed differ, even in their "underground edition" from their predecessors "under-the-ground". This difference lay in the fact that the core of the underground community was formed of people with no formal education, often with no high-school diplomas, let alone university degrees, and that the "rock'n'roll revolution" was a "revolt of the barbarians", no longer very tender or holy[9], rather than being a result of some intellectual, ideological-aesthetic discourse. These rocker "primitives" also formed the core of the Czech underground community, at least in the early 1970s when it crystallized and slowly started to realize its own existence as a community *sui generis*. And it was these people who gave it the energy and who were the bearers of the underground ethos.

The above-mentioned, however, only seemingly contradicts Jirous's definition of the underground as a result of a certain spiritual approach to life because such an approach might have been shared without reflection, wordlessly, spontaneously: matters of artistic orientation, expression, specific preferences were marginal – this can be demonstrated, for instance, by the diversity not only

9) The metaphor of the "barbarians" has become well established in Czech literature and culture, primarily thanks to Bohumil Hrabal, and needs no comment; however, it may be of interest that American literary historians soon started to use the same metaphor when dealing with the Beat Generation, e.g., LIPTON, Lawrence, *The Holy Barbarians*, New York: Julian Messner, 1959.

of the underground music of the period (musical experiments close to minimalism, and the concrete music of Zajíček and the DG 307 band, the art rock with touches of free-jazz by The Plastic People, or simple musical "traditional" of Karásek, to give just a few examples), but also of the underground literature (see, for instance, the first four underground samizdat anthologies from the mid-1970s, which shall be discussed later on).

Defining the underground in this way may also help to establish a demarcation line between, firstly, this specific Czech community and the communities "under-the-ground", which held similarly negative views of the majority society anywhere and anytime in history (regardless also of whether this was or was not under totalitarian regimes); and secondly, between the underground community and those who simply went with the flow, for whom underground was a fashionable thing in a sense that it was "in" to be "anti".

The Czech underground, thus, cannot be simply reduced to primitive rock music. Two more delimitations are needed in this respect.

A/ It is a fact that the Czech underground community consisted, primarily at the beginning, mostly of rock musicians and their friends – that is originally the fans of The Plastic People of the Universe and before that of The Primitives Group, and Knížák's Aktual, and that it was thanks to this community and its "rockers' revolt" that underground proved to be unusually and unexpectedly resistant in the following years. However, very soon different artists and intellectuals that later significantly enriched the Czech underground culture started to exercise their influence over the community. We can claim that the **new quality**, which was an attribute of the Czech underground culture, emerged as a result of the extraordinary cooperation of the "rock primitives" on the one hand and the artists and intellectuals on the other. This was quite a unique phenomenon and not only in the Czechoslovakia of that time – the worlds of the dissident intellectuals and of the rock "long-haired freaks" usually did not blend. In this way, the underground gradually ceased to be just a showcase of some sort of a provocative (pseudo) art, or this or that musical trend, but under the pressure of the totalitarian regime it also started to absorb impulses from previously alien domains. In the context of the upcoming "normalization era" with its idiotic intolerance and effort to sooner or later criminalize all that was beyond its control, and which at the same time from the early 1970s seemed like a permanent, constant phenomenon, the Czech underground community was first marginalized in society and later the normalization regime strived to make its future existence altogether impossible. On the other hand, though, mainly under the influence of Ivan M. Jirous and Egon Bondy, the group started to perceive itself as an alternative community and a cultural scene, as an underground both "*an sich*" and "*für sich*", not just a "counter-culture" of a kind but as a "second culture" that aims to be fully independent of the "first culture", which was continuously and systematically brought to uniform by the totalitarian regime.

However, we also need to note that such radical, even extremist ambitions could not in fact be accomplished, particularly after the Czech underground community was partly (never wholly) incorporated into the wider collective of Charter 77 in the year 1977; the main "regulation" of Charter 77, as is well known, was to open a discussion "with the power" on a strictly legal platform.[10]

B/ The spiritual attitude and values of the Czech underground (primarily those which were typical for the ambition to create a truly independent "second culture") also need to be contrasted against various sectarian, millenarian religious opinions and attitudes which may show certain similarities when compared cursorily, primarily when we realize how varied the sectarian movement is in the period of the so-called New Age.

When studied from a psychological perspective, the attitudes held by the Czech underground might be seen as some sort of a panic, an escapist solution when brought face-to-face with the incomprehensibility and extensive complexity of the so-called modern technical civilization, a side effect of which – at least in the Christian world – is also mass secularization.

Perhaps we could also agree with certain similarities detected between the underground culture and some negativist sectarian

---

10) The group around Charter 77, with its personal and social structure, in a certain way resembled the underground community, but it must be highlighted that its agents were in the majority of cases only prominent dissidents, intellectuals, latent leaders of a potential political opposition who also pursued their own goals. In this way, unfortunately, the unique homogeneity of artistic and intellectual plurality of the underground became blurred and faded within the Charter 77 community.

cults, at least in the way they renounce the "evil world" and deliberately resort to living in a "parallel" or even "illegal" world. More similarities can be found concerning the presence of the chiliast, nihilist, self-destructive attitudes as a manifestation of the deepest resignation to publicly combat the horrors of today's world.[11]

It must be stressed that these similarities are merely external and that on the inside the Czech underground community was structured in a distinctly different manner. For one, it totally lacked an indispensable charismatic religious leader and a structure of strict subordination, there was no analogy to the "chosen ones" who would allegedly survive the up-coming apocalypse. And last but not least, as a rule, sectarian fanatics are not interested in art, literature, and music: all this is part of the "sinful world" which is doomed.

In order to underline the difference, allow me one more parallel. On the one hand, there is a certain similarity between the radicalism of the Czech underground and the original leftist radicalism of the anarchists, or leftist aspirations which have not yet been deformed by being incorporated into political structures; on the other hand, there is a similarity between the different militant sectarian religious cults with extreme-right movements. Also here we must not be misguided by potential identical exterior traits. The original, genuine left pursued goals which were totally different from those of the extreme right – and that is also why it has never succeeded in achieving them.[12]

11) The fact that the underground community was perceived as a kind of "sect" by at least some intellectuals from the Charter 77 movement can be demonstrated by quoting one phrase from Václav Benda's essay *The Parallel Polis* from 1978: "[...] underground, which forms by far the most numerous part of the Charter has been able to politicize and overcome its sectarianism; however, the permanency of such a result is probably conditioned by our abilities to 'enlighten' these circles." PREČAN, Vilém (ed.), *Od morální k demokratické revoluci. Dokumentace*, Scheinfeld – Praha – Bratislava: Čs. středisko nezávislé literatury – ÚSD ČSAV – Archa, 1990, pp. 46–47.

12) The subject of where to look for the cultural and social legacy of the Czech underground of the 1970s and 1980s and regarding the possible interpretation and misinterpretation of where the Czech underground was placed within the traditional political spectrum was presented in October 2014 in the *Lidové noviny* newspaper (supplement *Orientace/Salon*, 11–12 October 2014) in a discussion *Ať si mladí udělají vlastní underground* [Let the Young Make their Own Underground], by Jiří Fiedor, Stanislav Komárek, Zbyněk Petráček, Jáchym Topol, Martin C. Putna and Břetislav

Thus, the radical attitudes of such an internally diversified community, as was the Czech underground in the 1970s, can be appreciated and adequately interpreted only bearing in mind the period when the community was established and existed. And only then can we truly understand how special it was among the different contemporary, and to a certain extent similar movements, labelled as "counter-cultural", "anti-commercial", "alternative" in the West or "dissident" and "parallel" in Czechoslovakia of that time. It was a specific mixture of radicalised rock revolt of the 1960s, the avant-garde, experimental art schools of the period including performances, happenings, land art and of course also pop-art, together with residues of free-thinking intellectual fermentation in Czechoslovakia in those years. And one more and very important difference: Czech underground community **renounced any kind of explicitly political ideas and objectives**.

The underground in the 1970s was also strongly influenced by the literary work of Egon Bondy (not so much by his ultra leftist political aspirations), which he had been creating "under-the-ground" since the late 1940s, and was open to both Christians and Marxists (of a purely anti-partisan, anti-Soviet breed); the underground was a safe haven for feminists and environmentalists, pacifists and admirers of the US Army, rock'n'roll and folk musicians, teetotallers and junkies, artists and experimental poets, samizdat publishers, followers of oriental religions and philosophies – and from time to time, naturally, StB agents could also be encountered there. When, after a few years, the underground community to a certain extent merged with the Charter 77 movement (which inadvertently proves the absurdity of any potential suspicion that the community had inclinations towards some sort of a sectarian quietism), it also started to be influenced by Václav Havel, primarily by his concepts of

Rychlík. This debate made it clear that different interpretations of the term "leftism" still exist in Czech society. Did the Communist Party of Czechoslovakia have anything in common with the political left in the normalization era, apart from (some) of its slogans? Wasn't it rather an ultra-conservative, fascist-like quisling clique, whose ideology was empty and whose interpretation of so-called socialism led to establishment of a crypto-consumerist society? If it was indeed so, it also has consequences for the interpretation of the social and political position of the opponents of the regime, among whom a certain place should be reserved also for the Czech underground.

"non-political politics" and the "power of the powerless" (although a possibility also exists that Havel was in his concepts influenced by his intense interest in the culture of the underground). It was a pluralistic community, open and striving to maintain and further develop the unalienated, authentic values, both generally human and artistic, under extremely unfavourable conditions in a country where a totalitarian regime was reinstated, which in fact continued in the Stalinist tradition.

Twenty years of existence of this specifically Czechoslovak community, which can justifiably be called the underground, introduced examples of almost all cultural and artistic trends specific to the alternative culture in the Western world of the period – and maybe sometimes generated some extras, something which was totally unique.

The main phases of its development and the leading ideas of the underground prior to its becoming part of the Charter 77 community were best summarized by Ivan M. Jirous[13] and Egon Bondy[14].

---

13) Jirous's work *Zpráva o třetím českém hudebním obrození* was written in 1975 and since then has been published many times in the Czech language as well as being translated into a number of languages. Probably the most important Czech edition in which the text is included is the anthology of Jirous's essayistic and publicist work JIROUS, I. M., *Magorův zápisník* (ed. Michael Špirit), Praha: Torst, 1997, pp. 171–198. For the latest (and textually most reliable) edition of *Zpráva o třetím českém hudebním obrození* see MACHOVEC, M. – NAVRÁTIL, P. – STÁREK, F. Č. (eds.), *"Hnědá kniha" o procesech s českým undergroundem undergroundem* ["Brown Book" on the Trials of the Czech Underground], Praha: ÚSTR, 2012, pp. 17–31. The text was published in its English translation by Paul Wilson (not specifically cited here) several times under the title "Report on the Third Czech Musical Revival". See e.g. in *Views from the Inside*, Praha: Department of Czech Literature and Literary Criticism, Faculty of Philosophy and Arts, Charles University, 2006; 2nd edition: Praha: Karolinum Press, 2018.

14) In the first place, the anti-utopian / dystopian novel *Invalidní sourozenci* [Disabled Siblings] (samizdat, Praha 1974), in which Bondy, in a poetic vision, tried to explore the possibility of establishing a fully autonomous subculture. This vision of his gained wide acceptance in the underground community at that time. (For now the latest Czech publication: BONDY, Egon, *Invalidní sourozenci,* Praha: Akropolis, 2012.) Throughout the 1970s and 1980s, Bondy was perhaps the most outspoken proponent of cultural autonomy of the underground and dismissed both compromises with the official culture and drawing closer to the culture of the prominent dissidents. At the same time, though – and this only became public in 1990 – in some periods

At the end of his "manifesto" *Zpráva o třetím českém hudebním obrození* [The Report on the Third Czech Musical Revival] he says, among other things:

of his life he was forced to cooperate with the StB to a certain level. A wealth of material exists about the cooperation and the avoidance thereof between Fišer-Bondy and the StB which has not been processed by experts, let alone assessed. Some comments came from Petr UHL in his extensive interview with Zdenko PAVELKA, *Dělal jsem, co jsem považoval za správné* [I Did What I Thought Was Right], Praha: Torst, 2013, some of which were rather critical (pp. 155–173) although Uhl defends Bondy in many aspects. However, in the same book he also says: "It never came to my mind to draw any conclusions from the fact that the State Security had listed someone in some category. It was a mendacious, conspiratorial organization, even towards individual StB members. [...] But if someone claims today in an effort to pretend that the documents of the State Security are truthful, that the organization was bureaucratic and well controlled from within and that is why Mr. XY 'for sure' must have been an informer and a snitch, then that person is not telling the truth. The relationship between the StB member and its victim – they were always victims, no matter in which category they were listed or what position they held and despite the fact that they often also acted amorally – should be explained by studies of oral history with the actual people concerned, before all of them pass away" (pp. 491–492). More recently Bondy's contacts with StB were treated by Miroslav VODRÁŽKA (sometimes signing his texts by a feminized version of his name: Mirka Vodrážková). Vodrážka interprets the matter differently from Uhl and strictly condemns Bondy, trying especially to put an end to the "Bondian myth" of a hero of underground culture. Subsequently, Vodrážka's texts roused sharp polemics See: VODRÁŽKA, Mirek, "Filosofický sendvič. Jak chutná Bondyho dílo?", https://www.advojka.cz/archiv/2015/10 /filosoficky-sendvic; VODRÁŽKA, Miroslav, "Pohromové myšlení současné české levice (k diskusi o tajné spolupráci Zbyňka Fišera alias Egona Bondyho)", http://www .bubinekrevolveru.cz/pohromove-mysleni-soucasne-ceske-levice-k-diskusi-o-tajne-spolupraci-zbynka-fisera-alias-egona; VODRÁŽKA, Miroslav, "O duchovním zelinářství", http://www.bubinekrevolveru.cz/o-duchovnim-zelinarstvi; MACHOVEC, Martin, "Ad Miroslav Vodrážka: Vodrážkův Bondy, Fišer, Kořínek... ale hlavně Vodrážkův Vodrážka", http://www.bubinekrevolveru.cz/martin-machovec-ad-miroslav-vodrazka-pohromove-mysleni-soucasne-ceske-levice-k-diskusi-o-tajne; PLACÁK, Petr, "Několik poznámek k otázce vztahu Egona Bondyho k minulému režimu" + "Jak feminista Vodrážka znásilnil básníka Egona Bondyho", *Paměť a dějiny* 9, no. 4 (2015); PLACÁK, Petr, "Cesta kanalizačními trubkami. Poznámky rázu literárního a psychologického (psychiatrického) k případu básníka Egona Bondyho a jeho vztahu k režimu v době normalizace", in KUDRNA, Ladislav (ed.), *Reflexe undergroundu*, Praha: ÚSTR, 2016.

The word underground has been used many times and the term second culture at least twice. To conclude, we should clarify what it refers to. The underground is not linked to any specific artistic movement or style although, for instance, in music it is mostly represented by rock music. The underground is a spiritual position held by intellectuals and artists who intentionally take up a critical stance towards the world they are living in. It is a declaration of war to the establishment, the existing political system. It is a movement which works primarily through artistic means but whose representatives realize that art is not and should not be the ultimate goal of artistic efforts.

And a few lines below:

It is a common and sad thing in the West, where the underground was theoretically formed and established as a movement in the early 1960s, that some artists after they had achieved acclaim and fame through it entered into contact with the official culture (we shall call it first culture for our needs), which gleefully accepted them and absorbed them like it absorbs new car bodies, new fashion or anything else. Here things are fundamentally different, **much better than in the West** [highlighted by the author of this article] because we live in an atmosphere of total agreement: the first culture does not want us and we do not wish to have anything to do with the first culture. In this way there is no temptation, which for every artist is a seed of doom: the desire for acclaim, success, awards and titles and, last but not least, material wellbeing which ensues from all of the above. While in the West, a lot of people who we might befriend here based on their thinking are living in confusion, here things have been clearly delimitated for once and for all. Nothing that we do can be to the liking of the representatives of the official culture because it cannot be used to create the illusion that all is in order. To be sure, things are not in order.

Of course, we do not have to agree with Ivan Martin Jirous that "here", that is, in Czechoslovakia in the 1970s, things were "much better than in the West" but he was right when he compared the (pseudo)values of the established societies on both sides of the Iron Curtain to the spiritual climate of the Czech underground "ghetto" of those years, which was undoubtedly much sounder than the spiritual climate of the majority societies. This community can be a model of the underground resistance, both for its radical ambition, at least for some time, to create a culture truly independent of the pseudo-culture of the totalitarian regime, without any compromises, and for the surprising variety of artistic and literary activities which emerged from this environment.

The latter of the two characteristics, the variety of the artistic activities, resulted from the former. Following the pressure of intolerance of the Czechoslovak "normalization" regime, people were driven to the underground "ghetto" who were often creative and who, under so-called normal circumstances, would be unlikely to encounter each other – and would probably have no reason to communicate with each other. In this respect, we can paradoxically thank the pro-Soviet regime of President Husák as it unintentionally became the co-author of the social and cultural variety of the Czech underground (it is obvious that this could also be said about the broader community surrounding Charter 77).

It would make no sense to demonstrate this variety of, for instance, underground literature, by presenting a short list. It suffices to mention the first underground anthologies from the 1970s.[15] At first sight these are rather heterogeneous conglomerates of texts of different poetics, for what is there in common between, for example, the fragile dreamy poetics of Věra Jirousová, drawing mainly on the work of Bohuslav Reynek and appraised by prof. Václav Černý,[16] and the satanic, nihilist, apocalyptic visions of the rocker Josef "Vaťák" Vondruška? What connects the "totally-realistic" poems, or

15) See primarily samizdat collections edited by Jirous in 1975: *Egonu Bondymu k 45. narozeninám invalidní sourozenci* [To Egon Bondy on his 45th Birthday from Disabled Siblings]; *Ing. Petru Lamplovi k 45. narozeninám* [To Ing. Petr Lampl on his 45th Birthday]. Also an anthology edited by Martin Němec in 1975: *Děti dvou sluncí* [Children of the Two Suns]. Finally an anthology edited by Pavel Zajíček in 1977: *Nějakej vodnatelnej papírovej člověk - Jiřímu Němcovi k 45. narozeninám a Martinu Jirousovi k jeho návratu z Mírova* [A Certain Dropsy Man of Paper. To Jiří Němec on his 45th Birthday and to Martin Jirous on his Return from Mírov Prison]. For a list of these and more collections see the bibliography "Nejvýznamnější samizdatové sborníky undergroundové literatury (1975-1989)", https://www.ustrcr.cz/data/pdf /projekty/underground/underground-samizdat-sborniky.pdf (quoted as of June 2019). 16) See the the first study by Václav Černý mentioned in the Footnote 7, pp. 900-908.

rather diary entries of the radical Marxist and Maoist Egon Bondy, with New Testament parables of the Protestant priest Svatopluk Karásek? What do the *zaum*, carefully polished, linguistically experimental verses by Andrej Stankovič or Eugen Brikcius, share with the sarcasm of the lyrics by Charlie Soukup? How to understand the spontaneous, "schizoid" texts of Fanda Pánek, full of so-called vulgarisms or even blasphemies? On the outside, formally, there are not many similarities, but the authors for whom the underground community was a natural background were connected by what was totally lacking in the official culture: the feeling of unity, mutual tolerance, the awareness that in the spirit of defiantly gained "complicity" something new was hopefully being created – something authentic, unalienated. And it is probably this aspect which was responsible for the specific values with which the underground community of the 1970s and 1980s contributed to Czech, or even world culture.

In conclusion, let me give you one example of how the variety and plurality of opinions, ideas and artistic approaches within the Czech underground community was reflected in the life of one of its main protagonists – the founder of the originally "Prague psychedelic band" called The Plastic People of the Universe, musician Milan "Mejla" Hlavsa (1951–2001).

In 1968, Hlavsa was one of many Prague teenagers with long hair, like many of his peers he played rock'n'roll in different amateur bands. Incidentally, he came across a record by the New York band The Velvet Underground, which was not yet very well known abroad, and their music made a great impression on him. The frontman of the band, Lou Reed, became his idol. Hlavsa put together a band with which he played songs by The Velvet Underground, but he named it after a song by another of the pioneers of the American underground, *Plastic People* by Frank Zappa, adding "of the Universe" to the title – perhaps as an allusion to John Lennon's song *Yer Blues* from the *White Album*. And by mere chance, the young art historian Ivan Martin Jirous came to see one of the gigs by The Plastic People and was captivated, immediately started cooperating with the band, wrote articles about them for artistic journals, and promoted the band's music and performances among his fellow art historians, artists and authors.

However, following the Soviet occupation in August 1968, so-called normalization started – and artists and writers who were not willing to submit to the regimentation of cultural life were very soon deprived of the possibility to work in their profession; pushed to the margins of society, their names were erased from the history of literature and arts. In the field of popular music in particular there were only a few who were able to resist and who did not disgrace themselves by complying with the requirements of the "normali-zation" regime – and soon Hlavsa's "Plastic People" became a true symbol of such resistance. However, the stronger the oppression was, the more the solidarity among the oppressed grew. Different "ghettos" and paths to the underground were established and these were the only possible way to create dissent. They were no longer a handful of crazy rockers, eccentric students and suspicious phi-losophers: in this way, solidarity was gradually stirring with the rep-resentatives of the nation's oppressed elite.

Hlavsa and his friends from the underground were in touch with leading dissident intellectuals even prior to the establishment of Charter 77 – in particular with Václav Havel and Jan Patočka, while many others such as Ludvík Vaculík, Zdeněk Mlynář, Jaroslav Seifert and even Václav Černý (though in his case undoubtedly with some reservations) manifested their solidarity with the underground as they understood that persecutions inflicted on the underground by the regime in 1976 might soon concern them as well. In 1977, the ma-jority of the underground musicians and artists joined Charter 77 out of solidarity, although the original thinking of the underground was not very close to the "legalist" principles of Charter 77, and consequently due to police terror and the manifested solidarity the underground community, disintegrated to a large extent at the turn of the 1970s and 1980s and it was only with difficulties and thanks to the younger generation that it was able to activate again in the 1980s. And as The Plastic People were not even allowed to play private concerts, they resorted to making "studio" records which were then distributed through samizdat means, or rather "magnitizdat".

For Hlavsa, the revolution in November 1989 probably came just in time as he had been fatigued by police terror in the years leading up to it and consequently finally inclined towards certain conces-

Lou Reed and Milan Hlavsa play in the White House in 1998; photo: Alan Pajer

sions, compromises – just to be able to play the music he loved.

One of the consequences of the change of the regime after November 1989 was a total disintegration of the underground community, which to a certain extent lost its *raison d'être* in the newly established state of freedom. The Plastic People stopped playing together even before, as early as 1988, which brought about much bitterness and disappointment. Hlavsa joined other bands and it looked like this chapter in the history of Czech independent culture would come to an end once and for all.

However, in 1997 Hlavsa managed to get The Plastic People together again, this time as a living legend. After that they often played at home and abroad, already as a completely professional band and releasing new music records.

In 1998, they were offered a great opportunity thanks to President Havel. They were invited by President Clinton to play for him and President Havel in the White House. Hlavsa accepted, but he also had one wish: he asked for the idol of his youth, former leader of The Velvet Underground to play with him in the residence of the US president. His wish was granted and so on 17 September 1998, to quote Bohumil Hrabal, the "unbelievable came true". Not

just The Plastic People, but also Lou Reed played in the White House! It is hard to imagine that any representative of American alternative culture or counter-culture would be able to smuggle the ill-famed New York rocker, worshipper of heroin and self-destruction, into the sanctuary of the US establishment.
Milan Hlavsa did it.

2006, 2015
Translated by Markéta Pokorná (OLDCHOOL)

3. CHARTER 77 AND THE UNDERGROUND

It is now a generally accepted, although not always sufficiently emphasised fact that the so-called trial of the Czech Underground in 1976 was one of the main impulses for the founding of Charter 77. The nineteen people arrested in March 1976, seven of whom (Havelka, Skalický, Stárek, Jirous, Zajíček, Karásek and Brabenec)[1] were convicted the following September, received the unequivocal support of the future leading Chartists, such as professor Patočka, Jaroslav Seifert, Václav Havel, Petr Uhl, and Zdeněk Mlynář.[2] And yet, Ivan Martin Jirous was the only defendant to have had a certain, albeit not very close, contact with one of the Charter founders, namely Václav Havel.[3] And it is also a well-known fact that, thanks to the solidarity of leading Czechoslovak dissidents – some of them famous abroad as well as at home – not only did a number of underground artists and activists receive much milder sentences than the despotic regime authorities had prepared for them, but also dozens and dozens of entirely unknown friends and supporters of the underground were prepared, a year later, not to leave their colleagues in the lurch, and on their account they abandoned the proverbial "merry ghetto" of the underground and joined the wider community of people working to "improve human affairs" (Comenius), even under the conditions of Husák's totalitarian "normalization" regime.

1) See "The Plastic People Of The Universe v datech", in RIEDEL, Jaroslav (ed.), *The Plastic People Of The Universe: Texty*, 2nd edition, Praha: Maťa, 2001; see also "The Plastic People Chronology" in the English translation of the book: *The Plastic People Of The Universe*, Praha: Maťa, 1999.
2) See two samizdat editions of *"Hnědá kniha" o procesech s českým undergroundem*, compiled and published in 1977 by Jaroslav Kořán and Václav Vendelín Komeda and in 1980 by Jaroslav Suk (Libri prohibiti collection); see its printed, enlarged, commented edition: *"Hnědá kniha" o procesech s českým undergroundem*, Praha: ÚSTR, 2012.
3) In the documentary film *The Plastic People of the Universe*, directed by Jana Chytilová (Czech TV 2001), Václav Havel states that he knew Jirous "a little bit from previous years, from the sixties", and only became better acquainted with him and the activities of the underground sometime around the end of 1975 and beginning of 1976, i.e. just prior to the "Second Festival of the Second Culture" held at Bojanovice and their arrest in March 1976. Before Havel met Jirous in person it was apparently František Šmejkal who recommended him to take an interest in the activities of the underground.

Before trying to elucidate the fairly complex relations that the underground established in 1976 and 1977 with the emerging community of Charter 77 signatories, I would like briefly to recall the history of the Czech cultural underground, which will make it easier to understand the mutual solidarity established in the crisis years.

Ivan M. Jirous probably provided the best explanation in his "manifesto text" entitled *Zpráva o třetím českém hudebním obrození* [Report on the Third Czech Musical Revival] dating from February 1975.[4] Jirous's *Report* is not addressed to "his own ranks" (i.e., poets, artists, and particularly rock musicians, and of course also their supporters), so much as to the wider community of Czech dissent, which was very fragmented in the mid-1970s. Being himself an intellectual he described in terms understandable to intellectuals what had been happening spontaneously for a number of years. Jirous's *Report* is also an attempt to appraise the author's own work, because it was **chiefly due to him** that one of the many groupings of the "rock and roll youth", that generation of very extravagant, non-conformist, young rockers, who, at the end of the 1960s wanted to fulfil their artistic ambitions irrespective of regime change, transformed itself by the mid-1970s into a richly structured community, which was initially pushed into the cultural underground by the doltishness of cultural policy during "normalization", but then reflecting the new situation is a given, and one that was liberating in a sense. So before 1975, the activities of the "psychedelic rock-band" The Plastic People of the Universe, a band which was then and still is a direct incarnation and synonym of the Czech cultural underground of the 1970s and 1980s, attracted the support of many creative people and intellectuals, who would hardly have been expected to have an interest in the rockers' primitivist art. Thanks to Jirous, a number of artists, particularly representatives of the so-called "Křižovnická škola" [Crusaders' School], including Karel Nepraš, Zorka Ságlová, Eugen Brikcius, Otakar Slavík and Olaf Hanel, were already interested in the Plastic People and had already taken part in some of their events, at some of which rock concerts merged into happenings organized by Brikcius

---

4) See *Magorův zápisník*, Praha: Torst, 1997, pp. 171–198 (in English published last in *Views from the Inside. Czech Underground Literature and Culture (1948–1989)*; 2nd edition, Praha: Karolinum Press, 2018. See also the last chapter of this volume.

and Ságlová, and somewhat earlier by Milan Knížák who although soon distanced himself from events organised by Jirous, continued to have a lasting spiritual and artistic influence on the underground community as is came into being. The "plastic underground" received a further very significant intellectual boost when that community became friends with the Catholic-oriented philosopher Jiří Němec and his wife, the psychologist Dana Němcová, and through them with a number of people connected with the defunct *Tvář* journal. It was Jirous who introduced the members of the Plastic People band at the beginning of the 1970s to the poet and non-conformist leftist thinker and philosopher Zbyněk Fišer alias Egon Bondy, whose verse from the 1950s and 1970s, as performed by the Plastics would be written in letters of gold in the annals of the Czech underground. Jirous also inspired the creation of several other underground bands or art and music ensembles in the early 1970s, some of which created works of lasting worth. We particularly have in mind the band DG 307, founded by the poet, musician and artist Pavel Zajíček. And it was also via Jirous that the Plastics community became close to graduates of the Protestant faculty of divinity such as Vratislav Brabenec or Svatopluk Karásek, and somewhat later Jan Kozlík, Aleš Březina or Miloš Rejchrt. And Jirous's above-mentioned *Report* was a reflection on that colourful underground community which had come into being quite unexpectedly and unprecedentedly.

However, Jirous was one of the first to be arrested in the critical year of 1976, and one of the first to be sent to prison, with the longest sentence of all: 18 months. So in addition to Jirous's *Report* there was a need for someone else to speak to people organising support for the imprisoned members of the underground community, and later to those who were coming up with the idea to found Charter 77 (to a great extent the same people), a vibrant personality who was relatively still at liberty. At this point one should stress the role played by three people above all: Václav Havel, Jiří Němec and Dana Němcová. Thanks to their personal contacts and their intellectual capabilities the latter two were able to convey the message about the underground into a language understandable not only to Václav Havel, but also to such diverse people as Ludvík Vaculík, Jan Patočka, Jaroslav Seifert, Jiří Hájek, Karel Kosík or Ladislav Hejdánek, and persuade them that it was not just worthy of their interest, but also of their involvement; that in the case of the trial of the Plastics et al., "*tua res agitur*". And **that** was successful as we know.

Now, let us explore the mutual relations between the initially underground community and the loose community around Charter 77 that was coming into being in the course of 1977. First, a couple of comments:

1) Unlike the later Charter 77 community, the underground community was essentially a group of close friends, and friends of friends, who were attracted to each other partly by a desire to "live differently", in their case as a non-conformist collective, in defiance of the "real socialism" of the "normalization" regime. It truly was a brotherhood and sisterhood of mostly young people who came together at rock gigs, concerts, festivals, seminars in private homes, poetry readings, or exhibitions, and also – quite frequently – in friendly company in pubs. Undoubtedly they were linked by a marked commitment to "passive resistance" and opposition to the world of politics reflected in adopting an anonymous lifestyle on the fringes of society. In contrast, the Charter community gradually came into being more as a fairly loose grouping of separate circles, united chiefly by their courage to stand up for human rights at a time of totalitarian tyranny. Obviously it was not possible prior to 1989 to hold a meeting for **all** of the Charter signatories, so it is highly probable that they did not know each other very well, and sometimes they had no interest in mutual acquaintance. Well, it is hard to imagine someone like the quasi-satanist underground pioneer of punk rock and a drug addict Josef "Vaťák" Vondruška, by profession a wall decorator, in discussion about the aims and orientation of the Charter with professor Václav Černý, Václav Benda or Pavel Kohout, for instance! Although they were all in the "same boat" so to speak, they were linked solely by the **civic courage** to enter the arena of their own *polis*, at a time when such an act was automatically regarded as criminal by those in power at the time. But it is evident from the above that social value preferences of the underground inevitably underwent considerable changes when that community was incorporated to a certain extent into the Charter 77 community.

2) When studying the structure of the Charter and trying to assess its social make-up, it is necessary to bear in mind that spe-

cific data about the number of signatories can be be very deceptive. The point has been made on numerous occasions that each signatory represented two, three or more non-signatories, who were *de facto* in total agreement with the activities of their signatory relatives. I have in mind, for instance, family members of signatories who often did not sign simply so that someone in the family should not be prevented from obtaining normal employment. In addition there were many people, particularly students, who were willing to sign the Charter, but refrained from doing so for their own safety at the request of "collectors of signatures" or rather after they had been warned by them. There were also cases of "non-signatories" who were active "Chartists" – dissidents, oppositionists. The following are three specific instances:[5]

a) Of the members of the Plastic People band at the end of the seventies, four (Hlavsa, Janíček, Kabeš, and Vožniak) never signed the Charter, while three (Brabenec, Brabec, and Schneider) did, although there was no difference of opinion among them, at least about this issue.

b) Jiřina Šiklová, one of the most active members of Czechoslovak dissent, and of the Charter 77 community above all, did not sign Charter 77 until the spring of 1989.

c) In January 2007, the historian Petr Blažek[6] finally published an article revealing the background to the collection of signatures in first wave after January 1977. It brought to light a whole num-

---

5) As far as the variety of such "non signatories" is concerned, see DRDA, Adam, "Ti, kteří nepodepsali (O lidech v opozici, ne-signatářích Charty 77)", in *Revolver Revue*, 33, 1997, pp. 215-224; MACHOVEC, Martin, "Polopatická impertinence", in *Kritická příloha Revolver Revue*, 8, 1997, pp. 231-235; MANDLER, Emanuel, "O hrdinech a o těch druhých", ibidem, pp. 218-231; HRDLIČKA, František – BRATRŠOVSKÁ, Zdena (eds.), *Jak chutná nezávislost. 33 životních ohlédnutí*, Praha – Olomouc, Czech Republic: Votobia, 1998; ČERNÁ, Marie, "Ti, kdo Chartu 77 nepodepsali", in *Lidové noviny*, 17th January 2017, p. 18. Concerning the case of Josef Mundil, see Anna Marvanová's article in JECHOVÁ, Květa (ed.), *Lidé Charty 77. Zpráva o biografickém výzkumu*, Praha: Ústav pro soudobé dějiny AV ČR, 2003, p. 106. The overall survey of the variety of oppositional trends in Czechoslovakia after the Soviet invasion of 1968 is found in OTÁHAL, Milan, *Opoziční proudy v české společnosti 1969-1989* [Oppositional Currents in Czech Society 1969-1989], Praha: ÚSD AV ČR, 2011.

6) See BLAŽEK, Petr, "Alchymie podpisové akce", *Lidové noviny* 20, no. 6 (8th January 2007), supplement Charta 77, pp. I-II; see also "Odpověď na nesvobodu. S Petrem

ber of oddities, but the most curious case of all that of the much revered and also vilified "guru of the underground" Zbyněk Fišer alias Egon Bondy, who would subsequently play a considerable role in the "underground fringe" of the Charter. Blažek clarifies a matter that was previously in doubt, and reveals that Fišer-Bondy **did** sign the Charter in December 1976, but at a meeting at Václav Havel's, "Jiří Němec tore up the paper with Bondy's signature, explaining that he did not regard him as legally competent. Uhl therefore created a duplicate, and made a note that it was to be held on deposit."[7] This fact allowed Fišer-Bondy in the following years to declare himself to be "an underground philosopher and poet", a colleague, and maybe even a friend of Václav Havel, and even take part as an actual Charter activist in Charter meetings (the so-called Fora) where the organisation of the Charter and its policy was debated,[8] while on other occasions he was an obdurate and hate-filled critic of the "shadow Charter establishment", cursing the Charter almost as collaborators and secret police stooges.[9]

Uhlem o ideovém rozpětí chartistů" [Conversation of Filip Horáček and Lukáš Rychetský with Petr Uhl], *A2* 3, no. 1 (2007).

7) This was confirmed by Ivan Jirous in the documentary film *Fišer alias Bondy* directed by Jordi Niubo (ČT 2000), where Jirous added that he considered it "a serious mistake". Jirous also evinced the opinion that the "censoring" of Bondy's signature by Charter 77 was "the reason for his bitterness and animosity" towards it. See also the reproduction of the duplicate in question in *Lidové noviny* 20, no. 6 (8th January 2007), supplement Charta 77, p. VI.

8) Fišer-Bondy actively participated in the 2nd (on 28th November 87), 3rd (on 17th January 88), and 4th Forum (on 14th May 88) of Charter 77; he even wrote a poem about the police raid that ended the 4th forum (dated 11th September 1988); see also: MACHOVEC, Martin, "Ediční komentář", in BONDY, Egon, *Bezejmenná*, 2nd edition, Praha: Akropolis, 2019, pp. 163–166.

9) Bondy added the following dedication to the heading of Part 8 of his samizdat *Poznámky k dějinám filosofie (Indická filosofie – pokračování)* [Notes on the History of Philosophy (Indian Philosophy – Continuation)] from 1981 (printed edition 1992 and 1997): "Dedicated to Petr Uhl and Václav Havel, who, while I was able to work, were held in prison." Most likely in 1984, i.e after Havel's release, Bondy wrote the essay *Kritika substančního modelu* [Critique of the Substantial Model] for Havel's philosophy anthology *Hostina* [Feast] (samizdat 1985, printed edition outside Czechoslovakia 1989). However, as early as 1985 Bondy's verse collection *Tragédie u Dvořáčků a jiné básně* (abridged in the two editions of his collected works under the title of *Petřiny*)

So was Jiří Němec right? And if he was, was he entitled to act the way he did in the case of Fišer-Bondy's signature? And was his motivation **really** what he said it was? When the Charter was signed in the spring of 1977 by Bondy's faithful pupil, the remarkable poet Fanda Pánek, however someone with a serious psychopathic disorder and whose personality was affected by drug addiction, no objections were raised. And there were most likely some other cases like Pánek's among the Charter signatories... So did Fišer-Bondy have grounds to be dissatisfied with the "leadership" of the Charter? These questions remain unanswered.

The above two comments give rise, among other things, to a more fundamental question, namely, who actually had or did not have the "right", even imply a "customary right" to take part in the shaping of the Charter, and subsequently who should or should not take

included a number of overtly rude texts about the Charter and Václav Havel, e.g. a poem dated 26th September 1985: "Prosral jsem životní šanci / že jsem v letech padesátých / nezpíval k tanci / Prosral jsem ji v šedesátých / že mi Literárky byly pro smích / Pak jsem ji prosral znova / že o Chartě jsem nenapsal / pochvalného slova / Proseru ji ještě do konce života / Jste pořád stejná holota" [I fucked up my chances in life / because I laughed at Literary News / Then I fucked them up again / when I failed to praise / the Charter / I'll fuck them up as long as I live / You're still the same rabble], or the poem dated 18th September 1985: "MLADÍKOVI OD DVOU SLUNCŮ L.P. 1985 // Čti – nečti / Dělej si co chceš / Nahnilost je sladká / to je tvůj život / Nadouvej si střeva důležitostí / osy světa od Hrádečku do Prahy a zpět /Čím míň let ti je tím dýl budeš moct blbnout / Už v sobotu pro tebe přijede aspoň Bundeskanzler / abys mu pomoh zařídit světovou politiku / neboť s Rusy už je amen / Američani je vymazali z mapy / Myslím / že alespoň celá střední Evropa na tebe čeká / pokud nedáš přednost zřízení Rakousko-Uherska / ovšem jen ruku v ruce se soudruhem Mlynářem ve Vídni". [TO A YOUNG MAN FROM THE TWO SUNS A.D. 1985 // Read – don't read / Do what you like / Rottenness is sweet / that's your life / Swell your guts with the importance / of the earth's axis from Hrádeček to Prague and back / The younger you are the longer you'll be able to act the fool / The Bundeskanzler is coming for you next Saturday at least / so you can help him regulate world politics / because the Russians are finished / the Americans have erased them from the map / I think the whole of Central Europe is waiting for you / unless you prefer establishment of Austria-Hungary / but only hand in hand with Comrade Mlynář in Vienna] (see E. B., *Básnické spisy III*, Praha: Argo, 2016, pp. 429, 435); however, Bondy had already made rude comments about the Charter in his prose work *677* (samizdat 1977, printed edition 2001) and most vehemently in his prose work *Bezejmenná* [Nameless] from 1986, which will be mentioned later.

part in discussions about its policy? Who was "welcome" at them? Only undisputed signatories? It is clear that the growing circle of actual signatories can be projected – initially fairly rapidly and then more slowly – onto a circle that was possibly twice as big: onto the "latent Charter support base" of "non-signatories". The same can undoubtedly be said about the underground community – or what in the 1980s should be referred to as **communities.** One sector of it overlapped with the Charter community, but its much larger support base never belonged to the signatories. The estimated **seven thousand** (!!) readers of the underground magazine Vokno, a figure established ex post by František Stárek,[10] its publisher, himself a leading Chartist, speaks for itself.

In addition to the above comments, the following is the result of our own "survey", which could help to clarify not so much the breadth or narrowness of the Charter 77 community, or the breadth or narrowness of the underground community, but rather the "social make-up" of the Charter, or the "generational diversification" within it, which were subsequently aired in controversies in the late 1980s over the form and policies of the Charter. On this matter there are two very specific figures which are of interest: a) the 242[11] original Charter 77 signatories from December 1976; b) the approximately 1,000 signatories from 1976–79.[12] Four leading Chartists, Petr Uhl,

10) Stárek's estimate is cited in Jana Růžková's thesis on *Vokno*, published as "Samizdatový časopis Vokno" in *Kritický sborník* 19, (1999–2000), pp. 193–231 (Bibliography section – estimation mentioned on pp. 195–196).

11) The number of 242 "first wave" signatories is given in the publication: PREČAN, Vilém (ed.), *Charta 77, 1977–1989*, Scheinfeld – Bratislava: Čs. středisko nezávislé kultury – Archa, 1990, p. 13; the number of 241 signatories is given in the feature about Charter 77 in *Lidové noviny* 20, no. 6 (8th January 2007), supplement Charta 77, p. III. (The same issue of *Lidové noviny* reproduced photographs of a total of 256 original "cards" with the signatures of the first signatories, i. e. there are 242 cards of the first signatories + 14 "cards" of signatories whose signatures were not supposed to be published at first, including Uhl's "duplicate" of the card signed by Zbyněk Fišer, i.e. Egon Bondy.)

12) From Charter 77's statements from 1977–79 it can be established that during that period a total 1018 people signed it. Specifically: by the end of 1977 (statements Nos. 1, 5, 8, 11 and 14) there were some 832 signatories [242 + 208 + 167 + 133 + 82] (the net figure of 167 signatories for Statement No. 8 is achieved by deducting 242 + 208 from 617 = 167); in 1978 (statements Nos. 17 and 20) 106 signatories; in

Jiří Gruntorád, František Stárek and Ivan Martin Jirous, were invited to express their opinion about the **proportion of "people from the underground" in the numbers given**.[13] It soon became clear, unfortunately, that a "survey" of this kind would not be possible without detailed preliminary research into the "personal histories" of the Charter 77 signatories, which has yet to be carried out. Only František Stárek has managed to make more extensive and specific comments on the matter.

People from the underground community were only represented minimally in the first wave of signatories of December 1976, and most of them were "underground celebrities" also known outside that circle. In addition to Jiří and Dana Němec, those signatories included Vratislav Brabenec, Věra Jirousová, Svatopluk Karásek, Jan Lopatka, Eugen Brikcius, Jan Šafránek, Aleš Březina, Olaf Hanel, and Jiří Daníček, in addition to some others who tended not to be known in dissident circles,[14] and finally – let us suppose – Fišer-Bondy. That proportion was natural and understandable.

1979 (Statements Nos. 25 and 27) 80 signatories; this accounts for the total of 1018 signatories for the initial period. Comparison with the number of new signatories 1980–1986: 1980: 48 signatories, 1981: 44 signatories, 1982: 36 signatories, 1983: 37 signatories, 1984: 25 signatories, 1985: 28 signatories, 1986: 31 signatories. At the end of the 1980s the number of new signatories once more increased sharply: 1987: 69 signatories, 1988: 111 signatories, 1989 (to 30th September) 291 signatories. These numbers are certainly not definitive as they do not take into account revoked signatures, the signatures of secret police agents, the so-called "signatures held on deposit" from the first wave, etc.

13) Our criteria for this classification are as follows: 1) people who prior to 1977 were **entirely or mostly** active in the underground community, and not in the circles of the known dissidents who subsequently set up Charter 77, with whom they subsequently came in contact particularly through the intermediary of Jiří and Dana Němec, or Ivan Jirous; 2) people who might have had (or did have) such connections, but being largely old artist friends of Jirous from the 1960s, were **mainly** active in the underground community in the early seventies (e.g. Andrej "Nikolaj" Stankovič, Věra Jirousová, Eugen Brikcius, Jiří Daníček), they were essentially intellectuals, university graduates, and qualified artists; 3) *sui generis* cases, such as Fišer-Bondy, Jiří and Dana Němec, and Jan Lopatka.

14) Jiří Mrázek, Jana Převratská, Miluše Števichová, Zdeněk "Londýn" Vokatý and Jan Schneider.

Some of the leading figures in the underground were still in prison, and none of the original "collectors of signatures" had any contact with the support base of the underground, that would require the assistance of Jirous who was still in jail. (According to Petr Uhl, Jiří Němec, then the only "collector" to have contacts with people from the Prague underground, decided at the time that at least in this **first wave** there would be no attempt to get the signatures of **those people** – again for fairly obvious reasons.) The overall proportion of signatories from the underground in the first wave was scarcely **6–7 percent.**

The very next wave, however, includes the names of the most active members of the underground community. In addition to Ivan and Juliana Jirous, they included Marie Benetková, Zbyněk Benýšek, Ivan Bierhanzl, Jan Brabec, Petr Cibulka, Jaroslav Kukal, Jan and Květa Princ, Miroslav Skalický, Karel Soukup, Andrej Stankovič, František Stárek, Ilja Storoženko, Petr Taťoun, Vlastimil Třešňák, Vladimír Voják, Dagmar Vokatá, Milan Vopálka, Josef Vondruška, Pavel Zajíček, and Jaroslav Hutka, who was getting much closer to the underground community at that time. But in addition there were dozens and dozens, possibly hundreds of supporters of the underground outside Prague, particularly in north and west Bohemia; these were people whose names meant nothing either then or now to the intellectuals who organized the Charter, and yet they showed solidarity with the Charter and deserve as much respect as the courage of the leading Prague dissidents. On the basis of the established criteria, František Stárek has managed to **identify** 164 signatories for the years 1977-79.[15] Ivan Jirous identified a fur-

15) The following is a list of **all** "underground signatories" from 1977-79 (i.e. including the seventeen in the first wave mentioned earlier), as provisionally identified on the basis of our "survey" by František Stárek (numbers in brackets refer to individual Charter statements where respective names are found: they are found only with the names that could be mistaken with other signatories of the same name found in other statements):

ther 7 signatories,[16] which amount to **22 percent** of the total for the given period, while the **overall proportion** of those signatories

Libor Albert, Ilektra Almeditu, Michaela Auerová, Vladimír Balabán, Ivan Bálek, Zdeněk Bartoš, Jozef Benedek, Marie Benetková, Zbyněk Benýšek, Ivan Bierhanzl, Pavel Blatný, Miloslav Boháček, Oto Bokroš, Jan Brabec, Petr Brousek, Zdeněk Buk, Ladislav Cerman, Vladimír Cerman, Petr Cibulka, Ivan Černega, Jiří Černega, Michal Černega, Hana Černohorská, Milan Daler, Josef Decastello, Blanka Dobešová, Antonín Dolejš, Jiří Doležal, Karel Duda, Bára Dvořáčková, Růžena Faitová, Luděk Farkaš, Jan Glanc, Viktor Groh, Richard Hamza, Karel "Kocour" Havelka, Jan Havlíček, Pavel Heřman, Štefan "Timpo" Hiroš, František Hochmann, Stanislav Homola, Miroslav "Alpín" Hrabáň, Jan Hrabina, Petr Hrach, Jan Hric, Jaroslav Hutka, František Chalupecký, Jiří Chmel, Hana Chmelová-Pípalová, Jaroslav "Šimako" Chnapko, Miroslav Ilek, Ivan Martin "Magor" Jirous, Juliana Jirousová, Zbyněk Jonák, Jaroslav Kabelka, Antonín Kamiš, Zdeněk Kazík, Jan Kindl, Michal Kobal, Josef Kordík, Jan Kozlík, Ivan Kožíšek, Jiří "Hubert" Kratochvíl (25), Karel Kraus (11), Vladimír Kroul, Jiří Křivský, Jiří Kubíček, Věra Kubíčková-Kabešová, Jaroslav Kukal, Jaroslava Kušnírová, Lilian Landová, Vendelín Laurenčík, Gabriel Levický, Jaroslav Linhart, Milan Linhart, Martin Litomiský, Vladimír "Salám" Macák, Pavel Macháček, Vratislav "Quido" Machulka, Ivan Maňásek, Vladimír Marek, Vlastimil Markytán, Petr Mašek, František Maštera, Michal Matzenauer, Jitka Matzenauerová, František Maxera, Otakar "Alfréd" Michl, Věra Mikulová, Jaroslav Mlejnek, Martina Mrázová, Vladimír Muzička, Pavel Myslín, Marcela Němcová-Kubínová, Markéta Němcová-Fialková, Pavla Němcová-Paloušová, David Němec, Ondřej Němec, Antonín Němejc, Vladimír Oborský, Jaroslava Odvárková, Jiří Olt, Pavel Opočenský, Věra Oppelová, Petr "Pinďa" Ouda, Josef Ouroda, Walter Pannc, František Pánek, Ladislav Papež, Viktor Parkán, Jan Pilnáček, Jaroslava Pilnáčková, Marcela "Mašina" Pinterová, Milan Píša, Ladislav Plíva, Antonín "Banán" Pojar, Jiří Popel, Jan Princ, Květa Princová, Petr Prokeš, Petr Ragan, Marie Raganová, Vratislav Riedl, Ivana Riedlová, Olga Rychtářová-Hochmannová, Zora Rysová, Zdenka Řeháková, Miroslav "Skalák" Skalický, Bohumír Slavík, Otakar Slavík, David Souček, Karel "Čárli" Soukup, Marie Soukupová, Andrej "Nikolaj" Stankovič, František "Čuňas" Stárek, Ilja Storoženko, Xenie Svobodová-Zavadilová, Jan Šafrata, Jan "Šejba" Šeba, Vlastislav "Wasil" Šnajdr, Petr Taťoun, Petr Tomíšek, Tomáš Toulec, Vlastimil Třešňák, Jiří Uhrín, Jan "Čágo" Unger, Jaroslav "Boví" Unger, Jaromír Urban, Jiří Vaněk (11), Josef Vaněk, Jan Velát, Vladimír Voják, Dagmar Vokatá, Josef "Vaťák" Vondruška, Milan "Dino" Vopálka, Lubomír Vydra, Robert Wittmann, Marian Zajíček, Pavel Zajíček, Ladislav Zatori, Jiří Zelenka, Jitka Zelenková, Pavel Zeman.

16) Jirous identified the following seven signatories from 1977–79 and one signatory from December 1976: Stanislav Borůvka, Luisa Geisslerová, Daniel Kumermann, Jan Litomiský, Martin Novák, Jiří Pallas (1), Jan Patočka jr., Tomáš Petřivý; Milan Kozelka subsequently drew attention to another four "underground signatories" from the same period: Jiří "Dak" Horák (17), Zdeněk Piras, Jana Pirasová, Jiří Mário Volf.

is **estimated** by Stárek and Jirous **at 40 to 45 percent**. (These estimates can be compared to the figures given by H. G. Skilling, as quoted by Milan Otáhal in *Opozice, moc, společnost 1969-1989*; Praha: ÚSD AV ČR - Maxdorf, 1994.)

Let us now consider the profile of the underground community in the 1980s, in respect to its relations with Charter 77.

It is necessary to recall at the outset that the entire Charter 77 movement lost some of its initial dynamism at the beginning of the 1980s, and a number of significant changes occurred in the community of its signatories. The years 1980-1986, i.e., up to the rise of Gorbachov, saw an addition of only 250 signatories to the initial figure of just over a thousand. The campaign of intimidation conducted by the regime and secret police, particularly the so-called *Asanace* [Decontamination] operation[17], aimed at forcing as many Charter 77 leaders and acitivists into exile, or jail them, was successful to a large extent. In addition, secret police agents joined the Charter ranks, as well as the - maybe even more morally deplorable - so-called "Charter tourists", who saw in the *Asanace* operation an opportunity to get a one-way ticket out of the country. In this connection it should be emphasised that the underground community that was partly incorporated into the Charter probably suffered more than any other "component" of the Charter from the campaign of intimidation. The following are the gravest instances:

a) Ivan Jirous was in prison during the periods 1977-79, 1981-85 and 1988-89. In addition, during the years 1985-87 he was placed under so-called "ochranný dohled" [protective surveillance], which virtually prevented Jirous from continuing his activity as the most agile organizer of underground cultural events. Although he continued to be probably the most important figure of the Czech underground, Jirous's **direct influence** on later underground and Charter developoments was naturally minimized. (Václav Havel, the main supporter of cooperation with the underground in the Charter leadership also spent the years 1979-83 in prison.)

17) Concerning operation "Asanace" see KOUTEK, Ondřej: "Akce ASANACE"; GREGOR, Pavel: "Vyšetřování akce ASANACE", *Securitas imperii*, 13, Praha 2006.

b) Constant police harassment also bore fruit subsequently. Some of the foremost underground artists, musicians and activists went into enforced exile, including Pavel Zajíček, Svatopluk Karásek, Vratislav Brabenec, Jiří Němec, Zbyněk Benýšek, Vlastimil Třešňák, Eugen Brikcius, Josef Vondruška, Karel "Kocour" Havelka, Miroslav Skalický, Karel "Charlie" Soukup, and Zdeněk "Londýn" Vokatý, as well, of course, as dozens of other less known people.

c) The last (albeit non-public) performances of the two best-known underground bands, The Plastic People of the Universe and DG 307, took place in 1979 and 1981. The country cottages where those final concerts were held were either confiscated and burnt down in terrorist operations by the secret police, StB (the Princes' house at Rychnov near Děčín, and the house of Jiří Velát at Kerhartice near Česká Kamenice), or at least confiscated from their owners (the house of Miroslav Skalický, Karel Havelka, and their friends at Nová Víska near Kadaň).[18] After Zajíček went into exile the band DG 307 fell apart; The Plastic People of the Universe continued to exist, but after 1981 gave no further performances under its name, not even in non-public venues.

d) A number of personalities who were very active in the underground community before March 1976 went into "internal exile", chiefly as a result of relentless police terror. By 1976, the underground community was far from identical to the circle of Plastic People fans from around 1970. In the words of Ivan Jirous "the faint-hearted abandoned it".[19] But far more testing times were to arrive at the end of the 1970s. We hasten to add that there could truly be many more reasons for aversion to the "Chartist incorporation" of the underground. Perhaps it should be recalled here that aversion

18) See the section: "The Plastic People of the Universe v datech" in RIEDEL, Jaroslav (ed.), *The Plastic People of the Universe: Texty*, 2nd edition, Praha: Maťa, 2001, pp. 22-23; see also Jana Chytilová's documentary film mentioned in Footnote 3.

19) In Chapter 5 of his *Report on the Third Czech Musical Revival* (Footnote 4; Paul Wilson's translation) Jirous writes about specific changes in the band's line-up at the beginning of the 1970s: "The group lost its professional status; weaker individuals left [highlighted by MM] and the core of the new Plastic People – around Hlavsa and Janíček – started off practically empty-handed with no equipment, only a few instruments and apparently nothing to fall back on [...]." That comment could apply *pars pro toto* for the whole of the underground community at that time.

to the Charter – at least at the beginning – particularly towards its ex-Communist leaders, was shared by former political prisoners of the 1950s.[20] For many "underground people", however, it was rather the case that they had an aversion to the *de facto* politicization of underground cultural activity, or a suspicion that certain leaders of the Charter simply wanted to use the underground "masses" as their "navvies" to achieve their latent political ambitions. So for various reasons, at least outwardly, some of Jirous' friends among the artists distanced themselves from the Charter-Underground community, such as Nepraš and Plíšková, as well as Milan Knížák, of course, who had adopted a critical stance towards the underground community much earlier, but also Jirous's brother-in-law, the photographer and film maker Jan Ságl, whose work before 1976 provided posterity with precious photographic documentation of underground art events.[21] By 1977 Fišer-Bondy had also withdrawn into a kind of internal exile when he started work on the enormous task, planned several years in advance, of writing his own history of philosophy, publishable in samizdat, which he entitled with excessive modesty *Poznámky k dějinám filosofie* [Notes on the History of Philosophy] (1977–1990).[22]

20) The author is grateful to Jiří Gruntorád for pointing out that the attitude of former political prisoners to Charter 77 can be gauged fairly objectively by the proportion of former members of K 231 club of the total number of signatories. Of particular interest is the discovery that in the first wave of signatures (from December 1976), which was in a certain sense "anonymous" as, apart from the "collectors" the first signatories did not know who their co-signatories were until the list was published, there was quite a high percentage of former members of K 231 club; this then fell sharply. Regarding the attitude of former political prisoners to Charter 77, see also the discussion "Byly to odlišné světy" [These were different worlds] (participants: Petr Blažek, Petr Koura, Petruška Šustrová, and Jan Wünsch), *Babylon* 16, no. 5 (2007), p. 8.
21) When working on his contribution to the publication *Alternativní kultura* (ALAN, Josef, ed.; Praha: NLN, 2001) the author spoke about this question with Jan Ságl, who said regarding his aversion to the linkage between the underground community and dissident circles something like: "Václav Havel came in one door and at that moment left by another." A similar formulation is found in Ságl's book *Tanec na dvojitém ledě / Dancing on the Double Ice*, Praha: KANT, 2013.
22) Bondy's *Poznámky k dějinám filosofie* [Notes on the History of Philosophy] were published in samizdat in the years 1977–1987; initially the author divided the work into thirteen samizdat instalments, the last of which, hypothetically the 14th instal-

e) The only further and relatively ongoing recording of underground activities, which was once so rich and varied, was left to samizdat (and "magnitizdat") projects, particularly, the magazine Vokno, which was first published in July 1979 predominantly due to the efforts of his editor František Stárek.[23] However, the secret police had some success here, as well. Stárek and his fellow editors were jailed from 1981 to 1985, and the magazine was not published during that period.

Thus at the beginning of the 1980s, the situation for the Charter and for the associated and non-associated underground communities seemed particularly hopeless. The underground community was *de facto* fragmented and shattered. The people who had most influenced underground activity were suddenly gone, the flock was scattered, biblically speaking, without a shepherd.

Things eventually changed in 1985 when Vokno resumed publication, Jirous was released from prison for the fairly lengthy period of three and a half years, and above all "the younger Czech underground generation" came on the scene, namely those associated with the newly founded magazine *Jednou nohou,* the future *Revolver Revue.* During that final phase of the Communist totalitarian regime, when unofficial events gained increasing momentum with each passing year, the Czech underground adopted a position distinct from that of the Charter. In a series of polemics on the pages of *Vokno, Revolver Revue, Infoch* and other samizdat periodicals it was again just Egon Bondy who attempted to draw a kind of "demarcation line" between the "young people in the underground", whose spokesman he seemingly felt himself authorised to be, and Charter 77, which he mockingly described as the "shadow Establishment".

ment, was never produced at the time in that form, because it was not completed until 1990. It was subsequently published as a printed edition in six volumes in the Vokno book series in 1991–1997.

23) In her aforementioned work (Footnote 10) Jana Růžková gives some specific data: issues 1 and 2 of *Vokno* came out in 1979, issue 3 in 1980, issues 4 and 5 in 1981. Issue 6 was confiscated in November 1981 and was never subsequently reconstructed and issued. Issue no. 7 then came out in spring 1985, i.e. after Stárek's release from prison in 1984, when he was still under so-called "ochranný dohled" [protective surveillance].

That phase of relations between the Charter and the underground community was recently studied by Luboš Veselý[24] and somewhat earlier by Martin Palouš[25]. To summarise the facts as we know them so far, of which the most important elements are (i) a controversy sparked in 1987 by the publication of *Dopis signatářům k 10. výročí Charty 77* [Letter to the Signatories on the 10th Anniversary of Charter 77], which, among other things set out the problems between the so-called "active core" of the Charter and its "passive majority", reflected on the Charter's "generational problem", and issued a call for the convening of a "Charter Forum"[26]; (ii) Anna Šabatová's unsuccessful attempt to have František Stárek appointed as one of the Charter 77 spokespersons, which was opposed by Petruška Šustrová, Václav Benda, and Rudolf Slánský, among others;[27] (iii) the so-called *Dopis 40 signatářů Charty 77 mluvčím* [Letter from 40 Charter 77 Signatories to Charter Spokepersons] drawn up by in August 1987 by Stárek in collaboration with Fišer-Bondy;[28] and the subsequent polemic on the pages of *Infoch* between Martin Palouš and Luboš Vydra, among others;[29] (iv) finally, the fact that all this eventually led to an agreement between Havel and Stárek to organize the so-called 2nd "Charter Forum" that was held on 28th

24) See VESELÝ, Luboš, "Underground (Charty 77)", in BLAŽEK, Petr (ed.), *Opozice a odpor proti komunistickému režimu v Československu 1968-1989* [Opposition and the Resistance against the Communist Regime in Czechoslovakia 1968-1989], Praha: Dokořán, Praha 2005.

25) See PALOUŠ, Martin, "Poznámky ke generačním sporům v Chartě 77 v druhé polovině osmdesátých let", in MANDLER, Emanuel (ed.), *Dvě desetiletí před listopadem 89* [Two Decades before November 89], Praha: Ústav pro soudobé dějiny AV ČR - Maxdorf, 1993.

26) See Charter 77 Document 3/87 (of 6th January 1987); see it also in PREČAN, Vilém (ed.), *Charta 77, 1977-1989*, Scheinfeld - Bratislava: Čs. středisko nezávislé kultury - Archa, 1990, pp. 307-322; see also OTÁHAL, Milan, *Opoziční proudy v české společnosti 1969-1989*, Praha: ÚSD AV ČR, 2011, pp.294-299.

27) See Luboš Veselý's above-mentioned study, pp. 115-116 (Footnote 24); see also KUČEROVÁ, Lenka, "Vokno do undergroundu" ("Cyklus Charta: rozhovor s Františkem Čuňasem Stárkem"), *Nový prostor* 4, no. 130 (2003), pp. 36-37.

28) See *Informace o Chartě 77* 10 , no. 10 (1987), pp. 8-10.

29) See Luboš Veselý's above-mentioned study, p. 118. In hindsight it may seem almost unbelievable that *Dopis 40 signatářů*, whose tone was friendly and almost deferential, could have provoked such a panic reaction among some of the leading Chartists.

November 1987, at which, as Veselý emphasizes, the influence of the radical "youth wing" – i.e., de facto the part of the underground supporting Stárek and Vokno – prevailed to a certain extent. To quote Veselý: "In the controversy over whether Charter 77 should convene public gatherings, the view of the more radical younger generation prevailed and a recommendation was made to the Charter spokespersons, Jan Litomiský, Libuše Šilhánová and Jan Vohryzek, that they should inform the appropriate authorities that a demonstration would be held to mark Human Rights Day on 10th December 1987."[30]

To these familiar facts, which nevertheless tend to be forgotten these days, it only remains to add a reflection on what role Egon Bondy, the self-appointed "shadow spokesperson" of the underground Chartist "faction" or wider underground support base, actually played in them. In his study, Luboš Veselý cites a source with the title *Výkaz preventivních opatření provedených útvarem čs. kontrarozvědky* [Report of preventive measures undertaken by Czechoslovak counter-intelligence],[31] which confirms the fact that in the second half of the 1980s Fišer-Bondy was repeatedly coerced by the secret police (StB) into a certain degree of collaboration, and was placed into the category of "důvěrník" [confidant] with the codename "Oskar". Veselý also quotes from that source the sentence: "In June 1987 OSKAR was directed to compile some material capable of creating controversy to be disseminated among Charter 77 circles. In July the text was prepared by OSKAR and was disseminated in August 87 by Charter 77 signatory František Stárek." Veselý also points out that by the 1980 a good number of underground and Charter activists realized that during police interrogations

30) See ibidem. The number of participants in what was in fact the first public appearance by the Chartists, albeit without official permission yet, which took place on the Old Town Square in Prague, was estimated at almost three thousand by František Stárek in the above-mentioned interview with Kučerová (Footnote 27), and he evidently considered that he and likeminded people in the Charter should take the credit for its organization.

31) In this connection Veselý refers to "a document produced by the 3rd section of Department 1 of Administration X of the National Security Corps (SNB) of 17th October 1987"; he does not state where the document is archived however, or whether it can be accessed by the public; see Veselý's above-mentioned study p. 117.

Fišer-Bondy "committed many indiscretions, although they knew nothing about his direct collaboration with the secret police". He concedes, however, that the *Letter from 40 Charter 77 Signatories* was truly Stárek's initiative, that Fišer's "controlling officer" could simply have "taken credit" for it, and most importantly, that if the StB were planning – particularly as part of "Operation Wedge"[32] – to sow dissension in the Charter community by using Fišer-Bondy, for instance, or by taking advantage of Stárek's enthusiasm – **they failed in their aim**, and in fact had the opposite effect. At its "2nd Forum", the Charter was markedly radicalised, and the "passive majority" became active. So it would only be a slight exaggeration to say that for the second time underground activists provided the dissident intellectuals with a stimulus that gave rise to major events – the events of 1987–88 that culminated in November 1989.

By now it is clear that Fišer-Bondy's actual contribution to those events will never be totally clarified, because part of his file, which documented his collaboration with the StB in that final period, was allegedly shredded. However, in this connection it is worth recalling a number of lesser known facts.

It is possibly no exaggeration to say that in the second half of the 1980s Bondy was the most active member of the old underground guard, being the only remaining underground intellectual who still felt like theorising about the "mission of the underground". Jirous simply didn't have the time or space to do anything like that, and all the others who could and should have had something to say about it were in exile. And it is undeniable that "Bondy the poet" enjoyed truly enormous authority among the younger underground generation, in spite of the fact that even in the period 1976–77 (when, as would eventually emerge after 1989, he really didn't collaborate with the StB, and on the contrary was classified as a "hostile person") he was willing to divulge far too much during police interrogations.[33] It was due to his natural plebeian behaviour, and

---

32) Regarding it see ŽÁČEK, Pavel, "Celostátní projekt 'Klín'" [Nation-wide Operation 'Wedge'] *Securitas imperii*, 1, Praha 1994, pp. 60–87.

33) The first person to draw attention to this was Ivan Jirous in 1979 in his essay "Zasadil jsem vám osiku, pane doktore!" [I've planted you an aspen tree, Doctor!] in which he writes specifically: "When they were 'closing the file' and I was reading the testimonies by over a hundred people, which it contained, the only testimony

his readiness to listen to absolutely anyone who visited him, even a totally unknown budding samizdat author, as Petr Placák, Jáchym Topol, and J. H. Krchovský, among others, have testified.[34] But it was also the legend about him, the legend of a poet who, as he himself said, was "in the underground since 1948", his uncompromising stance on matters of art and publication, his gift of perceiving problems from a perspective that was broader than just a few years or decades, and, when all is said and done, his charm, spontaneity, and diligence. It was his poetry that truly influenced almost every author of the underground. The pages of *Vokno* were always open to Bondy, so that at one time it looked as if Bondy was willing to turn the magazine into something like his "notebook"; he was also welcome at *Revolver Revue*. However, as his resentment against the Charter's "shadow Establishment" gradually increased and became almost paranoid, his "young friends" were no longer willing to mutely swallow it. Significant in this respect was his polemic with Ivan Lamper regarding just three chapters of Bondy's prose work *Bezejmenná* [Nameless] (samizdat 1986, printed edition 2001)[35]: "Na Žabinci" [In the Frogpond Pub], "Plovárna" [Swimming Pool] and "VOKNO". In passages inserted into texts with totally different subject-matter, Bondy – not for the first time, but now with extreme passion and indiscriminately – attacked the "shadow Establishment" of the Charter, and in particular its "pro-American wing"; he also criticised "the detachment of the local dissidents" from the current

that shocked me was Bondy's. He was the only one to betray every little thing to them. Not only did he tell them everything he knew, and everything they asked, he told them much more, and at that time I couldn't find the words to qualify his treachery." In the same essay, however, he had high praise for Bondy's poetry, prose, and philosophical essays. Those reflections should still be regarded as the starting point for any further study of Bondy's literary oeuvre. The essay is included in *Magorův zápisník*, Praha: Torst, 1997, pp. 419–430.

34) Bondy is spoken of in this way by Placák, Krchovský, Topol and several others, including in Jordi Niubo's documentary film *Fišer alias Bondy* (see Footnote 7); Krchovský writes about Bondy's intense influence on his work in the afterword to the publication of his juvenilia; see "Doslov (pokračovatele) autora", in /KRCHOVSKÝ/, J. H., *Mladost - radost...*, Brno (Czech Republic): Větrné mlýny, 2005.

35) The 2nd printed edition (Praha: Akropolis, 2019) of the book contains detailed comments on the facts and pseudofacts found in the three discussed chapters.

problems of Czech youth, having promoted himself to be their tribune; elsewhere he mocked those who were attached to civil liberties, and he developed a theory – which was a fairly overt defence of the Soviet system – that the "age of freedom" – i.e. the age of human rights – is over". Certain passages of those texts actually assume the form of pamphlets whose content is almost denunciatory. Lamper – under the pseudonym Horna Pigment – responded very vehemently on the pages of Issue 6 of *Jednou nohou / Revolver Revue* (1987) in an article "Zpívá hlasitě, ale falešně" [He sings loudly, but out of tune].[36] This was not only the first attempt to criticise Bondy by an author from the circle of underground journalists, but indeed **the first radical and detailed critique** of his attitudes to the Charter (and also his literary output of the previous years), which was possibly no less a shock for Bondy's devotees than the *Letter from 40 Signatories* was for leading Chartists a year later. The polemic had three interesting ramifications:

1) About a year after his critique of Bondy on the pages of *Revolver Revue*, Lamper spoke at a meeting of Chartist writers at Ivan Klíma's (1988),[37] where they discussed contributions to the samizdat magazine *Obsah*. Surprisingly, he criticised the writers as being elitist, attention-seeking, and inward-looking, using expressions that could have been borrowed from Bondy's "ideological arsenal". His arguments were suddenly fully in tune with the *Letter from 40 Signatories*.[38] These abrupt shifts of opinion in one of the most influential editors of the *Revolver Revue* are evidence, at the very least, of how rapidly and dynamically opinions about the actual mission of the dissident formations – the latent opposition in totalitarian Czechoslovakia in the late 1980s – started to polarize and be refined.

2) The text of the relevant passage (in the chapter titled "VOKNO") in Bondy's *Nameless* certainly does beg the question: where did the author's sudden hatred spring from, all that almost fren-

---

36) This article is included in the documentation section of the anthology ALAN, Josef (ed.), *Alternativní kultura*, Praha: NLN, 2001, pp. 550–556.

37) See the documentary film used in the 4th episode of Andrej Krob's TV serial *Samizdat*, Czech Television, 2002.

38) It is worth noting that among those present Karel Pecka reacted with irritation, Ludvík Vaculík with irony verging on self-irony, while Václav Havel was the only one to respond dispassionately and with understanding.

zied detestation of the Charter's leaders? (It must be noted that Bondy had only conciliatory words for his old friend Petr Uhl.) It also unfortunately begs the question: *cui bono?* in respect of it all. But maybe the study even of documents such as these can help clarify something of the internal mental development, and ideological diversification in the history of Czech dissent in general and the Charter in particular.

3) It is also remarkable that some of the wording of the *Letter to the Signatories on the 10th Anniversary of Charter 77* reacts to a certain extent to some of the rebukes voiced by Bondy in *Nameless*, although there is naturally no specific reference in the *Letter* to the passages in question. We have in mind the reflections on the need for "generational renewal", the effort to involve more of the Charter's "passive majority", such as by means of the proposed organisation of "Charter Fora". It cannot be ruled out, of course, that Bondy helped through his work to create different currents of opinion in the Charter, albeit his original intention might have been something quite different, that his infamous text helped write the last chapter in the history of the remarkable and sometimes contradictory symbiosis of the Charter 77 and underground communities.

2007
Translated by Gerald Turner

4. IDEOLOGICAL ORIENTATION AND POLITICAL VIEWS AND STANDPOINTS OF REPRESENTATIVES OF CZECH UNDERGROUND CULTURE, 1969-1989 (UNDERGROUND AND DISSIDENCE - ALLIES OR ENEMIES?)

The political, ideological orientation of Czech or Slovak representatives of the underground movement that existed in the country during the decades of totalitarian system can be adequately interpreted only within the framework of the political ideas of the entirety of Central and East European dissidence. As there have already been published many works written by eminent British, Canadian or American historians (some of whom will be quoted later on) who have dealt with these and related topics, let me only remind you of some of the obvious implications that seem to be relevant to us.

When looking back at the dissident movements that existed behind the Iron Curtain in the 1970s and 1980s, or even earlier, we cannot ignore:

a) The rich ideological variety that existed within each East European dissident group despite the fact that each of them were labelled by the Communist Party bosses and their henchmen as "hopeless efforts by isolated individuals in the pay of Western imperialists", as "anti-Soviet activity", "anti-socialist", "anti-working class plots" on the one hand – and on the other, in the West, as "democratic", "anti-totalitarian", "freedom-loving" movements – regardless of their actual aims and ambitions.

b) The fact, that in each Central and East European country in which a dissident movement existed at least in its embryonic phase, the political and ideological ambitions of such movement were largely subject to the political and social structure that existed in each of the respective countries before the establishment of the communist regime. Such revivals of local traditions in some cases rather contradicted what the West supposed were the freedom-loving, pro-democratic character of all dissident, anti-communist movements. Moreover, some of them were headed by the ex-Communist Party proponents and apparatchiks, which often lead to misunderstanding and bitterness on the side of more naïve western supporters of these movements.

c) The weak democracies in Central European countries, including today's Czech Republic and the truly pseudo-democratic system in today's Russia can be perceived as sad evidence of such historic developments.

Just a few examples: the complete lack of any experience with a pluralistic, democratic system in pre-revolutionary Russia enabled not only the smooth establishment of Stalinism with all its consequences, but also the ideological orientation of a number of its opponents. The Russian (or Soviet) dissidence comprised anti-Semitic, racist, chauvinistic tendencies, often idealizing the heritage of Russian Orthodox church, sometimes even denouncing "the rotten West" with the same vehemence as the Communist Party propaganda – suffice to recall Aleksandr Solzhenitsyn.

The dissident movement in Poland faced similar problems resulting from the country's pre-war political regime: the strong nationalistic, anti-Russian, anti-German, anti-Semitic, religious, Roman Catholic tradition often contradicted the ambitions of true democrats among Polish dissidents.

In Slovakia, there were attempts among the few local dissidents to glorify the Clerical Fascist regime that existed in the country during WW II.

The GDR dissidents, as far as their ideological orientation was concerned, were mostly subject to the political development in West Germany, or at least they had to put up with it, a fact that more or less guaranteed their democratic orientation. Nevertheless, there also existed another social undercurrent in the GDR, which resulted in a neo-Nazi movement in "neue Bundesländer" after German re-unification.

Seen in such a context, the Czech Lands, i.e., the Czech-speaking part of Czechoslovakia, with its relatively strong pre-war democratic, pluralistic tradition, was rather exceptional in the history of the dissident movement behind the Iron Curtain: the Charter 77 movement being perhaps the best example of such heritage. It is a well-known fact that Charter 77 united a large number of Czech and Slovak dissidents of the most varied denomination and of very different political backgrounds and affiliations, starting with former Communist Party members such as Ludvík Vaculík, Jiří Dienstbier or Pavel Kohout, or even ex-apparatchiks such as Jiří Hájek, Jaroslav Šabata or Zdeněk

Mlynář, through non-communists or democrats of Masaryk's persuasion (e.g., Jan Patočka, Václav Černý, Václav Havel), via genuine anti-communists (e.g., Karel Pecka and most of the former political prisoners of the 1950s), to Catholic priests (e.g., Josef Zvěřina) and even to some non-communist leftists (e.g., Petr Uhl or Jiří Müller) – but definitely no persons burdened with racist or fascist heritage.

Perhaps only such a rich variety of Czech and Slovak dissidents, who came to be united by their aversion and resistance to this totalitarian, fundamentally anti-pluralistic, anti-democratic, and, as a matter of fact, anti-socialist regime could be ready to incorporate the Czech musical underground community and its culture.

Since quite a lot of attention from the side of historians has already been given:

a) to the variety of cultural activities of the Czech underground community existing within the given delimitation: i.e., activities developing not only in rock music, but also in the field of literature, arts, samizdat book production, journalism and so on;

b) to the dominant ideas, main political views and standpoints of the best known representatives of Czechoslovak dissidence within the given period, especially to the most important and influential part of it, as it was represented by the Charter 77 movement, we would like to concentrate our attention on less well-known ideas, views and standpoints of "spiritual leaders" of Czech underground culture, which cannot by any means be identified with the views prevailing in the Charter 77 movement because at the very least the underground movement preceded the foundation of Charter 77 by several years.

Now, within the scope of Czech underground culture there occurs an issue of primary importance, that has to be answered first of all: What was really meant by the notion of "underground" by those who coined it? Because if the concept "underground" were only to serve as a label for a certain style of music or certain orientation in the arts and literature, we would hardly have any matter to discuss. However, the English term "underground" as it was being used in Czech culture undoubtedly referred to a specific world view, a specific orientation in life; it was to denote a specific system of values, all of which can be adequately interpreted and evaluated only within a concrete social and political framework.

What is mostly understood by the notion of "underground culture" in Czechoslovakia within the two decades between 1969–1989 follows from the characteristics, or if you like a delimitation, given by Ivan Martin Jirous, one of the leading figures of the Czech underground movement, in his manifesto *Zpráva o třetím českém hudebním obrození* [Report on the Third Czech Musical Revival], written and published in samizdat in 1975[1]. The English term of the so called "underground" can only be applied to a certain part of independent, anti-totalitarian, unofficial cultural activities: i.e., those that can be traced and identified in the community that had gradually gathered around the rock group The Plastic People of the Universe during the first half of the 1970s and which went on to be surprisingly productive until the end of the 1980s. Looking more closely at Ivan M. Jirous's *Report*, his "manifesto" of 1975, we can identify a survey of some previous ideas and views that the author found instrumental for the formulation of his own ideas with the help of which he managed to express the leading principles of the Czech underground movement. Thus, we should first discuss the ideas of Jirous' "underground forerunners" on the one hand, and those parts of the ideological background of the given era that generated such ideas and subsequently led to the main principles of Czech underground culture on the other.

It is undeniable that it was the entirety of the "cultural revolution" of the 1960s of which the Beat generation in the U.S., or the post-war French or German Existentialists were only early signals, that in its most radical modifications led to a certain kind of re-evaluation of traditional Western values. It was not just the 1960s in the West, but partially in what was then "the East", too, that saw massive changes in the established system of values. Let me only remind you of the immense role of the innovations in aesthetics and in the whole of the life-style as started by rock'n'roll music, the Beatles, the hippies, "flower power", the drug culture, that later generated

1) The text was first published in English (in Paul Wilson's translation) in *The Merry Ghetto*, a catalogue added to the record *The Plastic People... Prague. Egon Bondy's Happy Hearts Club Banned*, London – Paris: Boží Mlýn & SCOPA Invisible Production, 1978; most recently in *Views from the Inside. Czech Underground Literature and Culture (1948–1989)*, Praha: Ústav české literatury a literární vědy FF UK, 2006; 2nd edition: Praha: Karolinum Press, 2018.

more selfconscious anti-war movements, the so-called "sexual revolution", various anti-establishment movements, the ideas of cultural "autonomy", early environmentalist and ecological movements, left-wing, anarchistically oriented university disruptions, Abbie Hoffman's and Jerry Rubin's Yippies and so on – as far as the ideas of cultural "underground". And all of them could be understood as attempts at creating independent, "autonomous", non-alienated social "substructures".

Indeed, the 1960s represented a fantastic cultural and ideological ferment the importance of which was later on deliberately blurred by the world of show-business and fashion, although it is also a well-known fact that not all the ideas generated by the 1960s were necessarily those of an anti-dogmatic, anti-indoctrination character. Nevertheless the vague, but certainly not politically indoctrinated, brotherhood and sisterhood of long-haired hippies for the most part proved to be quite influential in promoting tolerance and re-evaluating values, in its effort to defy the political and cultural establishment of the day. And it was exactly such spontaneous ideas that formed the cultural background when the Czech underground movement began to take shape.

Therefore, if we were to trace the most important sources of ideas that gave the decisive impetus to the Czech underground movement, instead of studying various theories of the so-called "counter-culture" we had better look for the ideas rendered: e.g., in lyrics and music by Lou Reed, Ed Sanders and Tuli Kupferberg, or David Peel. Almost the entire world of Czech underground was predicated in songs such as *I'm Beginning to See the Light* by the Velvet Underground, *Everybody's Smoking Marijuana* by David Peel, or *Nothing* or *How Sweet I Roamed from Field to Field* by the Fugs. Had it not been such a spontaneous movement lacking any concrete political programme, the Czech underground movement, like other movements both in the West and in the East, would have never built on its strength and endurance and could never have become so varied.

However, as is usual in all social and cultural movements, even the so-called underground communities generated theoreticians who attempted to formulate the "guidelines" for such movements.

Ivan M. Jirous in his above-mentioned *Report on the Third Czech Musical Revival* mentions e.g., some of Jeff Nuttall's ideas in the book *Bomb Culture* (1968)[2], then, of course, he quotes the well-known, though somewhat enigmatic words by Marcel Duchamp about how "the great artist of tomorrow will go underground", and he also paraphrases some statements by Ralf-Rainer Rygulla whom he mentions directly in one of his articles written as early as 1969[3]. Yet one more important source of ideas that might have inspired him to formulate some of his own thoughts about the underground culture was the book *Do It!* by Jerry Rubin (1970)[4]. It is known from other sources that Jirous was acquainted with Rubin's book as early as the beginning of the 1970s. Since it is especially Duchamp and Rygulla whose ideas seem to be most influential, we should have a closer look at their texts quoted or paraphrased by Jirous, also because they no longer seem to be very well known nowadays.[5]

Marcel Duchamp himself recalls the moment when he uttered his famous statement in Philadelphia in 1961 in a conversation with Jean Neyens, which took place only four years later, i.e., in 1965, and in which he said: [...] on m'avait demandé "Où allons-nous?" Moi j'ai simplement dit: "Le grand bonhomme de demain se cachera. Ira sous terre." En anglais c'est mieux qu'en français: "Will go underground." Il faudra qu'il meure avant d'être connu [...][6].

Duchamp's idea actually emphasizes the necessity for artists, providing they really want to remain actual artists, to be unknown,

2) NUTTALL, Jeff, *Bomb Culture*, New York: Delacorte Press, 1968.
3) JIROUS, Ivan M., "The Primitives Group - česká tvář undergroundu", *Sešity pro literaturu a diskusi* 4, no. 30 (1969), pp. 49–50; see also idem, in *Magorův zápisník*, Praha: Torst, 1997, pp. 692–696.
4) RUBIN, Jerry, *Do It! Scenarios of the Revolution*, New York: Simon and Schuster, 1970.
5) Not only in Jirous's texts of the 1970s and 80s, but also in texts of any other Czech underground (samizdat) writers of those decades there is no mention of perhaps the most prominent theoretician of the western "counter-culture", Theodore ROSZAK, especially of his book *The Making of a Counter Culture* (New York: Doubleday, 1969). Roszak's ideas, the fact he saw the principal evil in modern technocracy rather than in communism, fascism or any other kind of traditional ideology, might have been close to Czech dissidents and underground writers.
6) See http://www.toutfait.com/issues/volume2/issue_4/interviews/md_jean/md_jean.html

to escape the attention of the world of commerce, of a market economy, but his idea perfectly corresponds with one of the principal concerns of the Czech underground community that had to try to escape the attention of other "devils" in the 1970s.

As far as Ralf-Rainer Rygulla is concerned, the passage that roused Jirous' interest is found in his epilogue written for an anthology of an Anglo-German collection of underground poetry published first in Darmstadt in 1968 under the title *Fuck You! Underground Gedichte*[7]. There he says among other things: "Der von Ed Sanders geforderte 'totale Angriff auf die Kultur' kann nicht durch systemimmanente Kritik erfolgen, sondern durch Kritik von außen, d.h. von Kriminellen, Süchtigen und Farbigen [...] Die Leute vom Underground haben erkannt, daß innerhalb der Legalität nichts mehr verändert kann." Jirous' concept of the so-called "second culture" was undoubtedly strongly influenced by some of Rygulla's ideas.

Now, as far as Jirous' *Report on the Third Czech Musical Revival* is concerned a few preliminary remarks seem to be necessary: Jirous wrote the text in February 1975: i.e., at a moment when the Czech underground movement was in full swing, so to say. Therefore, being one of the "fathers" of the entire movement, he probably felt obliged not only to offer a kind of the "theoretical defence" of the movement, but also to describe it in terms comprehensible to other formations or groupings of Czechoslovak dissidence, a fact which actually made out of his *Report* one of the first attempts at opening a dialogue within the whole of the Czechoslovak "unofficial world". Jirous' *Report* thus mostly contains a description of the variety of the underground community's artistic activities, and the "ideological aspects" are only included as an addendum: undoubtedly due to the fact that they did not play a very important role. Nevertheless, they are found there and can be summed up in the following quotation[8]:

I have often used the term "underground" and twice the term "second culture". In conclusion, we should make clear what this is. In Bohemia,

---

7) RYGULLA, Ralf-Rainer (ed.), *Fuck You! Underground Gedichte*, Darmstadt: Josef Melzer Verlag, 1968; 2nd edition: Frankfurt/M.: Fischer Taschenbuch Verlag, 1980.
8) See *Views from the Inside,* op. cit., p. 30–31.

the underground is not tied to a definite artistic tendency or style, though in music, for example, it is expressed largely through rock music. The underground is a mental attitude of intellectuals and artists who consciously and critically determine their own stance towards the world in which they live. It is the declaration of a struggle against the establishment, the regime. It is a movement that works chiefly through the various art forms but whose representatives are aware that art is not and ought not to be the final aim of an artist's efforts. The underground is created by people who have understood that within the bounds of legality nothing can be changed, and who no longer even attempt to function within those bounds. Ed Sanders of the Fugs put it very clearly when he declared a total "attack on culture".

This attack can be carried out only by people who stand outside that culture. [...] Two absolutely necessary characteristics of those who have chosen the underground as their spiritual home are rage and humility. Anyone lacking these qualities will not be able to live in the underground. It is a sad and frequent phenomenon in the West, where, in the early 1960s, the idea of the underground was theoretically formulated and established as a movement, that some of those who gained recognition and fame in the underground came into contact with official culture (for our purposes, we call it the first culture), which enthusiastically accepted them and swallowed them up as it accepts and swallows up new cars, new fashions or anything else. In Bohemia, the situation is essentially different, and far better than in the West, because we live in an atmosphere of absolute agreement: the first culture doesn't want us and we don't want anything to do with the first culture. This eliminates a temptation that for everyone, even the strongest artist, is the seed of destruction: the desire for recognition, success, the winning of prizes and titles and last but not least, the material security which follows.

In the West many people who, because of their mentality, would perhaps belong among our friends, live in confusion. Here the lines of demarcation have been drawn clearly once and for all. Nothing that we do can possibly please the representatives of official culture because it cannot be used to create the impression that everything is in order. For things are not in order.[...] The aim of the underground here in Bohemia is the creation of a second culture: a culture that will not be dependent on official channels of communication, social recognition, and the hierarchy of values laid down by the establishment; a culture which cannot have the destruction of the establishment as its aim because in doing so, it would drive itself into the establishment's embrace [...]

As Jirous is quite explicit in his characteristic of what he calls "underground" and "second culture" not much comment on the quoted passage seems necessary. It is obvious that Jirous was trying to compose a kind of "underground apology" by employing the theoretical arsenal of some of his predecessors. His concept of the "second culture" seems to be influenced by Rygulla's postulate: in its stress upon the necessity of its becoming absolutely independent of the so-called "first", i.e. the established culture, a fact which met with criticism on the side of some Czechoslovak dissidents, and even on the side of some of his underground colleagues. Also his preference for the "situation in Bohemia", i.e. in Czechoslovakia, must have raised a few eyebrows, to say nothing of his "millenarian", "chiliastic" vision of the future of the country ("lines of demarcation drawn once and for all").

However, the political and cultural situation in the mid 1970s in Czechoslovakia seemed so hopeless that Jirous' radical standpoints were welcomed by many of his friends as legitimate and justifiable. One of the natural consequences of such radicalism was of course the impossibility of opening any dialogue with the representatives of the "first culture", to say nothing of the "representatives of power". On the other hand, it became apparent that there was a danger of the underground community getting close to some religious sectarians living in seclusion from the majority of society.

Jirous' radical, almost extremist ideas were akin to the poet and philosopher Egon Bondy, who next to Jirous is probably the most influential of all Czech underground writers. Moreover, he was active in producing political and social theories and hypotheses. Bondy's case was unique and is relatively well-known today since dozens of his books have already been published in Czech, some of them also in translations into foreign languages[9]. Having published all his poetry and most of his philosophy since the late 1940s only

9) In English, see e.g. *The Merry Ghetto*, op. cit.; "Cellar Work" [an excerpt from a novella + selected poems], *Yazzyk Magazine*, no. 1 (1992); "Berta. Part Three. Section XXII" [an excerpt from a novella], *Yazzyk Magazine*, no. 4 (1995); *The Plastic People of the Universe*, Praha: Maťa, 1999; *The Consolation of Ontology. On the Substantial and*

in samizdat and having always declared himself a radical Marxist of an anti-Soviet line, i.e. first as a Trotskyist, later on as a Maoist, Bondy was an extremely rare bird in the world of Czechoslovak dissidence. His opposition to any kind of political establishment, his utopian / dystopian interpretation of radical leftist trends brought him to the underground community as early as the beginning of the 1970s – and he soon became a kind of a "living legend" there.

His provocative "anti-poetic", "totally realistic" poems were set to music by The Plastic People, and his dystopian novel *Invalidní sourozenci* [The Disabled Siblings][10], written in 1974, became a sort of a "holy scripture" for the Czech underground community of the 1970s. In the novel, Bondy presents his vision of a distant future, where there would be no more bonds and communication between the majority society and the minority society of underground people who would have managed to establish a community absolutely independent of a future version of the "first culture" of consumers and warmongers. In the situation of the country's isolation during the 1970s, Bondy's fiction exerted a powerful influence on the underground community with its prophetic, visionary aspects. No wonder Bondy was one of those figures of the underground community who could not cope with the "minimalist", law-obeying principles of Charter 77 and became one of its critics and even denounced the alleged "shadow establishment" of Charter 77 in the later years and instead was ready to offer his own, somewhat confused ideas of what we could call "undergroundism" by which he tried to renounce and denounce everything but the underground culture itself.[11]

Nonsubstantial Models, Lanham – Boulder – New York – Oxford: Lexington Books, 2001.

10) The novel was first published in Czech by the Toronto-based Czech publishing house Sixty-Eight Publishers (1981), and later three times in Czechoslovakia / Czech Republic (last time: Praha: Akropolis, 2012). It was translated into Italian as *Fratelli invalidi*, Milano: Eleuthera, 1993; into German as *Die Invaliden Geschwister*, Heidelberg: Elfenbein, 1999; also into Slovenian as *Invalidna sorojenca*, Vnanje Gorice: Police Dubove, 2017; parts of it were also translated into Polish and Hungarian.

11) Bondy did so in the 1980s in some articles that he published in the underground samizdat magazine Vokno, and was especially explicit about it in his novel *Bezejmenná* [*Nameless*], 1986; first published in samizdat in the same year, first published by regular printing presses only in 2001, next in 2019 in a commented edition (Praha:

Nevertheless even with such ideas, rather than with his own version of political radicalism of a Maoist orientation, Bondy did represent a part of the Czech underground community in its political or social ambitions, although it must be noted he became largely popular not because of these, but because of his excellent poetry, his sense of humour and self-irony otherwise so rare in thinkers of his kin. On the other hand, for a part of the more conservative figures of Czechoslovak dissidence, Bondy represented the very incarnation of the dreaded underground community with which the "decent dissidents" should have nothing in common.

However, it would be one-sided if Bondy's and Jirous' views were to be presented as only aimed at an apology of a kind of "splendid isolation" of the underground community, thus indeed echoing, recalling some kind of millenarian sectarians. In a number of his poems, even essays and treatises, Bondy provocatively and directly calls for an immediate overthrow of the totalitarian regime, of "Soviet Fascism" – and not only in Czechoslovakia or in the Soviet block, but everywhere in the world: he demands the immediate initiation of what used to be called "world revolution" and the establishment of real, "direct" democracy in the name of the salvation of all humanity, renouncing all versions of "class society" and "exploitation of human labour".

For example, in his text titled *Tzv. "Březnová báseň 1971", čtená na veřejném shromáždění* [The So-Called "March Poem 1971" – Read at a Public Gathering, 1971][12] he says among other things:

When I was twenty they executed Záviš Kalandra / who was then more to me than my own father / A few years later they nearly executed me / and now Petr Uhl and thirteen other comrades / have been convicted and

Akropolis): here his self-appointed defence or apology of "underground autonomy" and his criticism were mostly addressed to the supposed "shadow establishment" of Charter 77. On the other hand, his apology met with negative reactions from some underground essayists and reviewers themselves - e.g. Ivan Lamper or Alexandr Vondra at that time writing mostly for the underground magazine *Revolver Revue*.
12) See the Czech original in *Básnické dílo Egona Bondyho VII - Básnické sbírky z let 1971-1974*, Praha: Pražská imaginace, 1992, pp. 40-43; also in *Básnické spisy II - 1962-1975*, Praha: Argo, 2015, pp. 346-351; see the English translation by Anna Bryson + Jana Klepetářová, *Yazzyk Magazine*, no. 1 (1992), pp. 20-23.

are on their way to Jáchymov / again only because they are Marxists all of them / my comrades who with me / unmask the state-capitalist system – that creature of the Soviet Union – / and the colony that's called our own country / only because they are Marxists / and point the finger at the base alliance of international state capitalists / and our total enslavement [...] True – it is clearly impossible to start fighting with your bare hands and right out of nowhere / but whoever remains a human being / must be ready from this day and this hour / because the state-capitalist regime has to be destroyed / only don't ever again allow yourselves to be pushed around by professional apparatchiks – like in 1968 – / by those Svobodas, Dubčeks and Černíks / who (why should they?) don't really want to change a regime which created them – a regime they live off / You must always be aware that socialism / is no more and no less / than society organized for self-government / and so all powers are in your hands / if you will only use them / And take to heart at this moment / the words of Mao Tse-Tung / that liberation cannot come from above / people can only liberate themselves – and from below / while from above they gain nothing but the yoke [...] You sixty-year-olds – drag yourselves straight to the crematoria and take your place in the line / you forty-year-olds – may you watch your genitals rot away just like the genitals of your wives and nauseating lovers / you twenty-year-olds – go and hang yourselves right away / if you won't start preparing yourselves this very day and every day for war war war / war and war against the criminals / who otherwise will screw you any way they choose [...].

Looking back at such revolutionary proclamations we can hardly decide if their author really meant them or if he wrote them as a kind of a "reminder" of a "historic task of humankind" that would inevitably have to be accomplished one day in the future. One way or another, there is no doubt Bondy's voice was "crying in the wilderness" of Czechoslovak dissidence in the 1970s and 1980s and met with little understanding even from his underground fans and readers. Together with his later ideas of "undergroundism", as we have called them for our purpose, they were considered to be interesting, perhaps even inspiring – though mostly in the metaphoric sense of the word. Sometimes they were even mocked and parodied.

Nevertheless, even Ivan M. Jirous, although always remaining Catholic by faith, exhibited some understanding for Bondy's extremist political radicalism, thus contradicting somewhat his own postulates of creating the "splendid isolation" of an independent "second culture". He used the following quotation from Mao Tse-Tung as the epigraph of his *Report* of 1975: "In the great cultural revolutions there is only one way for the people – to free themselves by their own efforts. Nothing must be used that would do it for them. Believe in people, rely on them and respect their initiative. Cast away fear! Don't be afraid of commotion. Let people educate themselves in the great revolutionary movement."

Moreover, in the final passage of his *Report*, some parts of which have already been quoted, Jirous writes: "Briefly put, the underground is the activity of artists and intellectuals whose work is unacceptable to the establishment and who, in this state of unacceptability, do not remain passive, but attempt through their work and attitudes to destroy the establishment."

On the whole, we could probably agree with statements by Ivan M. Jirous, Milan Hlavsa, Vratislav Brabenec and by several other representatives of the Czech underground said on several occasions after 1989[13] – they argued that the Czech underground really had no political platform and no political programme. They really only wanted to do "their own thing" – play music for their limited audience, publish their texts in samizdat editions, and enjoy their own way of life. Unfortunately, however, they were compelled to become politically radicalised because of the totalitarian regime's intolerance and brutal oppression. However, their radicalism did not lead to a kind of a "world revolution" but rather to the activities of the defenders of human rights in Charter 77.

Jirous' and Bondy's ideological and political radicalism also found a necessary counterweight in Christian ideas (or perhaps their radicalism was channelled by them). They were rendered by other writers of the underground community, especially the protestant priest Svatopluk Karásek and his ex classmate, the musician and composer Vratislav Brabenec; Karásek used to address the underground community with his gospel songs, actually Biblical parables and similes set to music, making their eternal messages comprehensible, easy to

---

13) See e.g. the documentary film *The Plastic People of the Universe*; dir. Jana Chytilová, Czech Television (ČT) and Video 57, Praha 2001.

grasp, for everyone living his or her life in the underground "ghetto". It may be sufficient to quote only a few names of Karásek's songs to get some idea of their "ideological influence" Řekni ďáblovi ne [Say no to the Devil], 1974; *Vy silní ve víře* [You Who Are Strong in the Faith], 1970; *Kázání o zkáze Sodomy a Gomory* [Sermon on the Destruction of Sodom and Gomorrah], 1975; *Podobenství o zrnu a koukolu* [The Parable of the Good Seed and the Tares], 1977. Some verses of the last song mentioned are explicit enough:

> [...] As in the field, so in your own soul / Both good and evil are fast entwined / So we are both good, and we're immoral / Why, with both God and the devil sowed in your heart. // And if some meddlers were to appear / And swear to rid the world of sin / I'd say, 'You're joking! You'll be sorry! / There'd be none of us left in that field.' // Leave it to God to make the choice / About who are the good seeds and who the tares / We're good for grading potatoes / But at harvest time let God sort us out [...].[14]

These and similar words of the Bible helped the underground audience, despite the fact that it mostly consisted of non-Christians (i.e., "agnostics"), to identify their social position and to formulate their relation towards the majority society and the political establishment. Moreover, they proved to be instrumental for their worldview, and even helped them find their way to their own spiritual values and understand the so-called transcendental notions.

It could be said that the Czech underground community, when confronted with the brutal mechanisms of totalitarian oppression, started to identify its position in society with the early Christian gatherings of "the prosecuted" – no matter if the individual persons were official adherents of the Catholic or Protestant churches or not. Surprisingly enough, the Czech heirs of the rebels of the 1960s,

---

14) "[...] A jak v celém poli, tak i v duši tvé / je dobro se zlem fest prorostlé / tak sme dobrý i potvory / vždyť Bůh i ďábel přece v srdci tvém sil // Kdyby tak přišli ňáký nemehla / že náš svět zbaví od všeho zla / řek bych vy blázni, to sou fóry / kdo z nás by pak v tom poli zbyl // Kdo je zrnem dobrým a kdo patří na hnůj / do toho Bohu ty nefušuj / my můžem třídit brambory / a nás si po žních přebere Bůh [...]". English translations (by Paul Wilson) of the texts of most of Karásek's songs are found in a catalogue added to the record *Svatopluk Karásek: Say No to the Devil*, Upsala, 1979 (ed. Jaroslav Suk).

who in their defiance of any social establishment were mostly of an anti-religious orientation (it is enough to recall John Lennon's words about the fading popularity of Jesus Christ, to say nothing about the standpoints of people such as Mick Jagger or Frank Zappa) found their way not only to Christianity, but even to legal Christian churches. Thanks to Svatopluk Karásek and Vratislav Brabenec, the author of a very popular performance by The Plastic People entitled *Pašijové hry velikonoční* [Easter Passion Play], performed and recorded secretly in 1978[15] which once again rendered the most famous story in the Western world very much topical; the denizens of the underground were reminded not only of the centuries-long tradition of the *sui generis* "underground existence" of Czech Protestants – the so called Bohemian Brethren, whose church was banned between the 17th – 19th centuries, but also of genuine and original Christian values and even found its way to the Catholic Church, which lost its dominant position in Czechoslovak society as early as 1918, and was completely rid of its former power after 1948 and after centuries became oppressed again: this must have roused the sympathy or even the feelings of self-identification from the Czech underground community. Such a revival of Christianity in the underground community also led the underground to the platform of Charter 77 in which mutual tolerance was one of its leading principles, and Christian ideas were largely accepted.

Before we discuss the relationship of the underground community to the broader community of Charter 77, we should look at yet one more attempt at formulating a scholarly "theory" of the underground, in fact the only one that followed after Jirous' *Report* and preceded Bondy's self-appointed apologetics of the 1980s. We have in mind Jiří Němec's essay *Nové šance svobody* [New Chances of Freedom], 1979[16]. Němec, himself a philosopher, one of the best educated persons of his generation, could make use of his own

15) See the English translation in *The Plastic People of the Universe*, Praha: Maťa, 1999, pp. 87–97; the original record of the music has been released as a CD several times. See Discography in *Views from the Inside*, op. cit. See also Discography at the end of this volume.

16) The essay was published only in samizdat in Czechoslovakia (see *Vokno*, no. 2, 1979), and on the pages of Czech exile journals e.g. in *Svědectví* (Paris) 14, no. 62 (1980), pp. 221–229, also in the anthology *O svobodě a moci. Památce Jana Patočky*, Köln – Roma:

experience: he was both one of the leading figures of the underground movement from its beginnings, and one of the "founders" of Charter 77.

Moreover, he was one of the few Czech intellectuals who managed to gain the support of prominent Czech dissidents for Ivan M. Jirous and the underground musicians in 1976 when they were jailed and later sentenced to prison for allegedly "disturbing the peace". And it is also known, that the support of Václav Havel, Ludvík Vaculík, Zdeněk Mlynář, Jan Patočka, Jaroslav Seifert and a number of other dissidents who only a few months later established Charter 77 brought many underground people into the Charter community[17]. Feeling responsible for such an "incorporation" of the underground community into the community of Charter 77, Němec tried to uproot the prejudices of the supposed "intolerance" of the Czech underground and also pointed out how different its attitudes were from the "disengagement" of the hippies of the 1960s on the one hand, and how surprisingly close they were to Christianity on the other. Because, of course, it was obvious that not all Charter 77 intellectuals, especially ex-communists, jumped with joy having realized they found themselves in one group with the underground "filthy rockers" or even supposed drug-addicts.

As far as Charter 77 itself, there is no need to give a detailed description of its membership and leading principles. Numerous books in both Czech and English have already supplied us with such relevant information. Let me only remind you of the works by

---

Index - Listy, 1980, pp. 257-268; it was translated into Swedish and French; see also "Bibliografie Jiřího Němce", *Kritický sborník* 18, no. 4 (1999), pp. 63-94, esp. p. 70.

17) About the development in the relations between the underground community and Charter 77 movement see e.g. MACHOVEC, Martin, "Charta a underground", in DEVÁTÁ, Markéta - SUK, Jiří - TŮMA, Oldřich (eds.), *Charta 77. Od obhajoby lidských práv k demokratické revoluci 1977-1989. Sborník z konference k 30. výročí Charty 77*, Praha: ÚSD AV ČR, 2007. Its English translation is found in Chapter 3 of this volume.

Hubert Gordon Skilling[18], Vilém Prečan[19], Aviezer Tucker[20] and Barbara J. Falk[21] since they helped western readers most of all to understand the principal ideas of Central and Eastern European dissidence.

The platform that unified the rich variety of Charter 77 membership as it was outlined in the beginning of this paper is well-known, as well. Inspired by the fact that representatives of the Czechoslovak government had signed the Helsinki Agreement of 1975, the Charter signatories decided to urge the government merely to adhere to the laws that already existed in Czechoslovak legislation. We may term this approach a legalistic one. It was the guiding principle of Charter 77 even though it was apparent from the very beginning that its application was dubious: to ask a government that had established its power in violation of laws, some of whose members could even be charged with high treason, should strike one at the very least as imprudent. Yet one more contradiction is easily to be discovered between what could be said and published in Charter 77 documents (e.g., in petitions demanding a dialogue with representatives of power, in Havel's programme of the so-called "nonpolitical politics") and the real, actual, true aims of Charter 77. No doubt Charter 77's leaders knew they would be treated as the political opposition in the country even though they would deny and renounce such ambition. Indeed, they were thus treated, and in the long run they indeed established a germ of real political opposi-

18) SKILLING, Gordon Hubert, *Charter 77 and Human Rights in Czechoslovakia*, London: Allen and Unwin. 1981; idem, *Samizdat and an Independent Society in Central and Eastern Europe*, Columbus, OH: Macmillan, 1989.

19) PREČAN, Vilém (ed.), *Human Rights in Czechoslovakia: A Documentation*, Paris: International Committee for the Support of Charter 77, 1983; idem, *Independent Literature and Samizdat in Czechoslovakia in the 1970s and the 1980s*, Praha: Památník národního písemnictví, 1992; PREČAN, Vilém, "The Re-emergence of a civil society. Independent currents in communist Czechoslovakia in the 1970s and 1980", in *De tsjechische Republiek en de Europese cultuur*. Brussels: Koninklijke Vlaamse Academie van België voor Wetenschappen en Kunsten, 2000, pp. 57–66.

20) TUCKER, Aviezer, *The Philosophy and Politics of Czech Dissidence from Patočka to Havel*, Pittsburgh, PA: University of Pittsburgh Press, 2000.

21) FALK, Barbara J., *The Dilemmas of Dissidence in East-Central Europe: Citizen Intellectuals and Philosopher Kings*, New York – Budapest: Central European University Press, 2003.

tion without which they could hardly have attempted to overthrow the totalitarian regime in 1989.

It is a lesser known fact, however, that there were many Charter 77 sympathizers or fellow-travellers who never signed the Charter, and yet were in favour of it, and, moreover, worked for it, even when the reasons for their not becoming Charter 77 signatories could be different: some of these political "apostates" definitely wanted to remain less conspicuous and not lose a chance for efficient work useful for the entirety of the dissidence (e.g., Jiřina Šiklová, Josef Mundil or Milan Šimečka). Therefore it cannot be taken for granted that signing Charter 77 meant that the respective signatory was absolutely in favour of what was being done in the name of Charter 77 on the one hand, and, on the other, that non-signing implied any principal objections to Charter 77 ideas.[22] As far as the underground community of the mentioned rock musicians, poets and artists is concerned, it has been estimated recently that as many as 40 percent of the overall count of all pre-1989 Charter signatories came from the underground community and belonged, by the way, primarily to the working class.[23]

Many members of the underground, on the other hand, never signed Charter 77, and thus we can see the Charter 77 community and the underground community as two, partially overlapping circles in a complementary relation. Undoubtedly there were hundreds, if not thousands of underground people who remained outside Charter 77. A brief look at the attitudes to Charter 77 of the most well-known underground figures is illustrative: By the end of the 1970s, there were seven stable members in the most famous Czech underground rock band – The Plastic People of the Universe. Out of them, three signed Charter 77, whereas four others did not. Ivan M. Jirous did sign the Charter although its "legalistic" principles were in sharp contrast with the ideas he expressed in his *Report* of 1975 and elsewhere. Egon Bondy signed Charter 77 as well – and did so as early as December 1976, but his signature was immediately nullified by Jiří Němec, a fact which subsequently caused much bitterness[24].

22) See the details in the previous text (Chapter 3) in this volume: "Charter 77 and the Underground".
23) See ibidem.
24) See ibidem.

The reasons why people from the underground joined the Charter 77 movement might have been very different. Nevertheless, most of them probably signed it (at least in the first wave in December 1976 and during the following few months) to demonstrate their gratitude to those dissidents who organized support for their friends who were imprisoned in 1976 – and it probably mattered little to them if they disapproved of its "legalistic" aims or not[25]. After all, it is well-known that *the times they are a'changing*, and what might have seemed impossible and absurd as early as 1975 may have become possible some years later. The "millenarian" or chiliastic radicalism was mostly abandoned in the late 1970s and during the 1980s by the underground. Nevertheless, those who became Charter 77 signatories always formed the most radical fraction within the Charter movement. The apparent contradiction between the original underground ideas as mentioned above, and the "minimalist", "legalistic", compromise-seeking programme of Charter 77 proved not to be too drastic, and reconciliation between them was possible. František Stárek, one of the best-known underground journalists and editors, stated it clearly in an interview with the historian Milan Otáhal in 2003[26]:

I lived in the underground but perceived my signing of Charter 77 as an attitude of a citizen. That was my attitude of a citizen, same as others made their attitudes as citizens clear by entering the Communist Party for instance. Some factory workers might have expressed their attitudes as citizens by being Communist Party members, but I perceived my being a Charter 77 signatory, or being close to the Charter, as my own attitude.

Yet in the 1980s, there were at least two more important events in the history of Czechoslovak dissidence and Charter 77 on the occasion of which the underground community made its independent political views clear once again:

25) See ibidem.
26) See VANĚK, Miroslav - URBÁŠEK, Pavel (eds.), *Vítězové? Poražení? Životopisná interview I - Disent v období tzv. normalizace* [Winners? Losers? Biographic Interviews I - Dissidence in the Times of the So-Called Normalization], Praha: Prostor, 2005, pp. 857–889, esp. p. 882.

I) In 1987 the so-called *Dopis 40 signatářů Charty 77 mluvčím* [Letter from 40 Charter 77 Signatories to Charter Spokepersons][27] was issued and caused some indignation on the side of more "conservative" Charter signatories, especially ex-apparatchiks. The Letter was initiated by František Stárek, met with a warm welcome by Egon Bondy and was signed mostly by the Charter 77 signatories of "underground origin". It was a kind of a petition urging the Charter leaders, especially its spokespersons, to lend their ears to the supposed "passive majority" of the signatories who did not want to remain "passive" at all, to give younger Charter 77 signatories more opportunities to shape the movement as a whole, to make the Charter movement more pluralistic. The forty signatories of the *Letter* also supported the idea of summoning the so-called Charter "Fora", i.e. assemblies of as many Charter signatories as possible at which major issues would be discussed. Fortunately, Václav Havel and other Charter leaders immediately demonstrated understanding for such suggestions. In total, four Charter "Fora" were organized before November 1989, and through them the whole of Charter 77 became politically radicalised – almost at the last minute indeed! Charter leaders began accepting invitations to public rallies and demonstrations and began organizing them themselves. In this way, the underground signatories of Charter 77 contributed to the political profile of it and helped make it ready for the big political changes of 1989.[28]

II) In May 1988 Petr Placák, one of the representatives of a younger underground generation whose "press tribune" was mostly the samizdat magazine called *Revolver Revue*, wrote and published in samizdat his *Manifest Českých dětí* [Manifesto of Czech Children][29]

---

27) See the Czech edition of all Charter 77 documents: CÍSAŘOVSKÁ, Blanka – PREČAN, Vilém (eds.), *Charta 77: Dokumenty 1977–1989, I-III*, Praha: ÚSD AV ČR, 2007; *Dopis 40 signatářů* see in ibidem, III, pp. 287–290.

28) See the details in the previous text (Chapter 3) in this volume: "Charter 77 and the Underground".

29) Placák's *Manifesto* was published several times in samizdat during 1988-9, for the first time in *Informace o Chartě* (*INFOCH*), 1988, pp. 17–18, for the second time in Placák's own samizdat magazine called *Koruna* [Crown] (no. 2, 1989, pp. 2-3), here, however, both in Czech original and in its Latin translation (!!) under the title "Bohemorum liberorum declaratio". The text of the *Manifesto* was printed for the first time in Paris based Czech exile journal *Svědectví* 22, no. 85 (1988), pp. 269–270.

which quickly became well-known in the world of Czech dissidence and also roused indignation, even anxiety and misunderstanding. Petr Placák himself never signed Charter 77, but both his father and elder brother did. Furthermore, his father, prof. Bedřich Placák, was among the Charter 77 spokespersons for some time. Even before he published his *Manifesto*, Petr Placák gained a reputation in the underground as an excellent poet and writer (his novel *Medorek*, 1985, was awarded the dissident Jiří Orten Prize in 1989). Placák soon made friends with Egon Bondy and Ivan M. Jirous and for some time even took part in secret rehearsals of The Plastic People as one of the band's musicians, and at last in 1988 he came out with a text which actually called for the reestablishment of the old Kingdom of Bohemia (i.e., proclaimed a kind of semi-utopian royalism, a monarchic regime as possibly the best political system). Placák's poetic vision, partially serious, partially ironic, met with keen interest from the youngest underground generation. Even Ivan M. Jirous signed the manifesto and in so doing "blessed it" on behalf of the entirety of the underground. On the other hand, most Charter 77 leaders were terrified: they were merely too serious and cautious to accept such a child of playfulness and imagination. But as Placák and his followers started organizing various anti-regime demonstrations, even the Charter 77 leaders willy-nilly had to accept such an unwelcome ally. In our survey of the political thinking of the Czech underground community, Placák's concept of monarchy is the final and perhaps the most original one. It enriched the struggle of Czech dissidents with something they had lacked for a long time: a sense of humour, irony, poetry, and very unconventional political (as well as ecological and even egalitarian) ideas. Therefore, I am closing this paper with a quotation from Placák's *Manifesto*:

We Czech children declare that St. Wenceslas' Crown, i.e. the Kingdom of Bohemia, persists!

We are getting ready for the coming of a new King, which is our supreme aim.

The King is Dei gratia, he is responsible to God for his country and for his people!

The King is the aegis for the weak against the ill will of the powerful and the rich!

The King is a guarantee, he protects woods, wild game and the whole nature against the ruling criminals who without any respect pillage and destroy the treasures of the land and the Earth, without giving back to the land what they had robbed from it!

The King is the Law before which people, trees, animals, the land, the woods are equal and any act or conduct of one person at the expense of another is a crime! [...]

The Kingdom is a sacred heritage and the sacred heritage is the highest respect to everything – to every tree, brook, hill, to every single ant in the woods, to people, to their work, to the dignity of every single person!

The Kingdom is not the rule of a minority at the expense of the majority, or the rule of the majority at the expense of a minority!

The Kingdom is not the rule of a few thousand hoarders and money-grubbers, self-appointed ne'er-do-wells and parasites of the land and the nation!

The Kingdom is sacred!

If some of the words found it Placák's *Manifesto* were reminiscent of the ideas expressed by Duchamp, Rygulla, Bondy or Jirous, quoted above, it would probably not be coincidental but symptomatic, and it could serve as indirect evidence of the originality of ideas generated by underground communities that so far have been mostly neglected and ignored.

Prague – Bremen – Budapest – Austin – Rome
January – February 2010, April 2011

5. THE THEME OF "APOCALYPSE" AS A KEY BUILDING BLOCK OF UNDERGROUND LITERATURE DURING THE PERIOD OF "NORMALIZATION"

Firstly, some remarks regarding the two expressions in commas in the title of this text.

1) The Greek word *apokalypsis*, meaning "revelation" that we know chiefly from the New Testament, is often used in a non-religious sense in present-day Czech as a synonym for doom, perceived in a general or final sense, but in a partial sense too.

So the modern Czech literary variant of the Biblical or gnostic apocalypse definitely has no connotations of wild visions of "a star named Wormwood"[1] or a "a beast with ten horns and seven heads"[2], or of kings assembled at "a place called Harmagedon"[3]; the sense of it is simply a premonition of the end, or extinction.

2) The expression "normalization", which acquired a new, political meaning in Czech after 1969, is a very good example of the principles of Orwellian Newspeak, or what Bohumil Hrabal called "semantic confusion"[4], being introduced into everyday speech. There are other examples of such political and journalistic jargon from the early seventies, of "semantic shifts" due to pressure from the regime and the political situation. The spontaneous process of democratization in 1968 started to be described as "counter-revolution", which was intended to suggest, among other things, that the Stalinist putsch of 1948 was a "revolution"; the invasion of Czechoslovakia by troops of foreign countries was suddenly designated "fraternal assistance"; and the usurper regime and what was still at its core a totalitarian system was described as "democratic socialism".

The clear aim of the Czechoslovak puppet government, which was once more entirely in the hands of pro-Kremlin apparatchiks was not only to totally suppress the remnants of the efforts of

1) Revelation 8:11.
2) Revelation 13:1.
3) Revelation 16:16.
4) See Hrabal's text collage entitled *Sémantický zmatek* [Semantic confusion], in *Sebrané spisy Bohumila Hrabala*, vol. 15 – *Domácí úkoly*, Praha: Pražská imaginace, Praha 1995, p. 363.

democratization of 1968 and silence its representatives at all costs, but also to deprive people of their means of expression, and hence their scope for communication and mutual understanding.

Enforcing changes in the meaning of many well-used expressions, which were contingent on specific historical realities was also an attempt to alter the way people actually thought, because if something in Czechoslovak history in the period 1948–1989 was worthy of the description "normalization" then it was precisely that attempt at democratization in 1968, and not the years following the Soviet occupation. So perhaps it is not surprising that the poets and writers who sought in the 1970s to reflect in an authentic, unmanipulated and non-ideological manner on the time they were living in – one truly characterized by a new "confusion" as at Babel, if not of "tongues" then at least of one tongue – tended to update the theme of doom, or "apocalypse" in the broadest sense of the word.

It is a well-known fact that in 1968, the literary authors and musicians of the Czech underground of the seventies and eighties were definitely not among the foremost representatives of the democratization process of "renewal", either as politicians, columnists, or journalists. Broadly speaking, the latter were mostly members of the Communist Party with varying degrees of attachment to genuine democracy (i.e., people who were previously socially privileged, who had now become aware of the possibility, or rather the necessity of economic and political reforms). However, insofar as those literary authors and musicians of the future underground were mostly quite young, they took advantage of the much greater degree of freedom of those days to express their views and engage in artistic activity as much as possible. Nevertheless, the very fact that they did not get involved in the thick of political activity meant that they were subsequently capable of reflecting the frustration of the Husák regime's emerging "normalization" much more objectively than the foremost Czechoslovak writers, political commentators and journalists of the time – the future emigrés or so-called dissidents, who were, by and large, totally absorbed by the specific political message of 1968/69. Another paradoxical advantage of the authors and creators, who would subsequently become the main exponents of underground culture, was the fact that until the beginning of the 1970s they had either simply languished on the fringes of the Czech literary scene[5] (sometimes deliberately and consciously out of an aversion to anything that was fashionable, sometimes because of the subject-matter of the period was mostly alien to them, while their own subject-matter did not attract sufficient interest among the wider readership, but mostly because most of their texts were not publishable at all before 1968, and the subsequent period of relative democracy was too short), or they didn't manage to even enter Czech literary circles, or their first appearance in print was limited to a few magazine issues in 1968-69.[6]

These minor observations of a psychological and sociological nature, rather than from a literary and historical viewpoint, should be borne in mind if we are to adequately interpret the literary underground, particularly that of the 1970s. But another way of looking at it would be to conclude that the underground authors of those days were much less traumatized by 1968 than the former leading figures and future dissidents, who were suddenly – again in a very Orwellian sense – not only prevented from being published, but were actually "erased" from the history of Czech literature and culture. And one other factor should probably also be taken into account, namely that the frequent visions of doom, destruction, hopelessness, and sometimes self-destruction or at least disintegration or decay, as articulated by underground authors were truly much more universal than the reflections on personal frustrations from the pens of the "sixty-eighters" (suffice it to mention the well-known polemic between Milan Kundera and Václav Havel on "Czech Destiny"[7]) and are also only in apparent contradiction with

5) Such as Egon Bondy, Milan Knížák, Ivan M. Jirous or Andrej Stankovič, as well as the marginalized folk singers such as Jaroslav Hutka or Vlastimil Třešňák, and particularly the disdained rock musicians writing their own texts under the influence of the American underground music and literary scene of the time.

6) Such as Vratislav Brabenec, Svatopluk Karásek, Pavel Zajíček, and František Pánek, as well, of course, as the entire "younger underground generation" who wouldn't appear on the (samizdat) literary scene until the 1980s.

7) See Havel's essay "Český úděl?" [The Czech Deal?], in HAVEL, Václav, *Spisy 3 - Eseje a jiné texty z let 1953-1969*, Praha: Torst, Praha 1999, p. 888 (the notes also include the text of Milan Kundera's essay, "Český úděl", pp. 992-998).

the markedly joyful creative atmosphere so typical of the "merry ghetto" of the underground in the first half of the 1970s. That micro-community, was also the natural source of the "micro-climate" that allowed like-minded individuals and artists to survive better and support each other, a source of self-affirmation, and sometimes of "feedback". (The fact that the Czech underground was also a very heterogeneous community, even though its exponents were initially above all rock musicians and fans of that "accursed music" and of the specific value system and lifestyle associated with it, was more the outcome of a happy coincidence; this fact is anyway very familiar and need not be particularly emphasized.[8])

Now a few examples of "apocalyptic" themes in underground poetry:

Milan Knížák's experimental musical formation AKTUAL[9] was in many respects the forerunner of the Czech underground in the real sense of the word. In addition to ephemeral Czech bands such as the the Primitives Group or The Hell's Devils, it was Aktual that inspired The Plastic People of the Universe that came into being somewhat later, in autumn 1968, and is now the most acclaimed legend of the Czech underground, as well as the band DG 307, formed

---

8) See particularly: "Zpráva o třetím českém hudebním obrození", in JIROUS, Ivan M., *Magorův zápisník*, Praha: Torst, 1997, p. 171. Also: MACHOVEC, Martin, "Od avantgardy přes podzemí do undergroundu" [From the Avant-Garde via Unofficial Publishing to Underground: The Midnight Editions Circle, 1949–1955, and the Underground Circle of the Plastic People, 1969–1989], in *Pohledy zevnitř*, Praha: Pistorius & Olšanská 2008 (part of it in English is Chapter 1 of this volume); also: JANOUŠEK, Pavel (ed.), *Dějiny české literatury 1945-1989, vol. IV, 1969-1989*, Praha: Academia, 2008, esp. the chapter "Společenství a poetika undergroundu", pp. 279–295; the chapter "Próza undergroundu, okruh Revolver Revue", pp. 455–460.

9) The original recordings and some cover versions of Aktual songs were released on 2 CDs: *AKTUAL – ATENTÁT NA KULTURU*, Praha: Anne Records, 2003; *AKTUAL – DĚTI BOLŠEVIZMU*, Louny: Guerilla Records, 2005.

in 1973,[10] and several other underground bands including Umělá hmota [Artificial Material].[11]

A number of Knížák's texts[12] mostly from 1968 were written in an obviously ironic spirit of political provocation, or even blasphemy, such as: *I Love You and Lenin, The Kids of Bolshevism, Messiah The Bolshevik*, and *Bolshevik Gods*, others articulate a vision of a "new world", undoubtedly spawned by the utopia of American 60s "counter-culture", such as *The Apostles, How Divine it Would Be, Fuck and Don't Make War, Emissaries from the Cosmos, City of Actuals, The March of the Actuals*. The notions of fundamental "change", "transformation", and "purification" they contain already have something in common with "apocalyptic" moods. But Knížák's best-known texts of 1968 are probably *Assault on Culture* and *Be a Pig*. The latter includes the words: "Throw out your brain / Throw out your hearts / throw out all / that makes you human // Be a pig / Be a pig / Be a pig / Be a pig // A pig lives well / eats drinks and fucks / its life away".[13] This reflection of disgust at pseudo-humanity in the form of an appeal was without doubt already very radical.

Even before Egon Bondy became acquainted with The Plastic People and their community, he wrote many poetic and philosophical

---

10) The original recordings of DG 307 compositions were released on a number of CDs. The most valuable are: *DG 307 - HISTORIE HYSTERIE. Archiv dochovaných nahrávek 1973-75* [2 CDs], Louny: Guerilla Records, 2004; *DG 307 - SVĚDEK SPÁLENÝHO ČASU 1979/1980* [5CDs], Louny: Guerilla Records, 2013.

11) The group Umělá hmota soon split up in two groups: Milan "Dino" Vopálka's Umělá hmota II and Josef "Vaťák" Vondruška's Umělá hmota III. The original recordings are found on 4 CDs: *UMĚLÁ HMOTA II. VE SKLEPĚ - 1976/77* [2 CDs], Louny: Guerilla Records, 2003. *JOSEF VONDRUŠKA: THE DOM & UMĚLÁ HMOTA III - ROCK'N'ROLLOVÝ MILÁČEK* [2CDs], Louny: Guerilla Records, 2010.

12) A collection of Knížák's texts for Aktual were published in the volume: KNÍŽÁK, Milan, *Písně kapely Aktual*, Praha: Maťa, 2003. The English translations by Karolína Dolanská of some of Knížák's lyrics are found in a booklet added to the CD *Děti bolševizmu* (Footnote 9).

13) In Dolanská's translation. The original Czech text: „**Staňte se prasetem** // zahoďte mozky / zahoďte srdce / zahoďte všechno / co vás dělá člověkem // STAŇTE SE PRASETEM! / STAŇTE SE PRASETEM! / STAŇTE SE PRASETEM! / STAŇTE SE PRASETEM! // prase si dobře žije / jen žere a pije / a taky mrdá // STAŇTE SE PRASETEM! / STAŇTE SE PRASETEM! / STAŇTE SE PRASETEM! / STAŇTE SE PRASETEM!"

texts that could be interpreted as a modern parallel with apocalyptic or prophetic/admonitory literature. The evidence is also there to show that "thirsting for an apocalypse" or rather for a "radical social change", which simply must come about, even if it involves huge social upheavals or the actual extinction of existing civilisations, constituted an entire creative line of thought in Bondy's literary oeuvre from the 1950s. There is no space here, however, to deal with it in more detail, besides which this particular strand of his work would seem to have less of an impact on the underground of the 1970s.

Although Bondy's *Tzv. "Březnová báseň 1971", čtená na veřejném shromáždění* [The So-Called "March Poem 1971" – Read at a Public Gathering], from the collection *Zápisky z počátku let sedmdesátých* [Notes from the Beginning of the 1970s][14] was written before its author was accepted by the underground community as an "underground classic", in places its style clearly anticipates the texts he wrote in subsequent years, when the underground became truly entwined with his life and work. The text is actually one long litany: a series of curses and warnings, in which – truly in the manner of a Biblical prophet – the author indicts not only his neighbours, but all people indiscriminately:[15]

14) This collection was published in vol. 7 of *Básnické dílo Egona Bondyho*, Praha: Pražská imaginace, 1992, pp. 5–55 (the text cited is on pp. 40–42); the original samizdat edition dates from 1972; more recently in *Básnické spisy II – 1962-1975*, Praha: Argo, 2015, pp. 346–351.

15) Compare Gerald Turner's translation with Bryson's and Klepetářová's translation of the same part of the text as quoted in the previous text (chapter 4 of this volume). The original Czech text of this part of the poem goes as follows: "Ne – je jasné že nelze začít bojovat holýma rukama a zničehonic / ale kdo ještě je člověkem / musí se už od nynějška připravovat / protože režim státního kapitalismu musí být zničen / jen nesmíte znovu dopustit abyste se opět jako v osmašedesátém dali vláčet profesionálními aparátníky / Svobody Dubčeky a Černíky / kteří pochopitelně nemají zájem na tom aby se opravdu změnil režim jenž je vytvořil a z něhož žijí / Musíte si stále být vědomi že socialismus / není nic víc a nic míň / než samosprávná organizace společnosti / že tedy všechna síla je ve vašich rukou / jen když jich použijete / A pochopíte právě teď / co říká Mao Ce-tung / že nikdo nemůže osvobodit lidi shora / shora je je možno jen ujařmit / Za vašimi zády se ve skutečnosti třese vykořisťovatelská oligarchie / Sovětský svaz nepřežije osmdesátá léta / ale vy musíte být připraveni / I kdyby pozavírali všechny marxisty / nemohou pozavírat všechny vás // Nepíšu

[...] No – obviously we can't start to struggle with our bare hands and out of nowhere / but whoever is still human must as of now prepare themselves / because the regime of state capitalism must be destroyed / but you mustn't let yourselves be dragged along by the professional aparatchiks as you did in sixty-eight / the Svobodas, Dubčeks and Černíks / who understandably are not interested in a change of the regime they created and which gives them their livelihood / You must always be aware that socialism / is no more and no less / than the self-governing organisation of society / and so all power is in your hands/ so long as you use it / And at this moment you will understand Mao Zedong when he says / that no one can liberate people from above/ from above they can only be enslaved // In reality, behind your backs the exploitative oligarchy is shaking / the Soviet Union will not survive the nineteen-eighties / but you must be prepared / Even if they jailed all the Marxists / they can't jail all of you // I don't write poetry for you, and I've never wanted to write poetry / if you want poetry shit on your faces and smear it all over like skin cream / which precisely suits your souls / Because the brutality in which individual people are deprived of their freedom and even their lives is not the most terrible thing / the most terrible thing of all is the bestiality with which they force us to watch it and even applaud / If you're in your sixties go form a queue at the crematorium / if you're in your forties may your genitals and your wives' and vile mistresses' genitals rot away while you're alive / if you're in your twenties go off straight away and hang yourselves / unless from today you prepare every day for war war war / war and war on the criminals / who otherwise / won't waste time with you [...]

As they listened to such appeals, the young underground newcomers of the time tried to express their own feelings, which chimed

vám poesii a nikdy jsem vám nechtěl psát poesii / chcete-li poesii naserte si do ksichtu a pěkně si to rozmažte jako pleťový krém / který právě k vaší duši sluší / Nejstrašnější není totiž brutalita s níž jednotliví lidé jsou zbavováni svobody ba života / nejstrašnější je bestialita s níž nás všechny s klidem přinucují přihlížet ba tleskat / Šedesátiletí – jděte se přímo postavit do fronty před krematorium / čtyřicetiletí – ať vám uhnije zaživa vaše přirození i přirození vašich manželek a hnusných milenek / dvacetiletí – jděte se rovnou oběsit / jestliže nebudete ode dneška připravovat den co den válku válku válku / válku a válku zločincům / kteří jinak / s vámi nebudou dělat žádné cavyky".

in to a great extent with the thoughts quoted. A number of texts by Pavel Zajíček, written in the years 1973–75 for his experimental band DG 307,[16] express above all a yearning to destroy existing pseudo-values. The influence of Milan Knížák is quite evident in them, such as *Attack on History, Paper aPpsolute, Appearance, When, Degeneration, Sewer Called Fetishism*. There is a truly apocalyptic mood in the texts: *Returns* and *Purification*. *Returns* has the words "the return of time / without limit / the return of space / without possession / the return of the rock / to the cliff // everything as at the beginning / of creation / everything to the primordial transformation // the return of wild / nature / to obliterated cities / the return of iron to the earth / the return of stars / fallen long ago [...]".[17]

We note a similar mood at the end of *Purification*: "[...] every morning we should purify ourselves / every night we should make love / and at every moment we should be / prepared for the end".[18]

In Zajíček's early works, however, we can also hear utopian tones, paradoxically joyful visions of the world, in which it is possible to live in spite of all the horrors. These "post-apocalyptic" themes, which will be referred to later, are probably the most original contribution of the Czech underground ghetto to Czech literature. In Zajíček's poem *New Warriors*, which is actually a not particularly ironic paraphrase of Norbert Zoula's "working-class anthem" *Prison Song*, these aspects are particularly evident: "[...] new warriors are arising / in hope rejoicing / new warriors are arising / no whores demanding / new warriors are arising / enthused and understanding".[19] In the text *Explosion of Thought* a positive attitude to life after

---

16) See the volume Z[AJÍČEK], Pavel, *DG 307 (Texty z let 1973-1980)*, Praha: Vokno, 1990.

17) The Czech original: "**Návraty** // návraty času / bez omezení / návrat prostoru / bez vlastnění / návrat kamene / do skály // vše jako na počátku / tvoření / vše se do prvotního / promění // návrat divoký / přírody / do vyhlazenejch měst / návrat železa do zemský hmoty / návrat dávno / spadlejch hvězd [...]".

18) The Czech original: "**Očišťování** // [...] každý ráno bychom se měli očišťovat / každou noc bychom se měli milovat / každou vteřinu bychom měli bejt / připravený na konec".

19) The Czech original: "**Nový bojovníci** // [...] vstávaj nový bojovníci / v naději se radující / vstávaj nový bojovníci / žádný kurvy žádající / vstávaj nový bojovníci / nadšený a chápající".

"destruction" is also apparent: "[...] the explosion of thought / heats up the air / explosions of sympathy /a penetrating sound // how beautiful is / this destruction / how beautiful is /a common spirit".[20]

The fact that Knížák's, Zajíček's and above all Bondy's postulates expressed in poetic or quasi-poetic texts are more reminiscent of proto-communist than early-Christian visions, and that they tend to evoke slightly the refrain of Pottier's once popular song, namely: *C'est la lutte finale, / groupons-nous, et demain / L'Internationale / Sera le genre humain,* is certainly not fortuitous, because the Christian apocalypse and eschatology were revived repeatedly in the course of history, and sometimes what they inspired was used to surprising ends, but in the case of the Czech underground authors these reminiscences are always offset by a strong dose of irony and self-deprecation, which, moreover, is one of the other permanent features of underground literature as a whole, which we shall also mention later.

There are no ideological or theological references in the apocalyptic themes of František Pánek, another outstanding underground author, albeit one with a markedly psychopathic personality. Symptomatic in that respect is the opening text of Pánek's cycle from the 1970s and 1980s[21], the poem *Monarch God*:

In the frame of the graves through space / talons on the wings of the corpses / there appeared voices of predatory / riddles! // The cradle of the birth through the asshole / the glowing miracle so unique / the stroke of the end, the ideal / dung-beetle of mist, the ghost of nausea / the death's head moth, the monarch God. [22]

20) The Czech original: "**Exploze myšlení** // [...] exploze přemejšlení / rozpaluje vzduch / výbuchy soucítění /pronikavej zvuk // jak krásný je / todle ničení / jak krásnej je / společnej duch".
21) A complete collection of Pánek's poems in their original versions was published in PÁNEK, Fanda, *Vita horribilis 1972–1985*, Praha: Kalich, 2007 (Pánek's original samizdat collections were either untitled or came out under the title *U prdele* [I don't give a shit].)
22) The Czech original: "**Monarcha Bůh** // V rámu hrobů prostoru / drápy na mrtvol křídlách / zjevil se hádanek dravčích / hlasy! // Porodu prdelí kolíbka / zářící zázrak

In the text entitled *Ill Will* the vision of extinction is powerfully present:

Ill Will / To your life, dude, you've got the will / It's a dream / Like the brontosaurus / you'll just / die out, / dude. // Icarus / He flew up high, dude / Today same as yesterday / you fell / in the fucking shit, / you hog. // Vermin / You know fuck-all about it, you worm, / that in the grave of nature / you dig graves, / dude, / in your / fucking self.[23]

When Pánek's text *Eliášův oheň* [Elijah's Fire] or [St. Elmo's Fire] was set to music by The Plastic People, a poetic image in which a fundamental reassessment of values was established not simply by contrast but rather by creating a parallel or synonymity between a so-called lofty vision of "love begotten by God" and a so-called inferior vision symbolized here by "a bottle of rum already begun".[24]

The "primitive rocker", drug addict, and highly idiosyncratic naïve poet Josef Vondruška wrote lyrics that may probably be considered in the context of underground literature to be direct variations on "apocalyptic themes". The very titles of the poems or songs, that were set to music by the band Umělá hmota,[25] speak for themselves, such as *Strange Theatre*, *Living Corpses*, *Wild Angels*, and particularly *End of the World* – a text that was allegedly inspired by Bondy's prose work *Disabled Siblings*. Vondruška's *End of the World* includes the words: "[...] Sirens started to wail / migraines are

unikum / konce šlak, ideál / hovnivál mlh mdloby duch / smrtihlav monarcha Bůh".
23) The Czech original: "**Zvůli** // Zvůli / k životu máš vole vůli / je to sen, / jak brontosaurus / vymřeš / vole / jen. // Ikar / vysoko si vole lítal, / jako včera dnes / do hoven si / hlade / kles. // Hmyz / hovno červe víš, / jak v přírodě hrobě / hrobaříš / vole / sám / v sobě".
24) See *The Plastic People of the Universe* [texts of the songs, chronology, discography etc.], Praha: Globus Music – Maťa, 1999, p. 65, translated by Marek Tomin.
25) A selection of Vondruška's songs and poems from the 1970s was published in the volume: VONDRUŠKA, Josef, *Rock'n'rollový sebevrah* [Rock'n'roll Suicide], Brno (Czech Republic): "Zvláštní vydání...", 1993 (the text cited is called **Konec světa** in original and is on page 11; cited part in Czech original: "[...] Začly houkat sirény / šířejí se migrény / Celá zem se v peklo mění / je slyšet jen řev a klení / Lidé z toho strachem šílí / nejsou jim nic platný prachy / Vědějí že pojdou strachy [...]".

spreading / The whole land is changed into hell / only roaring and cursing can be heard / It makes people go mad from fear / pills are of no use to them / They know they'll die of fear [...]".

Two other authors from underground circles, Svatopluk Karásek and Vratislav Brabenec, are only seemingly unconnected with such apocalyptic themes. They both studied protestant theology and so one might expect that their treatment of apocalyptic themes would have an overtly Christian colouring. And this is undoubtedly the case of Svaťa Karásek's songs,[26] which include direct quotations from the New Testament (including Revelations), but they are selected and brought up to date in order to be most relevant to the burning issues of the "normalization" era. This is evident, for instance, in the texts *There was a Struggle*, *Say No to the Devil*, *Visit to Hell*, *It's Late*, and *Sermon on the Destruction of Sodom and Gomorrah*, whose closing several verses run as follows: "[...]When clutch of madmen embarks on ruining the town entire / a few brave people can save it in evil time. / God did not find those ten just men he sought: / With fire and brimstone his destruction wrought // In our town too those needed ten God seeks. / If he can't find them, then we're up shit creek."[27]

Religiosity is perhaps not so immediate in the case of Vratislav Brabenec[28] but is sublimated into a kind of ecologically tinged "pantheism"; it is a vision of the world from which the Christian God has already departed. Thus *Letter* from 1973, reads:

26) The texts of Karásek's songs were published in two different editions: KARÁSEK, Svatopluk, *Protestor znamená vyznávám* [Protestor Means: I Confess], Praha - Žďár n. Sázavou: EKK - Kalich, 1993; KARÁSEK, Svatopluk, *V nebi je trůn* [There is a Throne in Heaven], Praha: Maťa, 1999 (the latter has more reliable versions of the texts).
27) In Paul Wilson's translation. The Czech original goes as follows: "**Kázání o zkáze Sodomy a Gomory** // [...] Vždyť hrstka bláznů nakazí celý město, / pár statečných spasí město v dobách zlých. // Nenašel Bůh těch potřebnejch deset, / města se vzdal – život z něj odvolal. // I v našem městě hledá Bůh aspoň těch deset. / Nenajde-li – pak je vše v prdeli."
28) A collection of Brabenec's samizdat poems was published in BRABENEC, Vratislav: *Sebedudy* [Self-Bagpipes], Praha: Vokno, 1992 (the text of "Letter" is on p. 80-83). Later the collection was published again in an augmented edition: BRABENEC, Vratislav: *Sebedudy a jiné texty z let 1966-1987*, Praha: Kalich, 2010 (pp. 84-87).

[...] don't ask and sleep it's morning and we can't see anything / you're in the sea and there is no sun in the grave / and no death, it left them / it is now the life of a fly, flying and annoying / and revenging sins / I fly / I fly / the dead are coming and they wish me all the best / for the morning / pleasure of the sea is dreadful / is joy dreadful / do you know the joke about the fall / is hatred dreadful is love is murder the blaze / of a star / it's morning they have left they are carrying the worm to execution / and the wings of the murderer and they are carrying the murderer / each his own / it's murder the lamp blazing on the water / it's the star the murder shines [...].[29]

But Brabenec also had a powerful impact on the development of underground literature by his choice and arrangement of texts by other authors, or literary collages of a kind, which was one of the high points of Czech underground music. This relates not only to the New Testament texts in the *Easter Passion Play* cycle (1978) but also to the texts of Ladislav Klíma in the cycle entitled *How It'll Be After Death* (1979).[30] We need hardly add that both cycles evoked moments of extreme imperilment, and contained themes of confrontation with death and nothingness.[31]

---

29) The Czech original of the part cited: "**Dopis** [...] neptej se a spi je ráno a není vidět / jsi v moři a není slunce v hrobě / a není smrti odešla od nich / přišel muší život létat a trápit / a pomstít hříchy / létám / létám / přicházejí mrtví a přejí mi všechno / nejlepší k ránu / je radost moře hrozná / je radost hrozná / znáš vtip o pádu / je nenávist hrozná je láska je vražda záře / hvězdy / je ráno odešli nesou červa na popravu / a křídla vraha a vraha si nesou / každý svého / je vražda záře lampa na vodě / je hvězda vražda svítí [...]".

30) See the CDs: *THE PLASTIC PEOPLE OF THE UNIVERSE V. Pašijové hry velikonoční* (1978), (ed. Jaroslav RIEDEL), Praha: Globus Music, 1998; *THE PLASTIC PEOPLE OF THE UNIVERSE VI. Jak bude po smrti* (1979), (ed. Jaroslav RIEDEL), Praha: Globus Music, 1998.

31) Brabenec's arrangements of texts by other authors for musical performance by the Plastic People were published in the collected edition of texts set to music by the band; see *The Plastic People of the Universe: Texty*, Praha: Maťa, 2001 (2nd revised and augmented edition); in English in *The Plastic People of the Universe*, Praha: Globus Music - Maťa, 1999, pp. 87–107. The title of the Klímasque cycle *Jak bude po smrti* is translated by Marek Tomin as "Afterlife" here.

The crowning achievement of underground apocalyptic writing was probably Bondy's novel *Disabled Siblings* of 1974.[32] In the context of utopian, are rather "antiutopian", dystopian literature, this work is now fairly well known, and it has been written about not only within the context of Czech literature, but also on the German, Italian and Polish and other literary scenes, thanks to translations.[33] For the present context it is interesting as a vision of a "post-apocalyptic" world, in which the only possible option is to live to the full. It is evidently also Bondy's reflection on life in the "underground ghetto", and in fact also about its apotheosis. However the text of the work is so full of visions that it perfectly constitutes apocalyptic literature, with the opening theme of "the corpse of the world", again treated with a strong dose of irony, and also images of "celestial television", the threat of "rising waters", or the frequently prominent theme of "joyful self-destruction".

Echoes of apocalyptic moods, in the sense on reflection on the "normalization" years, are also very much present in the texts of the so-called "eighties" authors belonging to the younger underground generation mentioned earlier. They are mostly connected with the samizdat magazine Revolver Revue that was founded in 1985, but a number of its regular authors made their debut in samizdat in the late 1970s and early 1980s.

A prominent author of that younger generation was the poet and prose writer Petr Placák. The main figure of his prose work *Medorek* (the first samizdat from 1985)[34] is a sort of self-caricature

32) To this day there have been four Czech editions of Bondy's *Invalidní sourozenci*: 1/ Toronto: Sixty-Eight Publishers, 1981; 2/ Bratislava: Archa, 1991; 3/ Brno (Czech Republic): "Zvláštní vydání...", 2002; 4/ Praha: Akropolis, 2012. The last edition contains detailed comments.
33) See, for instance: BONDY, Egon, *Fratelli invalidi*, Eleuthera, Milano 1993; BONDY, Egon, *Die Invaliden Geschwister*, Elfenbein, Heidelberg 1999; BONDY, Egon, *Kuzyni inwalidzi* [an extract], in *Czeski underground. Wybór tekstów z lat 1969–1989*, Wrocław: Oficyna Wydawnicza ATUT, 2008; BONDY, Egon, *Invalidna sorojenca*, Vnanje Gorice (Slovenia): Police Dubove, 2017.
34) There were 4 samizdat editions of Placák's Medorek (each a different version) before 1989 and since then 3 printed (abridged) editions: PLACÁK, Petr, *Medorek*, Pra-

and irony, but also a prototype of the human monsters or freaks, who are apparently made to populate a dehumanised world. It has been compared, for instance to the figure of Oskar in Günther Grass's novel *Blechtrommel* [The Tin Drum]. The other characters in *Medorek* also display only a minimum of genuine human features. Placák's vision of the world is a picture of a satanic panopticum, a labyrinth, in which maybe only "the mad" can survive. And here again, in the spirit of the reappraisal of values under normalization, "black" is often substituted for "white". For instance the chapter entitled "In the Tomb" is possibly the most cheerful and optimistic chapter of the whole book, even though it ends in a massacre. Themes of extinction or coming to an end also figure frequently in Placák's poems,[35] such as in the undated text *The Raven:*

[...] I rose into the air on my enormous black wings / and with the long talons of my feathered legs I / caught hold of the highest branch of the highest tree / I dug my claws deep into its soul / I screamed in anger and the sun went down swiftly / a pale moon rose and infamous clouds sailed across the sky / crookbacked rats finally left their holes / the red sky was burning itself out, foul-smelling funerary candles / I sat on a gibbet lulled and reconciled / as far as the eye could see there was a huge snow-covered graveyard.

J. H. Krchovský (a pseudonym), who these days is probably now the most renowned Czech underground poet, alongside Ivan

---

ha: Lidové noviny – Česká expedice, 1990; PLACÁK, Petr, *Medorek + Starcovy zápisky*, Praha: Hynek, 1997; PLACÁK, Petr, *Medorek (anonymní román)*, Praha: Plus, 2010.
35) A selection of Placák's samizdat verse appeared in the publication, PLACÁK, Petr, *Obrovský zasněžený hřbitov* [A Huge Snow-Covered Graveyard], Praha: Torst, 1995; the cited text appears on pp. 47–48; the cited part of the poem in Czech original goes as follows: "**Havran** [...] vznesl jsem se na svých obrovských černých křídlech / a dlouhými drápy svých opeřených nohou jsem se zachytil / na nejvyšší větvi největšího stromu / zaryl jsem paráty hluboko do jeho duše / zlostně jsem se ozval a slunce rychle zapadlo / vyšel pobledlý měsíc a na oblohu vypluly zlopověstné mraky / přihrblé krysy konečně vylezly ze svých děr / červánky dohořívaly, smrduté zádušní svíce / seděl jsem na šibenici, ukolébán a usmířen / kam oko dohlédlo, obrovský zasněžený hřbitov".

M. Jirous and Egon Bondy, created an oeuvre[36] abounding in "monstrous" and "perverse" dreams of an "outcast", an "alien being" on this earth, scorning existing values, and articulating his longing for the earliest possible release from this earthly existence. In his verse Krchovský's "ideological theme" is greatly enriched by a very strong dose of self-deprecation and black humour, which actually adds a new spiritual dimension to his pessimistic agnosticism. Krchovský's poems have been put into music by The Plastic People and by other underground bands, also they have been translated by several translators; e.g., Justin Quinn, Marek Tomin, Craig Cravens, and have been published in various anthologies and CD booklets. The following example, in O. T. Chalkestone's translation, was originally a part of a samizdat volume *Bestiální něha* [Beastly Tenderness], 1981–82, and is also found in the volume mentioned in Footnote 36:

IF I WANT TO VANISH WITHOUT A TRACE / drowning in the river won't be my case / – I'll lay my lazy bones / in a bath full of acid at home // While I get the water running / I tame my anxiety mulling: / – how when I'm all dissolved / will I unplug the tub hole? // I'll employ mechanical power! / – linking the plug to the door knob with a wire / and when they open the door later / I shall need no undertaker // I am sure that all in all / the bath tub will retain my soul... / through the hole as I flow down / my soul asleep nirvana bound // A piece of shit cannot be soaped... / what there is not cannot be broke / only the pretty nothing that troubles the brain / will never go down the drain.[37]

36) An extensive selection of Krchovský's samizdat poetry continues to appear in reprints, but initially as: KRCHOVSKÝ, J. H., *Básně* [Poems], Brno (Czech Republic): Host, 1998.

37) From KASJAS, Piotr (ed.), *Anthology of Slavic Poetry*, [London, UK]: Kasjas Publishing, 2016, p. 121. The Czech original goes as follows: "CHCI-LI ZMIZET BEZE STOPY / nebudu se v řece topit / – uložím svou kůži línou / na dno vany s kyselinou // Zatímco si chystám lázeň / přemýšlím a krotím bázeň: / – jak, až budu rozežraný / vytáhnu pak zátku z vany? // Pomohu si mechanikou! / – spojím drátem zátku s klikou / a jak někdo chytne kliku / pohřbí mě i bez hrobníků // Jsem si jist, že každopádně / zůstane má duše na dně... / já vyteču stokou z vany / duše usne do nirvány // Hovno nelze umýt mejdlem... / to, co není, zničit nejde / jen to nic, co trápí hlavy / kanálem se neodplaví..." (KRCHOVSKÝ, J. H., *Básně*, Brno, Czech Republic: Host, 1998, p. 31).

The poems of Jáchym Topol[38] reflect the thinking of a "barbarian in the urban jungle", a Huxleyesque "savage" rejecting a priori the "laws" of the majority population, who no longer display the features of real people.

Jan Pelc's prose debut, which, with charming irony, he entitled *Děti ráje* [Children of Paradise] (1983), even though "Hell's children" would be a more apt description (and which subsequently formed part of a trilogy with the title *...a bude hůř* [...things'll get worse],[39] teems with individuals who are simply socially-detrimental, semi-bestial "monsters"; whereas the opposite is true, when viewed in the light of the hypocrisy of "normalization". In Pelc's presentation, the world of "normal people" is a totally alienate place – empty and cheerless; only in the "hell" of the outcasts is it possible to find authentic feelings, albeit at the cost of following a path to self-destruction.

Paradoxically *Magorovy labutí písně* [Magor's Swan Songs][40] the supreme verse collection of the "founding father" of the Czech underground, Ivan Martin Jirous, belongs – with regards to the years it was written – in the context of the younger underground generation. Jirous wrote the poems in prison in the period 1981–85, and it was in fact through them that – initially in connection with underground literature and later, in the nineties – that he became known as a poet *par excellence* in the context of Czech literature as a whole. Much has been written about Jirous's *Swan Songs*, and suffice it to mention it here, but this part of his oeuvre is quoted here only be-

38) Topol's selection of his samizdat poetry was published in TOPOL, Jáchym, *Miluju tě k zbláznění* [I Love You Like Mad], Brno (Czechoslovakia): Atlantis, 1990, subsequently reprinted several times.

39) Pelc's prose text *Děti ráje* (Part 2 of the trilogy *...a bude hůř*, but was probably the first part to be written) first appeared in print in the Paris-based Czech exile journal *Svědectví* (18, no. 72 (1984), pp. 673-724), and was subsequently reprinted in the Czechoslovakia in various samizdat editions. The complete, unexpurgated trilogy was eventually published years later: PELC, Jan, *...a bude hůř*, Praha: Maťa, 2000.

40) See the complete edition of Jirous's poetry: JIROUS, Ivan M., *Magorova summa* [Magor's Sum], Praha: Torst, 1998; 2nd, enlarged edition: Praha: Torst, 2007; 3rd, enlarged, complete edition in 3 volumes: Praha: Torst, 2015 (all three editions include commentaries, registers, indexes of names and bibliography).

cause of its supposed relevance to our reflection on the themes of destruction, extinction, and ruin. Of course such themes are present in *Swan Songs*, but we would be hard-pressed to find actual apocalyptic moods. Jirous's poetry has too much Catholic "earthiness", or rather his Christianity is anything but a yearning for a sudden ontological transformation after universal destruction. Nevertheless, the very fact that Jirous's spiritual poetry was written when the author was in Czechoslovakia's harshest prison, one that had even something in common with a death camp, is of itself quite revealing.

The occasional "apocalyptic" echoes in *Magor's Swan Songs* are neutralized by irony or hyperbole, and lack any vision of a global catastrophe as they tend to evoke concrete, sometimes drastic images of everydayness. Occasionally, they take the form of a "dialogue with God", virtually a prayer, by means of which the author begs for the destruction not to come, but to be averted. Thus for example in the four-verse poem: "All rednecks in Pelhřimov know / that because of uranium they'll destroy Křemešník in a single blow // God grant me one wish / let them find uranium under Hradčany rather than fish."[41] Or there is a part of a poem with the incipit *V neštěstí se vždycky hbitě* [Whenever tragedy knocks on my door]:

[...] Oh Lord, is it yet noon / Or is dusk upon the world so soon? / Is a bomb just a big knife? / Is the wind tearing the very last leaves / From the courtyard's hawthorn trees / Or will they turn again green? Do tell // Is there bark around heaven / As around earthly trees? / Or are you in your glory surrounded / By nothing but angelic spheres? / Is there fire in the heart of the void? / God, is that you in the void? [...][42]

41) The Czech original: "Ví v Pelhřimově kdejaký buran / Křemešník zbourají našli tam uran // Vyslyšet přání ať Pán Bůh dá mi / aby ho našli pod Hradčanami", in *MS*, Praha: Torst, 1998, 2007, 2015, p. 494. The English translation in *Up the Devil's Back / Po hřbetě ďábla. A Bilingual Anthology of 20th Century Czech Poetry* (eds. and translators Bronislava Volková & Clarice Cloutier), Bloomington, Indiana: Slavica Publishers, Indiana University, 2008, pp. 308–313.
42) The Czech original: "[...] Bože je teprv poledne / nebo pad na svět soumrak už? / Je bomba jenom velký nůž? / Poslední listí vítr rve / na dvoře z hlohů nebo se / zazelenají poznovu? řekni mi // Je kolem nebes taky kůra / jako na stromech na zemi? / Nebo jen kůry andělské / obklopují Tě v slávě Tvé? / Je oheň v srdci prázdnoty? / Jsi v prázdnotě to Bože Ty? [...]", in *MS*, Praha: Torst, 1998, 2007, 2015, pp. 329–330.

In conclusion, I would look to point to a connection between "underground apocalyptic writing" and the literary oeuvre of an author who definitely does not belong to this circle, although along with Ladislav Klíma, Josef Váchal, and Jakub Deml he has been perceived as a kind of *magnus parens* of Czech underground literature. That oeuvre could indeed serve as proof that the apocalypse was not simply the prerogative of some underground screwballs, as it were, but was probably an appropriate reflection of the years of "normalization". I am referring, of course, to Bohumil Hrabal's prose *Příliš hlučná samota* [Too Loud a Solitude], the first version of which was penned in the years 1973-74;[43] i.e., the same period as the most representative texts of the first wave of underground literature, and yet independently of them, as can be proven. I hasten to add that it is by no means my intention to compare the artistic qualities of Hrabal's text with the various "primitivist" writings of the underground "barbaians", let alone to establish any kind of chronological precedence. But it is necessary to emphasize a number of congruent themes:

They both comprise reflections on the crisis and hopelessness affecting Czech society in the nineteen-fifties, and particularly in the seventies and eighties, as well as an articulation of generalized human hopelessness, as well as explicit cosmic hopelessness. They both display a paradoxical joyfulness, which is achieved even at the cost of self-destruction, in both cases they reflect on the feelings of social outcasts; and finally, they both include similar, truly almost apocalyptic visions of some kind of "last judgement", hinted at in the words of Christ, Buddha, and Lao Tse. Another obvious similarity is the considerable use of irony and self-deprecation, stylistic and even noetic techniques that are favoured by Hrabal and most of the underground authors.

The English translation in JIROUS, Ivan M., *My itinerary has been monotonous for quite a while. Selected prison poems translated from Czech by Marek Tomin*, London: Divus, 2017 (pp. 32–33).

43) This (approximate) dating is given in an editorial comment by Milan Jankovič (on p. 243) on the 9th volume of Hrabal's collected works: *Sebrané spisy Bohumila Hrabala - Hlučná samota* (Praha: Pražská imaginace, 1994). The book was published in the English translation: *Too Loud a Solitude* (translated by Michael Henry Heim) San Diego - New York - London: Harcourt Brace Jovanovich Publishers, 1990.

Nevertheless, in the context of Hrabal's overall output *Too Loud a Solitude* is more of a one-off, at least as far as the themes mentioned are concerned. Absent from Hrabal's work is the theme of a "post-apocalyptic" life opportunity, which was used, and capitalized on to the maximum degree by his erstwhile friend and literary fellow-traveller Egon Bondy in *Disabled Siblings*, a theme which was probably an echo of life in the "underground ghetto".

One can only speculate whether that literary dimension is absent from Hrabal because by the 1970s he no longer had access to the underground community, but the fact remains that from the mid-seventies to the end of the eighties Hrabal's new texts were simply intensely varied evocations of a more or less idealised past, and he turned his back on raw narrative like the prophetic apocalyptic urgency of *Too Loud a Solitude* or certain texts of the underground authors. The fact they would never have published anything like that of his in pre-1989 Czechoslovakia is another matter, and there is no way we can deal with it here and now.

Prague – Udine – Rome
April 2009 – January 2010
Translated by Gerald Turner

It was certainly rock music, in addition to literature and poetry, which dominated the Czechoslovak underground scene of the so-called normalization period (i.e., the 1970s and 1980s). By now the Czech underground culture has already become a legend whose reputation has been widely recognized. If not hundreds, then dozens of underground samizdat books got into print after 1989, some of them have also been translated into foreign languages, and the underground music was released on dozens of CDs. Even though underground art and literature has already been adequately evaluated by art and literary historians, there are still gaps to be filled in.

The history of the artistic career of the "psychedelic rock band" called The Plastic People of the Universe, that epitomizes the whole of the Czech underground scene, is well known (in English see the texts of the songs, chronology, discography, etc. in Jaroslav Riedel's book,[1] in the anthology *Views from the Inside*,[2] and English *Wikipedia* "The Plastic People of the Universe").[3]

---

1) RIEDEL, Jaroslav (ed.), *The Plastic People of the Universe*, Praha: Globus Music & Maťa, 1999.

2) MACHOVEC, Martin (ed.), *Views from the Inside: Czech Underground Literature and Culture (1948-1989)*, Praha: Ústav české literatury a literární vědy FF UK; 2nd edition: Praha: Karolinum Press, 2018.

3) The volume *Views from the Inside* (MACHOVEC, Martin ed., 2006, 2018) also includes the most authoritative text as far as the notions of Czech "underground culture" or the "second subculture" of the 1970s are concerned, Ivan M. Jirous' interpretation, evaluation, and the way he used the above-mentioned notions forms the basis and framework for most of the research into the Czech underground culture. It is his "underground manifesto" *Zpráva o třetím českém hudebním obrození* [Report on the Third Czech Musical Revival] written in 1975 (in *Magorův zápisník*, Praha: Torst, 1997, pp. 7-31), which was published many times in samizdat and several times by regular printing presses after 1989, and also translated into several languages including English (first published in English in the catalogue *The Merry Ghetto*, released with the LP *Egon Bondy's Happy Hearts Club Banned*, London – Paris: Boží Mlýn & SCOPA Invisible Production, 1978). The importance of the Czech underground movement in the civil rights struggle in Czechoslovakia, the impulse it gave to the establishment of the Charter 77 movement, was probably first acknowledged abroad by prof. Skilling (SKILLING, Gordon H., *Charter 77 and Human Rights in*

Some of the less well-known aspects of the music of The Plastic People and some other Czech underground bands, especially those which make us consider Czech underground music a serious art phenomenon, are traced in this treatise. These bands undoubtedly overcame the modest aesthetics of mere entertainment, of which rock music and rock shows are generally considered to be typical examples. In its best achievements, Czech underground music managed to create innovative works worthy of interpretation in terms of art, theatre performance, and literature. Its consciously and deliberately subversive expression of an anti-totalitarian view (though not necessarily directly a political view) only contributed to such status, but this alone would have never sufficed for a high artistic standard.

It is widely acknowledged that the Plastic People, at least at the beginning of their artistic career in 1969–1971, gained reputation as a sort of a "vanguard" rock band whose shows were "psychedelic" indeed. But honestly stated, such up-to-date rock music hardly makes the Plastic People worthy of attention on the part of art historians. The 1960s saw a rich variety of rock shows in Western Europe and the US ranging from the gigantic stadium performances of show business superstars to underground music clubs with their ephemeral rock bands playing gigs of different quality. These gigs were quite comparable to the ones performed by the contemporaneous Czech band called The Plastic People of the Universe in "a faraway country of which we know little" (Sir Neville Chamberlain, Munich, Germany, 1938, speaking of Czechoslovakia), moreover, behind the barbed wires of the Iron Curtain.

Historians also recognize the fact that only some years later, in 1976, the police terror provoked by the independent activities of the Czechoslovak underground community gave the last – and maybe the most decisive – impulse to issue the initial Charter 77 petition and to establish the Czechoslovak dissident movement. In

Czechoslovakia, London: Allen and Unwin, 1981). Václav Havel in the book *Disturbing the Peace. A Conversation with Karel Hvížďala*, New York: Knopf & Vintage Books, 1990 [*Dálkový výslech* in Czech original, first published in samizdat in 1986], in this respect also stressed several times the important role of the Czech underground movement. *Wikipedia*, see: https://en.wikipedia.org/wiki/The_Plastic_People_of_the_Universe, Accessed in June 2019.

Plastic People in 1969. From the left: Josef Janíček – Pavel Zeman – Milan "Mejla" Hlavsa – Jiří "Přemysl" Števich – Michal Jernek; photo: Jan Ságl

this respect, the Plastic People and the underground community can be seen as one of the best symbols, even as the very incarnation of Czechoslovak political and moral resistance that in cooperation with other independent social forces finally managed to overthrow totalitarianism in 1989 and reestablish democracy in the country. This aspect, again, with all respect to it being undeniable, would not make the role of the underground rock musicians more prominent in the history of art at the beginning.

And yet, there indeed were moments in the career of the Plastic People and some more Czech underground rock groups in which the spontaneity, innocence, and naiveté of simple rock shows and stage gigs was deliberately and consciously overcome. And it is this fact which makes Czech underground music interesting and vivid to this day.

The Man with No Ears

In a ghastly white bathroom a horrid event took place
in a mirror that hanged on the wall
a head without a single strand of hair appeared
it was a man
his visage was most horrid
his bald skull bore two extremely warped ears

Two hours went by
the man looks into the mirror
takes out a box in which there is a syringe and some heroin
he shoots up his dose

Two more hours go by
the man looks into the mirror again
takes out a razor
and cuts off his extremely warped ears

The white bathroom like the morgue
is covered with blood
the box and the syringe lay on the floor
as well as the bottle with heroin,
two extremely warped ears and
the man with no ears[4]

(Michal Jernek, 1969)

---

4) In Josef Janda's translation. The Czech original: "**Muž bez uší** // V mrtvolně bílé koupelně se odehrál hrůzný výjev / v zrcadle, které viselo na stěně / se objevila úplně holá lidská hlava / byl to muž / jeho zjev byl hrůzyplný / na jeho holé lebce byly přirostlé dvě příšerně zkroucené uši // Uplynuly dvě hodiny / muž se dívá do zrcadla / vyndává skříňku / vytahuje injekční stříkačku a lahvičku s heroinem / sám si vpichuje svoji dávku // Uplynuly další dvě hodiny / muž se opět dívá do zrcadla / vyndává břitvu / a obě své příšerně zkroucené uši si odřezává // Bílá koupelna dělá dojem márnice / je pokropena lidskou krví / na zemi tu leží skříňka, injekční stříkačka, / lahvička s heroinem, / dvě lidské, příšerně zkroucené uši / a mrtvý muž bez uší". The English translation in The Plastic People of the Universe, p. 31 (see Footnote 1).

To better understand why and how such a simple and, as a matter of fact, quite traditionally conceived psychedelic rock sound and lyrics of The Plastic People changed into something more demanding and sophisticated, we have to trace at least **three encounters** experienced by the Plastics that gave the band the impulses necessary for the reevaluation of their primary artistic views.

First of all, they were impulses that came from their encounter with Milan Knížák's experimental music ensemble called AKTUAL.

Today, Milan Knížák is one of the best-known Czech personalities and has always been recognized as one of the leading figures in conquering new territories for modern art since the early 1960s, though he is often considered controversial and too ambitious in his experiments in fine arts, music, architectural design, literature, poetry, and art museum management. It was as early as 1963 that Knížák started organizing art happenings, events, and land art actions in Czechoslovakia. In 1967 Knížák also started experimenting with his musical ensemble, a sort of a pseudo-rock band called AKTUAL. Knížák composed most of the music and wrote most of the lyrics for the ensemble, which consisted of amateur enthusiasts, even non-musicians. Their music included experiments of all kinds. Besides features of rock music they made use of déclassé brass band evergreen songs and tunes, on the one hand, and the techniques and practices of minimal and concrete music, on the other. Beside traditional musical instruments they used sounds produced by buzzers, horns, the roar of a running motorbike engine, the rattling of broken glass splinters in a bucket, or even the sound of chopping wood logs onstage. Knížák's lyrics, always witty and easy to remember, thanks to their appropriate rhythm and rhymes, mostly mocked the venerated idols, the "sacred cows" of both Communist totalitarianism and of the Western consumerist "paradise". It is no wonder therefore that Knížák and his band AKTUAL managed to organize only about 6–7 gigs between the years 1967–1971. Most of their live performances were violently stopped before they reached the planned finale, and moreover, their audience hardly ever protested against such interventions. In 1970 and 1971 the ensemble AKTUAL played two gigs together with The Plastic People. Legend has it that The Plastic People members where the only ones among the audience, when AKTUAL was on stage, who really liked

Knížák's music. Later on, they also recalled how much they had been impressed by Knížák's Czech texts which lacked the usual banality and sentimentality of most contemporary Czech pop lyrics:

I Love You and Lenin

I LOVE YOU AND LENIN
I LOVE YOU AND LENIN
I LOVE YOU AND LENIN
I LOVE YOU AND LENIN

I love you for your hair
I love you for your smile
I love you for your tenderness
I love you for your dreams

I LOVE YOU AND LENIN
I LOVE YOU AND LENIN
I LOVE YOU AND LENIN
I LOVE YOU AND LENIN

I love Lenin for his goatee
I love Lenin for his bald head
I love Lenin for the revolution
I love Lenin for his up-sided world

I LOVE YOU AND LENIN
I LOVE YOU AND LENIN
I LOVE YOU AND LENIN
I LOVE YOU AND LENIN

(Milan Knížák, 1968)[5]

5) In Karolína Dolanská's translation. The Czech original: "**Miluju tebe a Lenina** // Miluju tebe a Lenina / miluju tebe a Lenina / miluju tebe a Lenina / miluju tebe a Lenina // miluju tebe pro tvoje vlasy / miluju tebe pro tvůj smích / miluju tebe pro tvý něžnosti / miluju tebe pro tvý sny // miluju tebe a Lenina / miluju tebe a Lenina / miluju tebe a Lenina / miluju tebe a Lenina // miluju Lenina pro jeho vousy / miluju Lenina pro jeho pleš / miluju Lenina pro revoluci / miluju Lenina pro jeho svět // milu-

AKTUAL in Mariánské Lázně, 1968. From the left: Milan Knížák – Josef Vereš – Jan
Maria Mach – Pavel Tichý – Ivan Čori

Assault on Culture

Wake father Koniash up
Let Jesuits arise from their graves
Thousands of books are to be burned
Wake father Koniash up

Tear down paintings, burn up your books
Destroy theatres with bulldozers

ju tebe a Lenina / miluju tebe a Lenina / miluju tebe a Lenina / miluju tebe a Lenina".
See KNÍŽÁK, Milan, *Písně kapely Aktual*, eds. MACHOVEC, Martin – RIEDEL, Jaroslav,
Praha: Maťa, 2003, p. 47; the recording of a cover version of the song was released
on a CD *AKTUAL. Děti bolševizmu*, Louny: Guerilla Records, 2005.

Destroy anything valuable
Make an assault on culture

Wake father Koniash up
Wake all the idiots up
The gifted ones must be killed
Wake father Koniash up

Tear down paintings, burn up your books
Destroy theatres with bulldozers
Destroy anything valuable
Make an assault on culture

(Milan Knížák, 1967)[6]

The second important impulse was due to an encounter with the art historian and poet Ivan Martin Jirous who, in the course of the following years, became one of the best-known representatives of Czech underground culture, and later also gained respect as a Czechoslovak political prisoner. Through Jirous, The Plastic People got into contact with a number of artists, mostly university and art academy graduates, who in the mid-1960s established an unofficial art group called *Křižovnická škola* [the Crusaders' School].[7]

---

6) Translated by M.M. The Czech original: "**Atentát na kulturu** // probuďte pátera Koniáše / ať vstanou z mrtvých jezuiti / tisíce knih je třeba spálit / probuďte pátera Koniáše // Rozkopte obrazy spalte si knihy / divadla ať srovnaj buldozéry / zahoďte všechno co má ňákou cenu / spáchejte atentát na kulturu // probuďte pátera Koniáše / probuďte všechny idioty / inteligenci je třeba zabít / probuďte pátera Koniáše // Rozkopte obrazy spalte si knihy / divadla ať srovnaj buldozéry / zahoďte všechno co má ňákou cenu / spáchejte atentát na kulturu". See KNÍŽÁK, Milan, *Písně kapely Aktual*, eds. MACHOVEC, Martin – RIEDEL, Jaroslav, Praha: Maťa, 2003, p. 39; the recording of the original version of the song was released on a CD *Atentát na kulturu*, Brno (Czech Republic): Anne Records, 2003. (Concerning páter Koniáš / father Koniash: Antonín Koniáš, 1691–1760, was a Czech Jesuit, preacher, missionary and censor. He was very active in re-catholicization project in Bohemia, wrote lists of "libri prohibiti", i.e. "banned books", and organized confiscations and public burnings of such books. In 19th century he became a symbol of religious, ideologic intolerance in the country.)
7) See the art catalogue JIROUSOVÁ, Věra (ed.), *Křižovnická škola čistého humoru bez vtipu* [The Crusaders' School of Pure Humor without Jokes], Hradec Králové – Praha:

Ivan Jirous and a number of his artist friends were excited by the vigorous enthusiasm of The Plastic People and their loyal audience and started collaborating with them in different ways. Jirous lectured them on Andy Warhol, pop art, and related subjects; others were inventive in making extraordinary stage decorations and crazy, fancy facepaintings for the musicians. The rock musicians themselves were soon involved in various artistic actions, events, and conceptual performances where their music was only a part of the whole libretto. It was especially the artists Karel Nepraš, Zorka Ságlová, Olaf Hanel, and Eugen Brikcius who showed a deep understanding for the musical ambitions of The Plastic People, and who, on the other hand, were also influenced by the bands' aesthetics and ideas that were rooted in the infamous mutiny of rock barbarians, in a reevaluation of values as coined by the generation of "flower power", of hippies.

Several examples of such cooperation follow:

1) The Plastic People and their friends took an active part in Ságlová's happenings *Throwing Balls* (1969) and *Homage to Fafejta* (1972). The first one was commented on by the author as follows: "In April 1969, after the ice had melted, we threw 37 balls of three different colours (blue, green, orange) into the lake, producing a floating sculpture taken by wind and waves. We left it on the surface of the water".[8] The second one, which the Plastics accompanied

Galerie moderního umění Hradec Králové - Středočeská galerie Praha, 1991; see also the art catalogue SLAVÍKOVÁ, Duňa (ed.), *Křižovnická škola čistého humoru bez vtipu*, Roudnice nad Labem (Czech Republic): Galerie moderního umění v Roudnici nad Labem, 2015-2016; SÁGL, Jan, *Tanec na dvojitém ledě / Dancing on the Double Ice*, Praha: KANT, 2013; MACHOVEC, Martin, *Jan Ságl / Tanec na dvojitém ledě / Dancing on the Double Ice / Popisky k fotografiím*, Praha: KANT, 2017.

The name of the "school" is based on the Czech adjective "křižovnický", which refers to the Knights of the Cross with the Red Star or the Military Order of the Crusaders of the Red Star. The artists chose the name by pure coincidence only - they used to meet in a pub called "U křižovníků" nearby a medieval Prague monastery (in Křižovnická street) that belonged (and after 1989 was returned) to the mentioned Roman-Catholic order.

8) See LAMAROVÁ, Milena (ed.), *Zorka Ságlová 1965-1995*, Praha: Galerie výtvarného umění v Litoměřicích, 1995; see also BUČILOVÁ, Lenka, *Zorka Ságlová. Úplný přehled*

Zorka Ságlová's happening "Throwing balls into the lake Bořín at Průhonice" (1968 concept, 1969 realization); in which members of the Plastic People and of the Primitives Group took part; photos: Jan Ságl

with their music, consisted of the participants inflating condoms and the subsequent throwing of the inflated "balloons" out of a window of a castle ruin. The point of the happening is found in the name of "Fafejta": Mr. Fafejta was a well-known condom manufacturer in prewar Czechoslovakia. The Plastics, in their early years, played *The Song of the Fafejta Bird about Two Unearthly Worlds* which probably inspired Zorka Ságlová to organize the happening.[9]

díla, Praha: KANT, 2009; KNÍŽÁK, Milan - POKORNÝ, Marek - VALOCH, Jiří, *Zorka Ságlová*, Praha: Národní galerie, 2006.
9) See more photos of the two events in SÁGL, Jan, *Tanec na dvojitém ledě / Dancing on the Double Ice*, Praha: KANT, 2013 (Footnote 7).

2) In 1974 Olaf Hanel organized two artistic events, *Homage to Bedřich Smetana* and *The Waking Up of the Blaník Knights*, both of them supported by an improvised, ephemeral band called Sen noci svatojánské band [The Midsummer Night's Dream Band] made up of some members of the Plastic People, in which the sculptor Karel Nepraš and the painter Miloslav Hájek played violin.

The first event made use of the famous main theme of one part of Smetana's symphonic poem *Má vlast* [My Country], i.e. "*The Vltava*". The Midsummer Night's Dream Band played the theme several times during one day starting nearby the Vltava's source high in the Šumava mountains and at last ending in Prague.

The second event, deliberately containing a politically subversive moment, was based on an old Czech legend about the sleeping knights inside Blaník Hill, some 50 kilometers southeast of Prague. According to legend, the knights will wake up and set off from the mountain, led by the Czech patron saint Wenceslas, to help the Czech people when their impoverishment and misery brought about by the "oppressor's wrong" reaches its climax. It is pointless to add that the performance of The Plastic People and their friends on top of Blaník Hill missed the desired effect: the noble knights inside went on sleeping.

3) In 1979 Eugen Brikcius created an event, or rather a "soap musical" as he called it, *Hello Fellow – Ave Clave*. Brikcius, one of the best-known Czech happening organizers (he had already started making them in late 1960s) and also an author of neo-Latin poetry, organized the event in a private apartment. The Anglo-Latin libretto, written and recited by Brikcius, was accompanied by the music of The Plastic People and composed by Milan Hlavsa just for this occasion. The event, however, ended abruptly because of a police raid: all the present persons' IDs were checked, and sixteen of them were subsequently arrested.

On such and similar occasions, the wild spontaneous rock music of The Plastic People was consciously channelled according to a previous scenario. As a matter of fact, such conceptual music only served the artistic aims set by others, but it undoubtedly helped broaden the horizons of Czech underground musicians themselves. As early as in 1973, The Plastic People themselves started introducing exper-

The happening "The Waking of the Blaník Knights", 1974, with
members of the Plastic People and Sen noci svatojánské band;
photos: Olaf Hanel

iments into their live stage music. Perhaps we should add that from
1973 onwards they could only give gigs outside Prague and other
large Czechoslovak cities (i.e., in village pubs, pretending to meet
only on the occasion of a wedding celebration and the like). By that
time their audience consisted mostly of devoted fans who were ad-
mitted only after presenting an invitation written by one of the band
members. Such growing anxiety, if not a kind of paranoia, reflected
the insane atmosphere in Czech society infected by the so-called normalization, actually a reestablishing of neo-Stalinism in the country.

The gig called *Do lesíčka na čekanou...* [Up to the Ranger's Watch...]
took place in pub in the village of Veleň nearby Prague in December 1973. The very name of the gig, quite unfit for a rock concert,
offers a clue to the adequate interpretation of the artistic shift that

The cover of the booklet mentioned in Footnote 10 with the photo taken in
the 1973 Veleň gig; photo: Petr Prokeš

occurred in the music of the Plastics: it quotes an old and notorious
Czech folk song, a favourite of drunk pub cronies.

Its simple minded lyrics say something about "a young ranger setting off to the woods to hunt only to be followed by his sweetheart –
the scene of their rendezvous in the woods being lit by moonlight".

The beginning of the gig shocked even the experienced and har-
dened audience of the Plastics: Pavel Zajíček, friend of the band and
the founder of another important underground ensemble called DG
307, started out by shouting the words "anti! anti!" and the like at
the audience. Meanwhile, the other musicians were sitting passively
on the stage, decorated with artificial trees as "woods", and were
having a snack. When the indignation on the side of the audience

seemed to have reached its climax, the shouting was stopped by an all-at-once, unison singing of the folk song *Do lesíčka na čekanou...* which was presented in the out-of-tune manner of the late night pub drunkards. Luckily, it was soon replaced by an improvised electronic, cacophonic composition called *Kohoutkova kometa* [Kohoutek Comet]. As this composition came to an end, the usual rock gig started at last, which, however, had some more surprises in store for the audience.[10]

This aforementioned surprise echoed the third important encounter of The Plastic People on their way underground: in 1973, they met with the texts of the legendary poet Egon Bondy whose name was officially non-existent before 1989. His ironic, mocking, and prophetic poetry of the 1950s and 1970s, which was only accessible in samizdat publications, enchanted The Plastic People. The Veleň gig also offered the first opportunity to present some of Bondy's poems set to music. The way in which the artistic career of the Plastics was to develop further on was not evident in the electronic experiments such as *Kohoutek Comet*, but rather the ritual-like, monotonous rock sound contrasting sharply with the prophetic message contained in the poet's verses of *Podivuhodný mandarin* [The Miraculous Mandarin] – replacing pop culture in favor of real literature and poetry. The "psychedelic years" and the primitive rock shows and lyrics of *The Man with No Ears* were now gone forever.

The Miraculous Mandarin

For your whole life you'll be spreading your legs to let in
The one and only the Miraculous Mandarin

You'll be stitching your outfit from uselessness and sin
You'll keep searching for the Miraculous Mandarin
With a blood road in your head and shadows in your grin
You'll keep longing for the Miraculous Mandarin

Many times you'll wish to gulp the gas like a gin
For again it wasn't the Miraculous Mandarin

---

10) See photos of the gig in the booklet added to a 2-CD set of the Plastic People of the Universe, *Do lesíčka na čekanou 1. 12. 1973*, Louny: Guerilla Records, 2006.

When at the age of forty you'll hang down your chin
You'll know the Mills of God have sucked you in!

(Egon Bondy, 1972)[11]

The other authentic step beyond the traditional territory of rock music was made in the same year of 1973 by the group DG 307, whose founder and lyricist Pavel Zajíček was musically backed by Milan Hlavsa, the leading figure of The Plastic People. The influence of Knížák's band AKTUAL is undeniable, but there are also considerable differences: the overall musical mood of DG 307 is gloomy and dark, close to prophetic reproaches and Christian parables. Knížák's ironies and mockery are mostly absent. The first important performance of DG 307 took place in a village pub of Postupice, September 1974, as a part of the so-called "First Musical Festival of the Second Culture".

Same as with the *Do lesíčka na čekanou...* gig, the audience was largely disappointed if not shocked by the experiments of DG 307. Obviously they were not aware of the fact of having witnessed the birth of one of the most famous musical legends of Czech underground culture.

St.

St. Paul
hounded all his life
St. Stephen

11) Translated by Jiří Popel for the English subtitles of Jana Chytilová's film *The Plastic People of the Universe*, Czech Television (ČT) and Video 57, 2001. The Czech original: "**Podivuhodný mandarin** // Po celý život budeš roztahovat klín / aby v něj vešel Podivuhodný mandarin // Budeš svůj šat šít z marností a z vin / hledat budeš kde je Podivuhodný mandarin // A v hlavě hukot krve a v očích noční stín / toužit jen budeš aby přišel Podivuhodný mandarin // Mnohokrát si budeš chtít pustit plyn /že zas to nebyl Podivuhodný mandarin // Až vyčerpáš se v čtyřicítce a budeš celá hin / poznáš že život je jen boží mlýn"; see *The Plastic People of the Universe, Texty*, 2nd edition, Praha: Maťa 2001, p. 60; see also BONDY, Egon, *Básnické spisy II. 1962-1975*, Praha: Argo, 2015, p. 386. The song with the text was released on a number of CDs. See for instance *THE PLASTIC PEOPLE OF THE UNIVERSE III. Egon Bondy's Happy Hearts Club Banned* (1974-75), ed. Jaroslav Riedel, Praha: Globus Music, 2001.

stoned to death
John the Baptist
beheaded
Jesus
crucified

is someone
chopping at your head?
have you not got
enough to eat?
fears for your health?
are your bones
disintegrating?
are they
plotting against you?
is someone
beating your chin with a stone?

What are you
afraid of then?

You know!

You are a crippled
cowardly animal
the main thing is you live high
off the hog!

St. Paul
hounded all his life
St. Stephen
stoned to death
John the Baptist
beheaded
Jesus
crucified

(Pavel Zajíček, 1974)

The cover of a booklet released with a 2 CD set with authentic recordings
of DG 307 music: DG 307 – HISTORIE HYSTERIE. Archiv dochovaných nahrávek
1973-75, Louny: Guerilla Records, 2004

What Are We?

Are we children
who can't grow old
or madmen
who don't know when to give up?

Why do we so often
hate each other?
Why do we build
castles of shit
on foundations of vanity?

Why don't we get together?
What are we afraid of?
What's so fancy about us?
What's so interesting about us?
We're carriers of fear and mistrust
We're prophets of dust

What do we want?
Where are we going?
What if we discover we're nowhere?
Will we shit ourselves over it?

Are we children
who can't grow old
or madmen
who don't know when to give up?

(Pavel Zajíček, 1974)[12]

When following the artistic careers of the Czech underground musicians in their ambitions at reaching the world of "real art", of "serious music", rid of all remnants of "pop entertainment", we may find the two artistic climaxes: *Pašijové hry velikonoční* [Easter Passion Play], performed by The Plastic People on stage in 1978, and

12) Both poems by Zajíček were translated by Paul Wilson and Ivan Hartel and published in the catalogue *The Merry Ghetto*, 1978. The Czech originals: "**Sv.** // sv. pavel / celej život stíhán / sv. štěpán / ukamenován / jan křtitel / sťat / ježíš / ukřižován // seká tobě / někdo do hlavy / seš snad hříčkou / popravy / máš nedostatek / potravy / vobavy vo svý / zdraví / bořej se ti / kostí základy / připravujou proti tobě / úklady / mlátí ti někdo / šutrem do brady? // čeho se tedy bojíš? // však ty víš! // seš zakrnělej / zbabělej živočich / hlavně že seš / prasácky dobře veleživ! // sv. pavel / celej život stíhán / sv. štěpán / ukamenován / jan křtitel / sťat / ježíš / ukřižován".
"**Co sme?** // sme dětma / který nestačily zestárnout / nebo šílenci / který nemůžou padnout? // proč se tak často nenávidíme? / proč na ješitnosti / pevnosti z hoven / stavíme? / proč se nepropojíme? / čeho se bojíme? // co je na nás vokázalýho? / co je na nás zajímavýho? / sme nosiči strachu / sme předzvěstí prachu // co chceme? / kam deme? / co až se vocitneme nikde / z čeho se tam posereme? // sme dětma / který nestačily zestárnout / nebo šílenci / který nemůžou padnout?" See Z[AJÍČEK], Pavel, *DG 307 (Texty z let 1973–1980)*, Praha: Vokno, 1990.

Dar stínum [Gift to the Shadows], performed by DG 307 in 1979.[13] In the post Charter 77 years, of which most of the underground artists, musicians, and poets were signatories, the atmosphere of Czech society was getting more and more depressive day by day. Also as a result of the "big trial" of the Czech underground of 1976, a number of underground activists, first of all Ivan M. Jirous, were repeatedly prosecuted and imprisoned. Many others were forced under police terror to leave the country and emigrate to the West with no chance ever to return.

Such overwhelming gloominess was adequately reflected by The Plastic People in 1978 when they set to music the words of perhaps the best-known story of the Christian world. The libretto is built on a choice of passages taken mostly from the New Testament Gospels that bring forth moments both eternal and topical. The Czech underground musicians thus not only followed the footsteps of innumerable medieval church "miracula," or Baroque oratories, *Passio Christi* compositions and performances, but, in their own way, they successfully managed to be innovative about it. We would even dare to compare their achievement with the innovations of the best composers of religious music of both the past and the present, and also with the writers who made the words of the Bible living and comprehensible again.

The performance took place at Václav Havel's country house Hrádeček in East Bohemia and only several dozen of the most

13) By the beginning of the 1980s the underground gigs and performances already roused the attention of Czech unofficial review writers, meaning those who did not lack academic background. See reviews by JIROUS, Ivan M.: "Kundy rty ústa tváře masky [Cunts lips mouths faces masks], 1980; "A hudebníky ve větvích nebylo vidět" [And the musicians couldn't be seen among the branches], 1981; "Jsou to divný kluci" [They're strange guys], 1981 – all of them in *Magorův zápisník*, Praha: Torst, 1997; see also a review by JIROUSOVÁ, Věra: "Koncert Plastic People na počest Ladislava Klímy" [Concert of the Plastic People in Honour of Ladislav Klíma], *Svědectví* 14, no. 62 (1980) (Paris); see also HAVEL, Václav, *Disturbing the Peace. A Conversation with Karel Hvížďala*, New York: Knopf & Vintage Books, 1990. In the 1970s and 1980s very little was written about Czech underground music from the point of view of musicology. Jiří Černý's article "O hudbě jakou hrají Plastic People of Universe a DG 307" [On the music played by Plastic People and DG 307], published first in samizdat editions of *"Hnědá kniha" o procesech s českým undergroundem* (1976, 1980), and finally in the printed, commented edition of the same title (Praha: ÚSTR, 2012), is an exemption.

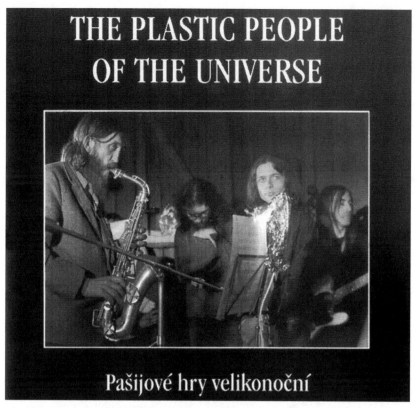

THE PLASTIC PEOPLE OF THE UNIVERSE

Pašijové hry velikonoční

The cover of the CD THE PLASTIC PEOPLE OF THE UNIVERSE V. Pašijové hry velikonoční (1978), Praha: Globus Music, 1998

trusted friends could come and see it. Nevertheless, those ones who expected a show, a real performance on stage, were disappointed again, this time because of a reason quite different from the one that caused their indignation at the *Do lesíčka na čekanou...* gig and the like – there were just the musicians, playing and singing their parts, emphasizing with their music the topical moments of the best-known of all human tragedies. *The Passion Play* by The Plastic People can thus be interpreted as the absolute opposite, antithesis of all attempts at making the New Testament message more accessible to consumerist society, such as Webber's and Rice's musical *Jesus Christ Superstar* for instance: no pleasing melodies, no shows, no cheap effects, and/or drastic tricks – first of all, no show! The matter proved to be too serious for the Czech underground of the late 1970s.

What Need Have We of a King

What need have we of a king in the Roman empire?
Pilate, our governor is sufficient for us and peace
and tranquility in the land
What need have we of a poor king, riding on an ass?
The people are led astray by your words about love for one's neighbour
What need have we of the healed?
Peace in the land, peace in the empire and Pilate is our governor
You blaspheme against the high priests
and call yourself a son in the house of David, king of Jews
and you stir up the people
you shall be put to death with thieves
and your deeds shall be forgotten and your words
as a thief is forgotten
for you blasphemed against the peace of the empire
we shall expose you to ridicule in robes of purple
and a crown of thorns
as a warning to future generations
Jesus of Nazareth, King of the Jews,
you blasphemed against the order of the world and the priests
and you presented yourself as a poor king on an ass,
as the lamb of God, as the promised Messiah and as Elijah
your deeds are numbered: what need have we of any further witnesses?
You have blasphemed against the order of the world in word and deed
What need have we of love or blind men who can see?
What need have we of the healed?
Peace and order in the Empire are more important to the priests
                                                    and the people
Crucify him!

(Biblical text, arranged by Vratislav Brabenec, 1978)[14]

14) Paul Wilson's translation. See *The Plastic People of the Universe*. Prague: Globus Music & Maťa, 1999. Czech original: "**Nepotřebujeme krále** // Nepotřebujeme krále v ustanovení římského impéria / dost je nám Pilát hejtmanem a klid v zemi klid / nepotřebujeme krále chudého na oslátku / lid obloumzněný tvým slovem o lásce k bližnímu / nepotřebujeme uzdravených / klid v zemi klid impéria a Pilát je nám hejtmanem / rouháš se nejvyšším kněžím / za syna z rodu Davidova za krále Židů se

The performance *Dar stínum* [Gift to the Shadows] took place in another country house, in the village of Nová Víska, northwest Bohemia, 1979.

Not only had the sound of the band abandoned all prophetic urgency, but in order to prevent interference of all intruding side effects, the musicians made themselves "invisible" for this occasion. The stage was hidden behind a curtain made of ragged bedsheets and only now and then could the audience have a glimpse of a musician or his instrument, but mostly it was only their "shadows" projected on the "curtain" which was never to rise. The "invisible" performance adequately symbolized the social and political situation of the country and, moreover, it took one more step in the musical and artistic development of the Czech underground.

The Way across Czecholand

I'll penetrate with my tongue
into your lotus flower
We'll set fires on the faded plains
on the way across Czecholand

With our fingers we'll open
rusty recesses
We'll set free the rays
of our presence
We won't drown
in the sea of light

stavíš / a bouříš lid / budeš popraven s lotry / a činy tvé zapomenuty budou i slova tvá / jako na zločin se zapomíná / neboť rouháš se ustanovením světským klidu impéria / ku posměchu vystavíme tebe v purpuru s korunou trnovou / na výstrahu pokolením příštím / Ježíši Nazaretský, králi židovský / rouhal ses pořádku světa a kněžím / za chudého krále na oslátku / za beránka božího se vydával / za Mesiáše jenž přijíti má za Eliáše / jsou sečteny skutky tvoje a není potřeba více svědků / rouhal ses pořádku světa a slova tvá a činy tvé / nepotřebujeme lásku a slepých kteříž vidí / nepotřebujeme uzdravených / je klid a pořádek impéria přednější kněžím i lidu / Ukřižovat!"

From the DG 307 "Gift to the Shadows" performance, 1979; photo: Jaroslav Kukal

With lime we'll burn down
the living graves
lining our ways
witnesses
of our corpse-like strays
We'll see a bright auspice

The iron circle of eternity

I'll penetrate with my tongue
into your lotus flower
We'll set fires
on the faded plains
on the way across Czecholand

(Pavel Zajíček, 1979)

Neither

Neither the sea, nor the land
neither the light, nor the dark
neither a snake, nor a bird
neither the silence, nor the roar
neither a vision, nor a blindness
neither nothing, nor everything
neither the freeze, nor the move
neither a body, nor a shadow
neither the fall, nor the flight
neither the stink, nor the aroma

Neither neither neither

Neither the sea, nor the aroma
neither the light, nor the shadow
neither the freeze, nor a vision
neither the flight, nor the silence
neither the dark, nor the stink
neither the fall, nor a bird
neither a blindness, nor a snake
neither a body, nor a nothing
neither the move, nor the land
neither everything, nor the roar

(Pavel Zajíček, 1979)[15]

15) Both cited texts from *Gift to the Shadows* were translated by M.M. Their Czech originals: "**Cesta českem** // proniknu jazykem / do tvýho lotosovýho květu / zapálíme ohně / na vyhaslejch pláních / cesty českem // otevřeme prsty / rezatý skrýše / vypustíme paprsky / naší přítomnosti / v moři světla / se neutopíme // spálíme vápnem / živoucí hroby / při cestách / svědky / mrtvolnýho bloudění / spatříme jasný znamení // železnej kruh věčnosti // proniknu jazykem / do tvýho lotosovýho květu / zapálíme ohně / na vyhaslejch pláních / cesty českem".
"**Ani** // ani moře ani pevnina / ani světlo ani tma / ani had ani pták / ani mlčení ani řev / ani vidění ani slepota / ani nic ani vše / ani zmrazení ani pohyb / ani tělo ani stín / ani pád ani let / ani smrad ani vůně // ani ani ani // ani moře ani vůně / ani světlo ani stín / ani zmrazení ani vidění / ani let ani mlčení / ani tma ani smrad /

From the DG 307 "Gift to the Shadows" performance, 1979; photo: Jaroslav Kukal

It is worth mentioning one more factor that contributed to the underground "Gesamtkunstwerk": the underground concerts and gigs were quite unique and unrepeatable. We have in mind particularly the anxiety that was always present in the souls of all participants in underground actions – both the musicians and the audience. Police raids could be expected any time and indeed they often occurred. The unwelcome guests then played roles of

ani pád ani pták / ani slepota ani had / ani tělo ani nic / ani pohyb ani pevnina / ani vše ani řev". See Z[AJÍČEK], Pavel, *DG 307 (Texty z let 1973-1980)*, Praha: Vokno, 1990. The original recordings were released on *DG 307 - SVĚDEK SPÁLENÝHO ČASU 1979/1980* [5CDs], Louny: Guerilla Records, 2013.

their own, according to their own "librettos" and "scenarios", perhaps not those of a *deus ex machina* but rather those of a *diabolus ex machina*. The fear roused by such expectable interference consequently contributed to changes and modifications of the underground artists' attitudes and ambitions, and in cases when such expectations proved to be unjustified only made all the participants enjoy the underground actions much better than any "normal situation" could ever offer.

The Czech (or Czechoslovak) underground movement has so far been mostly recognized as an important and integral part of the Czechoslovak civil rights struggle of the 1970s and 1980s. Moreover, it has been appreciated for its specific social position and for the sociopolitical role it played before the collapse of the totalitarian regime.

In his text *Zpráva o třetím českém hudebním obrození* [Report on the Third Czech Musical Revival], written in 1975, Ivan M. Jirous characterized not only the principal ideas and the social position of the Czech underground movement, but also the role of artists in the society (perhaps not only) of those years.[16]

The fact that the heritage of Czech underground music is still alive, and has still something to say, is indirectly confirmed by a high number of musical releases of records.[17] Czech underground literature, on the other hand, has already gained wide recognition at home and abroad as well.[18] With a few quoted examples we tried to point out the fact that the Czech underground musicians occasionally managed to generate music of a value that went far beyond the aesthetics of "pop entertainment". They joined their musical efforts with visual artists and introduced serious topics into their music, with texts by remarkable writers and poets (Egon Bondy, Ladislav Klíma, Vratislav Brabenec, Pavel Zajíček, biblical texts, etc.). Thus they performed "art rock" not only relevant to the history of

16) See the English translation in the 2nd edition of *Views from the Inside*, Praha: Karolinum Press, 2018.

17) See chosen discography at the end of this volume, also in the 2nd edition of *Views from the Inside*, Praha: Karolinum Press, 2018.

18) See JANOUŠEK, Pavel (ed.), *Dějiny české literatury 1945-1989* [The History of Czech Literature, 1945-1989]. 4 vols. Praha: Academia, 2007-2008.

political resistance behind the Iron Curtain or the history of rock music of the twentieth century, but also for the history of contemporary visual and performative arts.

Prague – Budapest – Leiden
January 2009–2011

7. THE TYPES AND FUNCTIONS OF SAMIZDAT PUBLICATIONS IN CZECHOSLOVAKIA, 1948-1989

Both in Czech literary history and, as far as we know, in the literary histories of other ex-Soviet satellites as well there is a tendency to claim what is more or less obvious: that samizdat[1] books, periodicals, leaflets, and recordings of music and the spoken word (magnitizdat) were necessary and vital in Soviet bloc countries. The Soviet elimination of unrestricted, uncensored publishing inevitably led to samizdat as an attempt to retain the continuity of pluralistic, democratic values under conditions essentially hostile to them. The need for communication and exchange of opinions results in the circulation of printed-like material, mostly typewritten copies, which reach only a limited number of readers.

When freedom and democracy are established, the value of samizdat is at last liberated from its nonliterary, extraliterary function, and it is up to editors and publishers to issue the samizdat materials or not, and literary historians and bibliographers can choose to describe them in their own terms. Literary texts may be interpreted and evaluated *an sich*, and the printed texts may then find their proper places on library shelves, mostly left to find their way to general oblivion. At the same time, bibliographers can describe these texts according to their own criteria with the help of

---

1) As far as the origin of the term *samizdat* is concerned, in 1953, Nikolai Glazkov (1919-79) actually used the term *samsebyaizdat* (e.g., for the title *Полное собрание стихотворений. Книга первая. МОСКВА-1953-САМСЕБЯИЗДАТ* [Collected Poems. Volume 1. MOSCOW-1953-SAMSESBYAIZDAT]; see the reprint of the typewritten title page in EICHWEDE, Wolfgang (ed.), *Samizdat. Alternative Kultur in Zentral- und Osteuropa: Die 60er bis 80er Jahre. Dokumentationen zur Kultur und Gesellschaft im östlichen Europa*, Edition Temmen, vol. 8, Bremen: Forschungsstelle Osteuropa an der Universität Bremen, 2000, p. 276.

The word SAMSESBYAIZDAT was later shortened to the now well-known form. See also HAMERSKY, Heidrun (ed.), *Samizdat: Alternative Culture in Central and Eastern Europe from the 1960s to the 1980s*, Bremen: Research Centre for East European Studies at the University of Bremen, 2002; EICHWEDE, Wolfgang, "The Conception of the Exhibition", in HAMERSKY 2002, pp. 15-19, esp. p. 16; DANIEL, Aleksandr, "Wie freie Menschen", in EICHWEDE 2000, pp. 38-50, esp. p. 41; BOCK, Ivo - HÄNSGEN, Sabine - SCHLOTT, Wolfgang, "Kultur jenseits der Zensur", in EICHWEDE 2000, pp. 64-77, esp. p. 65.

the newly coined word *samizdat*. Perhaps the most challenging of all the jobs concerning samizdat is that of archivists and librarians: what to keep and what not to keep in the archives? How does one distinguish a true samizdat from a (typewritten) manuscript and from a fake?

Yet another difficulty seems to arise in the consideration of samizdat: which are "totalitarian regimes"? Are they only to be identified with the various Communist, mostly Stalinist, systems in their rich variety? Probably not. And if not, could we find samizdat predecessors in, say, Nazi Germany, Fascist Japan, and Italy? Or faced with the alarming lack (if not the total absence) of civil liberties in a large number of other countries during the past century, shouldn't we look for samizdat there as well? What about the authoritarian, paternalistic regimes and military dictatorships in today's Latin America, Africa, and Asia? What about the Muslim theocracies and semitheocracies? Is there no need in all of these for a certain kind of "samizdat"? And – last but not least – what about the almost innumerable "independent", "alternative", "underground" publishing activities in our contemporary democratic world, which respond to the so-called information explosion in their own ways? Isn't there at least some continuity with the former samizdat? But we will not pose further questions of this kind. Suffice it to say that the rough, approximate definition of samizdat can no longer suit our purposes.

It is worth noting, however, that the research carried out so far in the field of Czech, Slovak, and other Central and Eastern European samizdat, no matter how valuable, has been based on a vague and limited literal interpretation of the term and consequently has been mostly confined to the description of major editions of samizdat series (e.g., Edice Petlice [Padlock Editions], Edice Expedice [Dispatch Editions], and a few more samizdat editions in the case of Czechoslovakia) and their role in spreading "banned literature".[2]

2) On the history of Central and Eastern European samizdat, see especially SKILLING, Gordon H., *Samizdat and an Independent Society in Central and Eastern Europe*, Columbus, OH: Macmillan, 1989, esp. the chapter "Samizdat in the USSR, China, and Central Europe", pp. 3–40; see also KONRÁD, György, "Looking Back at Samizdat", in HAMERSKY 2002 (Footnote 1), pp. 7–10; EICHWEDE, Wolfgang, "Archipel Samizdat" [Archipelago Samizdat], in EICHWEDE 2000 (Footnote 1), pp 8–19; BOCK, Ivo – HÄNSGEN, Sabine – SCHLOTT, Wolfgang, "Kultur jenseits der Zensur" [The Culture

One of the first steps in this rather vague research into Czech samizdat was made by the late professor Gordon H. Skilling, and most Czech students of samizdat seem to follow in his footsteps. We have in mind essays and studies by Vilém Prečan, Jiří Holý, Tomáš Vrba, Jiří Gruntorád, Jan Pauer, and a few enthusiastic bibliographers (e.g., Prečan, Gruntorád, Johanna Posset, Jitka Hanáková), whose merits are undeniable.[3] Nevertheless, at least the rough delimitation of

beyond Censorship], in EICHWEDE 2000 (Footnote 1); HAMERSKY, Heidrun (ed.), *Samizdat: Alternative Culture in Central and Eastern Europe from the 1960s to the 1980s*, Bremen: Research Centre for East European Studies at the University of Bremen, 2002; ALAN, Josef (ed.), *Alternativní kultura. Příběh české společnosti 1945-1989* [Alternative Culture: The Story of Czech Society, 1945-1989], Praha: Nakladatelství Lidové noviny, 2001; ŠRÁMKOVÁ, Vítězslava (ed.), *Tabuizovaná literatura posledních dvaceti let* [The Taboo Literature of the Last Twenty Years], Praha: Ústav pro kulturně výchovnou činnost, 1990.

3) Concerning the basic research into Czech samizdat in English, see especially PREČAN, Vilém, "Bibliography of the Czechoslovak Samizdat: Samizdat Periodicals 1977-1988", *ACTA* 2, no. 5-8 (1988), pp. 64-82; PREČAN, Vilém, *Independent Literature and Samizdat in Czechoslovakia*, Praha: Památník národního písemnictví - Ústav pro soudobé dějiny ČSAV, 1992; PREČAN, Vilém, "The World of Czech and Slovak Samizdat", in HAMERSKY 2002 (Footnote 1), pp. 11-13; SKILLING, Gordon H., *Charter 77 and Human Rights in Czechoslovakia*, London: Allen and Unwin, 1981; SKILLING, Gordon H., *Samizdat and an Independent Society in Central and Eastern Europe*, Columbus, OH: Macmillan, 1989; MACHOVEC, Martin, *A Brief Report on Present Knowledge of Czech Samizdat Phenomena 1948-1989*, Praha: Libri Prohibiti, 2004, libpro.cts.cuni.cz/clanky. htm.; MACHOVEC, Martin, "Czech Underground Literature, 1969-1989: A Challenge to Textual Studies", in *Voice, Text, Hypertext: Emerging Practices in Textual Studies*, edited by Raimonda MODIANO, Leroy F. SEARLE, and Peter SCHILLINGSBURG, pp. 345-357, Seattle: University of Washington Press and Walter Chapin Simpson, 2004. In Czech, see especially GRUNTORÁD, Jiří, "Samizdatová literatura v Československu sedmdesátých a osmdesátých let" [Samizdat Literature in Czechoslovakia of the 1970s and 1980s], in ALAN 2001 (Footnote 2), pp. 493-507; HANÁKOVÁ, Jitka, *Edice českého samizdatu 1972-1991* [The Editions of Czech Samizdat 1972-1991], Praha: Národní knihovna České republiky, 1997; POSSET, Johanna, *Česká samizdatová periodika 1968-1989* [Czech Samizdat Periodicals 1968-1989], Brno (Czechoslovakia): Továrna na sítotisk a společnost R&T, 1991; VRBA, Tomáš, "Nezávislé písemnictví a svobodné myšlení v letech 1970-1989" [The Independent Literature and Free Thinking 1970-1989], in ALAN 2001 (Footnote 2), pp. 265-305; MACHOVEC, Martin, "Šestnáct autorů českého literárního podzemí", *Literární archiv PNP*, 25, 1991, pp. 41-77. In German, see especially PAUER, Jan, "Charta 77. Moralische Opposition unter den

the subject matter has been made, the samizdat makers themselves have given their evidence in a number of documentary writings, memoirs, and films,[4] and now seems to be the best time to test some new criteria.

We will attempt to classify samizdat publications, keeping in mind not only the ambiguity of the notion of a totalitarian regime[5] but also the fact that we are trying to interpret phenomena whose legal status was always quite doubtful, never certain.

As far as the totalitarian systems themselves are concerned, historians and other researchers should not view them as one indivisible, unchanging monolith. Regarding Czechoslovakia, it is common to distinguish between (1) the establishment of the Stalinist regime after 1948 and its peak in the early 1950s; (2) the weakening of harsh Stalinism in the 1960s; (3) the almost complete breakdown of the monopolistic position of the government of the Communist Party

Bedingungen der Diktatur", in EICHWEDE 2000 (Footnote 1), pp. 52–63; POSSET, Johanna, *Tschechische Samizdat-Periodika 1968–1988*, Master's thesis, Wien: University of Vienna, 1990; ZAND, Gertraude, *Totaler Realismus und Peinliche Poesie. Tschechische Untergrund-Literatur 1948–1953*, Wien: Peter Lang, 1998.

4) *Samizdat: A Fifteen-Part TV Documentary*, directed by Andrej Krob, Česká televize, Praha (2003).

5) For the purpose of this article, I will resist the temptation to cite at length from Hannah Arendt (*The Origins of Totalitarianism*, New York: Harcourt Brace Jovanovich, 1973) and other theoreticians of totalitarianism (Raymond Aron, *Democracy and Totalitarianism*, Ann Arbor: University of Michigan Press, 1990; Carl J. Friedrich and Zbigniew Brzezinski, *Totalitarian Dictatorship and Autocracy*, Cambridge, MA: Harvard University Press, 1965) and instead will offer my own attempt to reach a better understanding of the notion, no matter how commonplace this offering may sound. I would suggest that the criterion may be less political and more economic, at least as far as Stalinist or neo-Stalinist totalitarianism is concerned (and probably the fascist variety as well). A political system may be considered totalitarian if its economy (and, of course, its political structure) consists of a complete, "total", control of productivity, in which any individual or free enterprise would be a disturbing element. The economic basis is the essence of totalitarianism and is derived from a philosophy or ideology – in this particular case, Marxism in one of its dogmatic interpretations. A system so structured simply cannot admit a single exception, a single attempt to put its guidelines into doubt, for if it did, its ideology would lose its absolute purity and power – and consequently the whole economic and political system would collapse; witness 1989 in Central and Eastern Europe.

in 1968–69, during which we need not expect, then, to find intensive, massive samizdat publishing; (4) the so-called "normalization" period of the 1970s and early 1980s, that is, the reestablishment of totalitarianism, sometimes referred to as "post-totalitarianism";[6] and (5) the years of "perestroika" and "glasnost" – the gradual degeneration of (post-)totalitarianism. As is generally known, however, in other Soviet bloc countries the chronology of change did not always coincide with that of Czechoslovakia.[7] What, however, unified the political systems in all those countries was the pragmatic definition of citizenship and the fact that notions of law, legislature, and legality changed semantic identities.[8] The frontiers between what counts as "legal", "illegal", and/or "punishable" are deliberately blurred – as the very notion of the law loses its original meaning and purpose. It seems therefore a little out of place to ask what is "legal", "official", *lege artis*, "semilegal", or "illegal" in totalitarian systems.

There is no doubt, however, that even the most liberal, most democratic states have to restrict basic liberties (e.g., freedom of speech) in a definite but undoubtedly legal way. We simply know what is and what is not "legal", what is "illegal", and what is "punishable". In totalitarian regimes as defined above, the basic civil liberties, especially the freedoms of movement, of speech, and of enterprise, are restricted in a much more radical way than in any democratic state (all ideas competing with or contradicting the ruling ideology, philosophy, pseudophilosophy, religion, and pseudoreligion **must** be banned).

6) See HAVEL, Václav, "The Power of the Powerless", in *Václav Havel, or, Living in Truth. Twenty-two Essays Published on the Occasion of the Award of the Erasmus Prize to Václav Havel*, ed. Jan Vladislav, pp. 36–122, London: Faber and Faber, 1986; HAVEL, Václav, "Moc bezmocných" [The Power of the Powerless], in *Eseje a jiné texty z let 1970–1989 / Dálkový výslech. Spisy 4* [Essays and Other Texts 1970–1989 / A Long-Distance Interrogation. Works, vol. 4], pp. 224–330, Praha: Torst, 1999.

7) See KENNEY, Padraic, *A Carnival of Revolution: Central Europe 1989*, Princeton, NJ: Princeton University Press, 2003); FALK, Barbara, *The Dilemmas of Dissidence in East-Central Europe: Citizen Intellectuals and Philosopher Kings*, Budapest: Central European University Press, 2003; EICHWEDE 2000 (Footnote 1), esp. p. 12.

8) See PŘIBÁŇ, Jiří, *Disidenti práva. O revolucích roku 1989, fikcích legality a soudobé verzi společenské smlouvy* [Dissidents of Law: On the 1989 Velvet Revolutions, Fictions of Legality, and Contemporary Version of the Social Contract], Praha: Sociologické nakladatelství, 2001; PŘIBÁŇ, Jiří, *Dissidents of Law: On the 1989 Velvet Revolutions, Legitimations, Fictions of Legality, and Contemporary Version of the Social Contract*, Aldershot, U.K.: Ashgate, 2002.

It is always the will (or occasional goodwill and mercy) of leaders in these systems that determines what is and what is not allowed. Samizdat publishers (and, of course, dissident activists) who tended to ignore the absurd legislation in totalitarian regimes (occasionally going so far as manifesting openly their activities and identities) behaved in a way appropriate for democracies, whose laws most of them would probably be inclined to observe.

Given the ambiguity of the law in totalitarian systems, any attempt to classify various samizdat activities fails if it approaches them as merely textual material, as literary products, or – most of all – as works of art. It is necessary to take into account various extraliterary, extralingual, extraaesthetic functions of these samizdat activities as well as their social, political, and psychological dimensions. To reiterate one of the most elementary notions of textual studies, it is the texts that we deal with, texts in their various forms and sometimes with very specific functions. Traditionally, texts written by hand are called "manuscripts". However, at a certain stage in the development of writing skills and technology, typewritten texts may also be considered manuscripts. On the other hand, typewritten texts are, in their own way, close to printed material, and it is precisely the ambiguity of the typewritten texts that also makes samizdat materials interesting for textual studies.

In the Czechoslovak context in 1948–89, samizdat mostly consists of typewritten materials. More advanced technology, such as manifolding, hectography, ormig, stencil copying, seriography, photography, Xerox copiers, or even offset printing and the use of real printing machines, to say nothing of computer printing (which only began to be used in 1989), was quite rare.[9] This limitation was due primarily to the fear that frequent use of these machines might arouse the undesired interest of the secret police.[10] There were typewritten copies that were the only versions of a text, so, as

9) The use of printing machines in clandestine printing offices was quite frequent only with the Czechoslovak branch of Jehovah's Witnesses (the Bible and religious texts' printing); see ADAMY, Herbert, *Byl jsem manažerem ilegální továrny* [I Was a Manager of an Illegal Factory], Praha: Ostrov, 1999. Some Slovak Catholic samizdat publishers also made full use of the offset printing machines; see Footnote 43.

10) See VRBA, Tomáš, "Nezávislé písemnictví a svobodné myšlení v letech 1970-1989", in ALAN 2001 (Footnote 2), pp. 265-305.

a matter of fact, they might count as manuscripts. Yet there were also – though quite rare – handwritten and hand-rewritten copies of an original text which were made for circulation among samizdat readers. And there was printed material, usually costly, rare biblio-phile editions of literary texts and reprints of graphic sheets made with the help of slightly more advanced technology (block printing machines enabling casework) which produced prints indistinguish-able from printed books. Ultimately, there were additional copies of all three of the above-mentioned samizdat types made with the help of manifold writers and jellygraphs.

Thus we can try to offer the first, tentative definition of samizdat materials: **in Czechoslovakia samizdat usually consisted of type-written copies of texts, not necessarily multiplied or duplicated but mostly in about six to twelve copies, produced by their au-thors or by editors or typists with the aim (be it conscious or unconscious, deliberate or indeliberate) of dissemination and circulation among readers, regardless of how few they might have been – family members, close friends, acquaintances, or any other persons – without prior imprimatur from the author-ities of the totalitarian state.**

This definition would probably apply to the USSR as well, but if Poland were included, the first criterion of our definition would probably have to be changed as follows: they are typewritten or printed copies of texts... mostly in several hundreds or thousands of copies, and so forth. However, although the word samizdat was never used in Poland[11] (and it was quite unknown in Czechoslovakia in the 1950s and scarce and exotic in the following decade),[12] Polish samizdat publishing was probably the most massive of all of the So-viet bloc countries, and relatively advanced printing technology was

11) See SKILLING, Gordon H., *Samizdat and an Independent Society in Central and East-ern Europe*, Columbus, OH: Macmillan 1989; BRUKWICKI, Jerzy, "'Neuer Himmel, neue Erde.' Die Symbolik der Solidarność 1980 bis 1989", in EICHWEDE 2000 (Footnote 1), pp. 124–128; SZARUGA, Leszek, "Untergrundpresse in Polen. Ein Beschreibungsver-such", in EICHWEDE 2000 (Footnote 1), pp. 130–134.

12) See SKILLING, Gordon H., *Samizdat and an Independent Society in Central and Eastern Europe*, Columbus, OH: Macmillan 1989; BOCK, Ivo, "Der literarische Samizdat nach 1968", in EICHWEDE 2000 (Footnote 1), pp. 86–93; PREČAN, Vilém, "The World of Czech and Slovak Samizdat", in HAMERSKY 2002 (Footnote 1), pp. 11–13.

much more available there than elsewhere. (The same change in our definition would probably be necessary if we were to trace any contemporary samizdat activities.)[13]

So far almost no attention has been given to the textual or semantic content of samizdat (both literary and nonliterary) publications.

According to the above definition, even utter graphomaniac prattling, babbling rubbish must be granted the status of a samizdat publication, provided it meets all the given criteria; and in theory it would be punishable as a result. However, the more copies made and the more "political" the contents of the disseminated texts, the greater the risk of prosecution for their originators. Typewritten periodicals or casual typescripts produced by high school students, though quite frequent in Czechoslovakia in 1948–89, were the exception that proved the rule, and their originators were rarely prosecuted if ever.

Despite the fact that the Czechoslovak copyright law of 1965 stated that an author could use his or her manuscript as he or she chose, one was liable to be prosecuted and jailed without ever taking part in any samizdat publishing but merely for having written a text, manuscript, or letter[14] perceived as "antistate", "antigovernment",

13) VRBA 2001 (Footnote 2, 3, 10) offers a much narrower classification of Czech samizdat. He distinguishes between "samizdats" and "editions", i.e., unofficial publications bearing most of the signs of a regular book or periodical edition – such as format; bookbinding; high-quality paper; title page, half-title page, etc.; the occasional occurrence of a frontispiece; the frequent use of masthead, printer's mark, imprint; relatively high-quality typewritten copies; standard, uniform graphic design; pagination; etc. Altogether, what I would call a series of editions of established samizdat is not samizdat for Vrba but only those publications that I call "wild samizdat".

14) Such were the cases of innumerable petitions and open letters sent by Czechoslovak citizens to the president of the country or to the representatives of the executive and legislature in which they only demanded that the country's own laws be respected and kept: for which they were often interrogated by the police, even prosecuted. Actually, the Charter 77 movement started with such a letter in December 1976; the Výbor na obranu nespravedlivě stíhaných (VONS; Committee for the Defense of the Unjustly Persecuted) petitions are another good example. See SKILLING, Gordon H., *Charter 77 and Human Rights in Czechoslovakia*, London: Allen and Unwin 1981; CÍSAŘOVSKÁ, Blanka - PREČAN, Vilém (eds.), *Charta 77. Dokumenty 1977-1989* [Char-

"antisocialist", "anti-Communist", and so forth.[15] One could even be prosecuted without having written anything, much less disseminated it, but simply for one's thoughts, beliefs, or convictions, when expressed orally in public places, or - more likely - for one's social class affiliation. But after the harshest years of early Stalinism in Czechoslovakia in the early 1950s, such danger was relatively small.

SAMIZDAT CLASSIFICATIONS

As we seem to have defined samizdat - especially with regard to its role in totalitarian Czechoslovakia - as a historical phenomenon in terms of politics, history, law, and social science, we can now try to make further progress in its classification.

I. According to the motivations for publishing and distributing samizdat

(a) A sort of "inner need" for the truth, for opposing the totalitarian political system by creating "little islands of truth in a sea of lies".[16]

In establishing, so to speak, a "miniature plurality of opinion", mostly deliberately inconspicuous "cells of freedom", samizdat producers and distributors shared "the solidarity of the shattered", responded to their conscience as "men of the spirit".[17]

ter 77: Documentary 1977-1989], 3 vols., Praha: Ústav pro soudobé dějiny AV ČR, 2007; BLAŽEK, Petr - SCHOVÁNEK, Radek (eds)., *VONS.cz, Webové stránky o dějinách Výboru na obranu nespravedlivě stíhaných (1978-1989)* [VONS.cz, website on the History of the Committee for the Defense of the Unjustly Persecuted (1978-1989)], www .vons.cz, esp. www.vons.cz/ informace-o-charte-77, 2007; BLAŽEK, Petr - PAŽOUT, Jaroslav (eds.), *Nejcitlivější místo režimu. Výbor na obranu nespravedlivě stíhaných očima svých členů. Diskusní setkání 19. října 2007* [The Most Irritable Spot of the Regime: Committee for the Defense of the Unjustly Persecuted as Seen through the Eyes of Its Members. A Discussion Meeting of October 19, 2007], Praha: Pulchra, 2008.

15) For this reason, the editors of Edice Petlice and Česká Expedice (Bohemian Expedition) inserted into their editions the warning "Výslovný zákaz dalšího opisování rukopisu", abbreviated as "VZDOR" ["DEFIANCE"] - i.e., "Any recopying of this manuscript is expressly forbidden."

16) A paraphrase of Václav Havel's terms "living in truth" and "living in a lie," which later became popular journalistic clichés; see HAVEL 1986, 1999 (Footnote 6).

17) Concerning the system of values, especially the basic moral notions of Czech dissidence of the 1970s, see PATOČKA, Jan, *Heretical Essays on the Philosophy of*

This need to maintain truth coincided with the authors' need to continue their writing and to maintain their role of writer, denied them after 1948 and for a second time after 1968. To be sure, for most of the theoreticians of samizdat, only such authors are identified as those worthy of being labelled with the honorary title of a "samizdat writer".[18]

(b) Solidarity with friends and colleagues.

Some authors[19] did not seem to be keen on playing the role of a "living conscience of humanity" (or of a nation);[20] they simply chose to write in their own way, pursuing their own aesthetic

History, Chicago: Open Court, 1996; SKILLING 1989 (Footnote 2), esp. pp. 128-131; PAUER, Jan, "Charta 77. Moralische Opposition unter den Bedingungen der Diktatur", in EICHWEDE 2000 (Footnote 1), pp. 52-63; TUCKER, Aviezer, *The Philosophy and Politics of Czech Dissidence from Patočka to Havel*, Pittsburgh: University of Pittsburgh Press, 2000; SEDLACKOVA GIBBS, Helena, *Moral Politics and Its Others: The Charter 77 Dissident Movement in Czechoslovakia (1977-1989)*, UMI Microform 3089390, New York: Department of Comparative Literature, New York University, 2003, esp. pp. 70-115, chap. 2, "Patočka's Legacy: The Dissident as 'the Man of the Spirit'"; SUK, Jiří, "Podrobná zpráva o paralelní polis. Nad korespondencí Václava Havla a Františka Janoucha" [The Detailed Report on the Parallel Polis: The Correspondence between Václav Havel and František Janouch], in HAVEL, Václav - JANOUCH, František, *Korespondence 1978-2001*, Praha: Akropolis, 2007, pp. 9-29 ; HAVEL 1986, 1999 (Footnote 6).

18) See especially SKILLING 1981 (Footnote 3); SKILLING 1989 (Footnote 2); PREČAN 1992 (Footnote 3), PREČAN, Vilém, *Nezávislá literatura a samizdat v Československu 70. a 80. let* [Independent Literature and Samizdat in Czechoslovakia of the 1970s and 1980s], Praha: Ústav pro soudobé dějiny ČSAV, 1992; PREČAN, Vilém, "Independent Literature and Samizdat in Czechoslovakia", in *Literature and Politics in Central Europe: Studies in Honour of Markéta Goetz-Stankiewicz*, edited by Leslie MILLER, Klaus PETERSEN, Peter STENBERG, and Karl ZAENKEL, Columbia, SC: Camden House, 1993, pp. 91-107; PREČAN, Vilém, "The World of Czech and Slovak Samizdat", in HAMERSKY 2002 (Footnote 1); PAUER, Jan, "Charta 77. Moralische Opposition unter den Bedingungen der Diktatur", in EICHWEDE 2000 (Footnote 1), pp. 52-63; GRUN-TORÁD, Jiří, "Samizdatová literatura v Československu sedmdesátých a osmdesátých let", in ALAN 2001 (Footnote 2), pp. 493-507.

19) Such solidarity may have been typical of some of the authors of the underground circle of the rock band The Plastic People of the Universe, e.g., Věra Jirousová, Jiří Daníček, Eugen Brikcius.

20) "The living conscience of humanity" became a popular journalistic cliché and was probably derived from the notion of the "moral politics", as characterized, e.g., by SEDLACKOVA GIBBS 2003 (Footnote 17).

ends, which may not have been unacceptable to totalitarian censorship and ideological surveillance. Their samizdat editions or circulating manuscripts may have been motivated by human solidarity with such happier writers' colleagues whose books could no longer be published for different reasons. It was mostly because these colleagues were known in public as "dissidents", that is, opponents of the Communist totalitarian regime, and their works as bearers of politically critical, explicitly formulated standpoints incompatible with government guidelines. (However, the reasons for banning books from libraries and denying their authors any further publishing possibilities were sometimes quite incomprehensible, being merely the result of the "revenge logic" of the representatives of oppressive systems; the truly political, ideological reasons – to say nothing of the aesthetic ones – rarely if ever operated.) The "solidarity authors" could probably publish at least some of their works in state-controlled publishing houses, pretending to comply with government guidelines. Nevertheless, they voluntarily shared the fate of their proscribed colleagues by publishing their works only in samizdat.

In a way, such authors were close to the "grey zone" writers, that is, the ones publishing (or, when artists or actors, exhibiting or performing) officially but covertly sympathizing with the samizdat authors and sometimes proving it by supporting them in a financial or other material way.[21]

21) The term "grey zone" was probably first used by Josef Škvorecký in one of his English-language essays (ŠKVORECKÝ, Josef, "Prague Winter", *American Spectator* 9, 1983, pp. 19–23). He used it as a metaphor for a considerably large part of Czech and Slovak people, who, though remaining "silent", i.e., not joining the "dissidents" in their protests, disagreed with the Communist Party guidelines and thus represented a hidden threat to the totalitarian regime: "On the outside, these 'conformists', the 'grey zone' of real-socialist society, have become 'normalized,' as the Party lingo has it; that is, they have conformed to the post-1968 political climate. They express their thoughts and feelings only in intimate circles of the most trusted friends, otherwise they follow the nauseating rituals of 'socialist progressivity'" (ibidem, p. 23). Indeed, the "grey zone" artists, writers, journalists, students, etc., largely helped overthrow the Czechoslovak Communist dictatorship in November 1989 (see also SUK 2007, Footnote 17). Perhaps the best-known representative of the "grey zone"

(c) Taking part in samizdat publishing as a result of moral, personal influence.

Some samizdat writers, young in the 1970s and 1980s and hence unable to write and publish during the 1960s – the preceding years of relative freedom – deliberately followed the example of their older friends, colleagues, and sometimes parents. Such was the case of most Czech underground poets, especially those of the "third underground generation":[22] Jáchym Topol, Petr Placák, J. H. Krchovský, and some others who were inspired by the example of the "second underground generation" (Ivan Martin Jirous, the whole circle of musicians, poets, and artists that gathered around the rock band The Plastic People of the Universe in the 1970s) or even by the best-known representative of the "first underground generation", Egon Bondy, who started publishing exclusively in samizdat as early as 1949.

(d) Taking part in samizdat publishing for its own sake to get a chance, so to speak, "to enter the territory of an adventure", of "the punishable", of running the risk of being pro-

writers of the 1970s and 1980s (though not the most typical one) was Bohumil Hrabal, one of the most popular and most published Czech post–World War II writers. However, his case was quite extraordinary. He started publishing in samizdat with Egon Bondy and others in the early 1950s, became very popular after 1963, when he started publishing some of his books in state-controlled publishing houses, was listed among the "banned authors" after 1969, and was at last pardoned in 1974: prior to 1989 nevertheless, his best books, *Obsluhoval jsem anglického krále* [I Served the King of England] (1971), *Něžný barbar* [Tender Barbarian] (1973), and *Příliš hlučná samota* [Too Loud a Solitude] (1976), in their unexpurgated forms, could only be published in samizdat. Concerning Hrabal, see ROTH, Susanna, *Laute Einsamkeit und bitteres Glück. Zur poetischen Welt von Bohumil Hrabals Prosa*, Bern: Peter Lang, 1986; PYTLÍK, Radko, *The Sad King of Czech Literature: Bohumil Hrabal - His Life and Work*, Praha: Emporius, 2000.

22) On the three underground generations, see MACHOVEC, Martin, "Šestnáct autorů českého literárního podzemí", *Literární archiv PNP*, 25, 1991, pp. 41-77; KOŽMÍN, Zdeněk - TRÁVNÍČEK, Jiří, *Na tvrdém loži z psího vína. Česká poezie od 40. let do současnosti* [The Hard Bed of Wild Wine: Czech Poetry from the 1940s to the Present Time], Brno (Czech Republic): Books, 1998 (here esp. TRÁVNÍČEK, Jiří, "Tři generace českého undergroundu" [Three Generations of Czech Underground], pp. 236-244).

secuted, even jailed; a kind of "adrenaline sport". Likewise with the drive to find a way out, to escape "totalitarian boredom".

(e) A wish to become a prominent socialite, a VIP of a certain kind; to gain weight or importance from the fact that one is taken for "an enemy of the state" by a totalitarian regime. (Such motivation was probably not so frequent in Czechoslovakia, but we learn that it was quite common in the Soviet Union,[23] especially when such writers[24] published their samizdat – or even nonsamizdat – writings in one of the Russian publishing houses abroad as "tamizdat".)

(f) Graphomania of all kinds, subdividable in turn:

(f1) Traditional, simple graphomania as manifested by the production of worthless texts which otherwise would not be published. It thus finds the most natural outlet in samizdat editions, which have the advantage of giving their originators the chance to emphasize their own importance. On the other hand, taking part in regular a literary competition under so-called normal conditions would

---

23) As far as a general survey of the history of samizdat in the USSR is concerned, see KISSEL, Wolfgang S., "Samizdat als kulturelles Gedächtnis. Terror und GULag in der russischen Erinnerungsliteratur der sechziger Jahre", in EICHWEDE 2000 (Footnote 1), pp. 94-104.

Concerning samizdat VIPs in the USSR, see PUTNA, Martin C. - ZADRAŽILOVÁ, Miluše, *Rusko mimo Rusko. Dějiny a kultura ruské emigrace 1917-1991* [Russia outside Russia: History and Culture of the Russian Exile 1917-1991], vol. 2, Brno (Czech Republic): Petrov, 1994, p. 130: "Russia has always been a country of bizarre paradoxes. Therefore it cannot be much surprising that, in the Brezhnev years, tamizdat editions were considered to be much more prestigious than publishing in one's home country. Even utterly conformist writers, publishing abundantly at home [in Soviet state-controlled publishing houses], did not despise publishing in foreign forums [in Russian publishing houses] as such a way of publication gained them reputation and temporary glory" (the author's own translation).

24) On the author's demand, Miluše Zadražilová (see Footnote 23) mentioned, e.g., Bella Achmadulina, Fazil Iskander, or Vasily Aksjonov as authors officially publishing in the USSR yet trying to publish abroad (i.e., in tamizdat) for reasons of prestige (PUTNA and ZADRAŽILOVÁ 1994, Footnote 23). Among Russian samizdat authors with the same ambitions, Zadražilová mentioned Igor Cholin and other representatives of the "Lianozovo circle".

leave such authors no choice except "self-publishing" at their own expense.

(f2) A more refined kind of graphomania, not necessarily producing mere rubbish, is rather a response to totalitarian restrictions, to the impossibility to publish, according to the slogan "The more you deny our existence, the louder we shall cry". One might also consider the generally insane conditions and social climate under totalitarian systems in order to adequately interpret the manic-depressive states of mind of writers and artists provoked by the established insanity. This motivation is also related to the well-known counterproductive effects of repressive manipulation and surveillance.

(g) An effort to fill in gaps in official, government-supported publishing.

Because some out-of-print books were unlikely to be reprinted, many were photocopied in public copy-making offices, though there were not too many of these in the 1970s and 1980s (about a dozen in Prague). Retyping of already published texts was rare, but it did occur. Well-known examples are Jirous's retyping all available Czech translations of Franz Kafka's works in the mid-1960s and Bedřich Fučík's and Vladimír Binar's editions of the collected works of Jakub Deml, Jan Zahradníček, and Jan Čep in the 1970s and 1980s.

Photocopying of typewritten texts was more frequent in the case of books which were to be published in state-controlled publishing houses but whose releases were delayed for one reason or another, sometimes for years, even though the text was more or less "innocent". Such was the case with J. R. R. Tolkien's *The Lord of the Rings* in Czech translation by Stanislava Pošustová: it was completed as early as the beginning of the 1980s but was published by regular printing presses only ten years later. In the meantime, possibly hundreds of copies of its typewritten text circulated.

Other well-known examples of filling in the gaps were innumerable editions of Ladislav Klíma's philosophical works; Petr Holman's six-volume *Frekvenční slovník básnického díla Otokara Březiny* [Word Count Dictionary of Otokar Březina's Poetical

Works] (1986); and Bondy's thirteen-volume *Poznámky k dějinám filosofie* [Remarks on the History of Philosophy], written and published in samizdat in 1977–87.

h) Unconscious participation in samizdat publishing.

There could have been "samizdat publishers" who were quite unaware of the possible penalization of their activities. The arbitrariness and willfulness of the representatives of the totalitarian state in interpreting articles of the penal code could have led many people mistakenly to believe that their typewriting and distributing of various texts were legal.[25]

II. According to the originator

(a) The author of the text in person.

In such cases, it is sometimes rather difficult to distinguish the "original manuscript", possibly with its various subsequent versions, from those that were deliberately retyped with the aim of their distribution for circulation. (Only the relative absence of corrections can make us believe that the typewritten copy is a final one and is intended to circulate as samizdat.) The "author's samizdat" can further be divided into three groups:

(a1) Copies bearing the author's real name, sometimes even in the form of a signature. Such was the case of Jaroslav Seifert's or Jaromír Hořec's samizdat editions of their own work. (Hořec sometimes signed his works with his own name, sometimes with one of his pseudonyms.) In such cases, the author is identical to the samizdat publisher.

---

25) A good example of such samizdat production is the copying of Miloslav Švandrlík's 1969 best seller, the antimilitarist, anti-Stalinist parody *Černí baroni aneb Válčili jsme za Čepičky* [The Black Barons, or As We Soldiered under Comrade Čepička]: though never actually one of the "banned books" in the 1970s and 1980s, it nevertheless disappeared from public libraries in the early 1970s and was never published again before 1989. Moreover, its sequel, or "second part", existed only in typewritten copies before 1989: both being photocopied and even retyped by thousands of Czech readers, this was probably the most popular book with the Czech general reading public during the two decades (see ŠVANDRLÍK, Miloslav, *Černí baroni aneb Válčili jsme za Čepičky*, Praha: Mladá fronta, 1990).

(a2) Copies published under a pseudonym. The best-known example of such an approach in Czech literature is probably the case of the underground poet and philosopher Bondy, whose real name, Zbyněk Fišer, is unknown to most readers.[26] The reasons for the use of a pseudonym, as far as samizdat editions are concerned, were certainly not only artistic or aesthetic but mainly political. Let us recall here other uses of pseudonyms that became legendary in the history of Czech literature (though not necessarily because of their bearers having been as politically unacceptable to the totalitarian regime as Bondy). Examples would be Ivan Wernisch's Václav Rozehnal,[27]

26) Zbyněk Fišer chose the pseudonym "Egon Bondy" as early as 1949 (see Footnote 30) and wrote under it not only until 1989 but until his death in 2007. The case of his pseudonym was extraordinary in the history of Czech literature for several reasons. First, during four decades (1949–1989) he published under it only in samizdat, so that officially he was a non-existent writer, an Orwellian "no-person" indeed. (He actually published a text elsewhere under his pseudonym – the novel *Invalidní sourozenci* [The Disabled Siblings] – as early as 1981, nevertheless it was published by the Czech Sixty-Eight Publishers, based in Toronto, Canada.) Besides, Bondy's close friend Hrabal modelled one of his literary figures – a poet named "Egon Bondy" – on the real person Egon Bondy (see Hrabal's officially published short stories *Taneční hodiny pro starší a pokročilé* [Dancing Lessons for the Advanced in Age], first published in 1964, and *Legenda o Egonu Bondym a Vladimírkovi* [A Legend about Egon Bondy and Vladimírek], first published in the volume *Morytáty a legendy* [Murder Stories and Legends], in 1968). Thus "Egon Bondy" became a literary "myth" twenty years before he actually made his official debut in Czechoslovakia. See JANOUŠEK, Pavel (ed.), *Slovník českých spisovatelů od roku 1945* [Dictionary of Czech Writers since 1945], vol. 1, A–L , Praha: Brána, 1999, p. 56; see also *Slovník české literatury po roce 1945* [Dictionary of Czech Literature since 1945], "Egon Bondy", http://slovnikceske-literatury.cz/showContent.jsp?docId=915&hl=egon+bondy+ (accessed in June 2019); see also the bibliography of Bondy's works in MACHOVEC, Martin, *Bibliografie Egona Bondyho (se soupisem rukopisné pozůstalosti a archivované korespondence)* [Bibliography of Egon Bondy (With the Catalogue of the Manuscript Estate and Archived Correspondence)], Praha: Libri Prohibiti, 2006–2018, http://www.libpro.cz/docs/bibliografie-egona-bondyho-2018_1530980541.pdf (accessed in June 2019).

27) "Václav Rozehnal" was one of the pseudonyms of the renowned Czech poet Wernisch, who could publish only in samizdat in the 1970s and 1980s. Rozehnal's samizdat publications, such as the collection of poems *Z letošního konce světa* [Concerning This Year's End of the World], misled even the editors of the first samizdat dictionary

Jiří Hásek's J. H. Krchovský,[28] Václav Jamek's Eberhardt Hauptbahnhof,[29] and last but not least, perhaps the first Czechoslovak samizdat edition after 1948, Bondy and Jana Krejcarová's 1949 anthology of surrealist poetry, *Židovská jména* [Jewish Names].[30] There the very Jewish-sounding

of Czech writers: the entry "ROZEHNAL, Václav" is found in it, presenting the "writer" as a real living being (see BRABEC, Jiří, GRUŠA, Jiří, HÁJEK, Igor, KABEŠ, Petr, LOPATKA, Jan, *Slovník českých spisovatelů* [Dictionary of Czech Writers], Toronto: Sixty-Eight, 1982. Concerning Wernisch, see JANOUŠEK, Pavel (ed.), *Slovník českých spisovatelů od roku 1945*, vol. 2, M–Ž , Praha: Brána, 1998, p. 682.

28) Hásek started publishing his poems under the pseudonym "J. H. Krchovský" in the late 1970s. As he became one of the best-known and most popular representatives of "the third underground generation", his ironic pseudonym also became famous ("Krchovský", derived from a Czech-German slang word "krchov", i. e. German "Kirchhof", means approximately "Mr. Churchyard" or "Mr. Boneyard", thus mocking the morbidity and necrophilia of the totalitarian regime). Later, Krchovský's elaborate, refined, ironic, neodecadent poetry gained him not only recognition from critics, reviewers, and literary historians but also large popularity with the Czech reading public: he is probably the bestselling contemporary Czech poet. See KRCHOVSKÝ, J. H., *Básně*, Brno (Czech Republic): Host, 1998; JANOUŠEK 1999 (Footnote 26), p. 446; TOPOL, Jáchym, "The Story of Revolver Revue. Contribution to a Closer Understanding of the Last Samizdat Generation" in MACHOVEC, Martin (ed.), *Views from the Inside. Czech Underground Literature and Culture (1948–1989)*, 2nd edition, Praha: Karolinum Press, 2018, pp. 79–91.

29) Jamek's German-sounding pseudonym "Eberhardt Hauptbahnhof" (i.e., "Eberhardt Main Station") is of a kind similar to "J. H. Krchovský": the author attacks with his funnysounding pseudonym the hypocrisy of Czech pseudopatriotism in its Communist or anti-Communist versions. Moreover, his collections of poems published in samizdat in Edice Petlice (1988, 1989) belong to the best achievements of Czech samizdat, dissident poetry; see JANOUŠEK 1999 (Footnote 26), p. 319.

30) *Židovská jména* was produced by its two editors and its coauthors at the beginning of 1949. Most of its copies were soon confiscated by the police, but one copy survived, was retyped in the 1960s, and was the source of the first official publication of the anthology in 1995. Though the participants chose their Jewish-sounding pseudonyms deliberately to express their protest against a new wave of anti-Semitism in the post–World War II Soviet Union and Czechoslovakia, only Fišer's pseudonym – Egon Bondy – survived and entered the history of Czech literature. See MACHOVEC, Martin (ed.), *Židovská jména 1949* (with contributions by Egon Bondy, Sarah Silberstein [Jana Krejcarová], Isaak Kuhnert [Jaroslav Růžička], Nathan Illinger [Karel Hynek], Gala Mallarmé [Jana Krejcarová], Benjamin Haas [Jan Zuska], Dina Š. [Libuše Strouhalová], Edmond Š. [Vladimír Šmerda], Herbert Taussig [Zdeněk Wagner], Pavel Ungar [Vratislav Effenberger], Arnold Stern [Oldřich Wenzl], Szatmar Neméthyová

pseudonyms of the collaborating authors – by which they wanted to protest against a new wave of anti-Semitism in the Soviet Union and Czechoslovakia – were asking for prosecution, as it were.

(a3) Anonymous "author's samizdat", hardly identifiable as self-initiated editions of the author's own text.

(b) The publisher of samizdat books and periodicals (often identical to the editor and sometimes even to the typist).

This subgroup of so-called established samizdat is sometimes considered to encompass all samizdat publishing (see works by Skilling, Prečan, Pauer, and others) because of the effort made by the editors to imitate "real books" or periodicals with the limited means and resources of typewriting: every single volume is numbered, bears the name of the edition, often even bears the real name of its editor, contains the imprint information, and so forth. In some cases, this sub-group can be identified with the preceding subgroup, the author of the text in person (IIa), in which the author doubles as the publisher. But in most cases such samizdat publishers (in Czechoslovakia the best-known representatives were probably Ludvík Vaculík, founder of Edice Petlice, and Václav Havel, founder of Edice Expedice) edited and disseminated texts by other authors. By including their names, often even with their own handwritten signatures in most of the copies of the well-known series of editions,[31] the publishers took full responsibility for their samizdat activities.

[Anna Marie Effenbergerová]), Praha: Nakladatelství Lidové noviny, 1995. On *Židovská jména* see MACHOVEC, Martin, "Židovská jména rediviva. Významný objev pro dějiny samizdatu", *A2* 3, no. 51-52 (2007); DRUBEK, Natascha, "Sich (k)einen Namen machen: Die Židovská jména der Honza K.", *Slovo a smysl / Word & Sense* 14, no. 28 (2017); DVORSKÝ, Stanislav, "Židovská jména – bájení a skutečnost", *Souvislosti* 28, no. 3 (2017).

31) Besides Edice Petlice and Edice Expedice, GRUNTORÁD 2001 (Footnote 2, 3) mentions, e.g., Edice Půlnoc [Midnight Edition], Kvart [Quarto Editions], Česká Expedice [Bohemian Expedition], Krameriova Expedice [Kramerius's Expedition], Kde domov můj [Where Is My Homeland Editions], Prameny [Sources Editions], Hermetická Edice [Hermetic Editions], Vokno [Window Editions], Proti všem [Despite Everything Editions], Prostor [Space Editions], Pražská imaginace [Prague Imagination Editions],

Three more divisions are identifiable here, according to the publisher/author relations.

(b1) The publisher was allowed to publish the book (or the periodical contribution) by the author of the text.

(b2) The publisher was not allowed to publish the book (or the periodical contribution) by the author of the text, but the text was published anyway, against the author's will, with readers sometimes informed about it, sometimes not. Such was the case of the magnitizdat editions that Petr Cibulka often put into circulation in spite of the authors' explicit objections.[32] Diametrically opposed was the case of Milan Jelínek's attempt to publish Milan Kundera's book *L'art du roman* [The Art of the Novel] in Czech translation. This having been explicitly forbidden by its author in a phone call, Jelínek respected Kundera's veto and did not publish the translated book in samizdat.[33]

Popelnice [Garbage Can Editions], Duch a život [Spirit and Life Editions], Theologia [Theology Editions], Přátelé [Friends Editions], and others.

32) See VANICEK, Anna Naninka, *Passion Play: Underground Rock Music in Czechoslovakia, 1968-1989*. Master's thesis, North York: York University, 1997; MÜLLER, Miloš – CIBULKA, Petr, "'Přál bych si, aby tady moc byla pro občana.' Rozhovor s Petrem Cibulkou" ['I Would Like the Power to Be Granted to Citizens of This Country': An Interview with Petr Cibulka], *Sklepník* 1, 1994, pp. 47-52. VANICEK, 1997, p. 131, argues in the chapter "Controversy over Distribution Practices": "Cibulka distributed the vast majority of music without the knowledge or consent of the musicians who had recorded it. He decided on this approach after speaking with many musicians who were adamantly opposed to their recordings being circulated in such a way: 'I found that the majority are cowards and are paranoid about having their music distributed unofficially. After conducting many excruciating interviews, I realized that if I left it to the artist, I wouldn't be able to issue almost anything [...] Those who were indifferent or pleased were definitely a minority.' This approach obviously presents large ethical problems, a point that did not go unnoticed at the time; it reveals the differences of opinion with regard to oppositional work. One of Cibulka's main goals was to circulate materials at all costs. He was willing to suffer the consequences of such activity, and did indeed suffer throughout the years. What he also did was impose his vision of reality on everyone who became a part of his activity, however inadvertently."

33) Prof. Milan Jelínek, one of the Brno-based samizdat editors, recalls in the television documentary on samizdat that, in a phone call from Paris, his old friend Milan Kundera strictly forbade him to "publish" in samizdat his book *L'art du roman* in

(b3) The publisher was allowed to publish yet only in secret, *sub rosa*, under the condition that he or she would pretend to have been forbidden by the author (i.e., the preceding situation [b2]), so as to keep the latter safe from penal prosecution. Such was the case of Bohumil Hrabal's books, published by Vaculík in his Padlock Editions.

(c) The anonymous publisher, often the person who only typed the handwritten manuscript and so mostly indistinguishable from a typist.

These cases are found in the realm of so-called "wild samizdat", which was, of course, the safest, the most frequent, and – from the point of view of textual studies and textual criticism – the "worst of all", as the role of publisher was often identifiable with that of self-appointed editor. Almost innumerable copies of "wild samizdat" are now found on the bookshelves of the Prague samizdat library and archives, Libri Prohibiti, and are a nightmare for today's editors and readers: some of the self-appointed publishers/editors of "wild samizdat" did not hesitate to exercise their own creativity and imagination when retyping texts by other authors, thus generating not only copies of copies of copies but also textual versions of versions of versions and so forth.

(d) The typist.

This subgroup sometimes overlaps with the subgroup of the anonymous publisher (IIc), so that we are again dealing with "wild samizdat" publishing, but for several reasons we have to establish it as a distinct subgroup. For cases existed where carefully retyped samizdat copies belonged to the subgroups in which copies bore the author's real name (IIa1), where copies were published under a pseudonym (IIa2), or under the name of the publisher of samizdat books and pe-

---

Czech translation; Kundera might have been worried about that, nevertheless Jelínek indicates he was more likely to have forgotten about how difficult the publishing situation back in Czechoslovakia was. Moreover, the case provides early evidence that Kundera has always been rather reluctant to publish his French-written books in his old home country (in 2008 the Czech reading public still has no access to Kundera's complete works). See part 8 (on Moravian samizdat) of the Czech television documentary series *Samizdat*, mentioned in Footnote 4.

riodicals (IIb); such retyped copies were made simply with the aim of giving more readers a chance to read the same material that the originator had produced by mere retyping (at the same time such typists could avoid the danger incurred by resorting to public copy-making offices). Here, unlike the subgroup the anonymous publisher (IIc), the originator consciously renounces any ambition of editing the retyped text and engages in "mere retyping".

(e) The products of the activities of the Czechoslovak state security service (StB) aimed at spreading disinformation, that is, the samizdat fakes.

In certain cases, suspicion arose that samizdat readers were chosen as a target of secret police provocation. Police agents provocateurs distributed real or fake samizdat in order to learn what their victims would do with them, especially whether they would further distribute them. Although little research has been done in this area so far, it can almost be taken for granted that such cases were rather rare, and so far there is no direct evidence of the Czechoslovak state security service producing its own fake samizdat for the sake of provocation or disinformation.[34]

III. According to traditionally recognized types of printed material

This part of our classification does not seem to pose any difficulty and is a natural part of the work of archivists and librarians of samizdat literature. Here, the following may be distinguished:

(a) Books of fiction, nonfiction books, reference books, books with reproductions.

(b) Anthologies of texts (fiction, poetry, essays, articles, nonfiction, etc.).

(c) Collections of poems by an individual author.

(d) Periodical volumes.

(e) Leaflets, separate sheets, loosely joined sheets.

---

34) See, e.g., the samizdat periodical *Informace o Chartě 77* [Information about Charter 77], 14 (1987): a fake letter (probably a product of the Czech secret police) by Čestmír Císař, published in the samizdat magazine *Diskuse* [Discussion], is mentioned there. I thank Jiří Gruntorád for the information concerning the hypothetical "samizdat fakes".

(f) Magnitizdat issues (tape recordings, cassette recordings), sometimes accompanied by various additional printed matter.

IV. According to the date of production and of issuance, if different

Here again the situation seems to be quite simple:

(a) Issues of texts dated according to when they were written and/or when they were first published in samizdat.

(b) Undated samizdat publications (frequent in "wild samizdat").

(c) Antedated samizdat publications, rarely occurring, usually for reasons of safety. A legendary case is one of the very first Czech samizdat examples, from the "presamizdat" period, namely, the typewritten surrealist anthology *Roztrhané panenky* [The Lacerated Dolls], dated 1937 but actually published in 1942.[35] More frequent were cases of "wild samizdat", where the dating of individual samizdat issues was often mistaken for – or deliberately replaced by – the author's own dating of the text itself: the year when the text was written replaces the dating of the samizdat edition (i.e., the year when the text was only rewritten or reedited by an editor or a typist).

(d) Postdated texts, frequently "wild samizdat" issues for which the dating of the text itself was replaced by the dating of the samizdat issue.

V. According to the textual content of samizdat publications, that is, their internal features (linguistic and generic)

Here again the situation is simple:

(a) Texts written in the language of the country where the samizdat publishing took place.

(b) Translated texts.

Both subgroups can be further divided by genre.

(1) Fiction (prose, poetry, drama, essays, entertainment, etc).

(2) Nonfiction.

35) Concerning the anthology of surrealist poetry *Roztrhané panenky*, see KUNDERA, Ludvík, *Spisy L. K.*, sv. XVII /A/; *Spisy L. K*, sv. XVII /B/ – *Různá řečiště /a/*; *Různá řečiště /b/* [L. K.'s Collected Works, vol. XVII /A/; L. K.'s Collected Works, vol. XVII /B/ – Various Riverbeds /A/; Various Riverbeds /B/], 2 vols., Brno (Czech Republic): Host, 2005. (/A/, pp. 172-174, /B/, pp. 93-100); see also part 8 of the television documentary series *Samizdat*, mentioned in Footnote 4.

(2a) Political, informative, juridical texts.

(2b) Documentary texts.

(2c) Philosophical, religious, psychological texts.

(2d) Specialized, scientific texts, including literary criticism, literary history, for example, *Slovník českých spisovatelů* [Dictionary of Czech Writers] (Brabec et al. 1982, see Footnote 27); art history, for example, a number of Petr Rezek's editions; lexicographic, linguistic texts, for example, Holman's *Frekvenční slovník básnického díla Otokara Březiny* mentioned above.

Until recently, it was assumed by Czech bibliographers that, in the Czechoslovakia of 1948–89, political texts and books of fiction and philosophy were the most frequent samizdat materials.[36] However, according to a recently published testimony,[37] these were outnumbered by printed religious texts, including the Bible in a new Czech translation:[38] they were produced in secret, clandestine printing offices run since the mid-1970s by the outlawed religious organization Jehovah's Witnesses, whose samizdat activity was reportedly financed by the voluntary gifts of the sect's Czech and Slovak members. The Czechoslovak Jehovah's Witnesses reportedly published millions of samizdat copies in fourteen secret, literally underground printing offices, using cyclostyle and even offset technology. Theirs was a unique samizdat production, developing in perfect isolation and in no communication with other samizdat activities.

---

36) See especially HANÁKOVÁ 1997 (Footnote 3); PREČAN 1988 (Footnote 3); POSSET 1991 (Footnote 3).

37) See Footnote 9. Unfortunately, there is no other reliable source of information that would verify the data found in Herbert Adamy's book. The secretive, clandestine character of the sect's inner life only aggravates the unreliability of the given data.

38) The translation of the Bible for the use of the members of the Jehovah's Witnesses sect is anonymous. However, the preface of its 1991 edition (of course, already a printed, bound book) says it was translated from English, not from the original languages; its imprint assigns the copyright to "Watch Tower Bible and Tract Society of Pennsylvania" and describes its translation as the "New World Translation of the Holy Scriptures / Czech (bi 12-B)".

VI. According to the chronological order of samizdat publishing in Czechoslovakia (with regard to the main political changes)

(a) Presamizdat period, 1939–45, the years of the Nazi occupation of the Czech territory (very rare publications).

(b) Protosamizdat period, 1948–56, the period of Stalinism (rare publications).

(c) The gradual decay of protosamizdat, 1956–67 (the more space for uncensored publishing in legally printed books and periodicals, the smaller the need for samizdat publishing).

(d) Nonsamizdat period, roughly between spring 1968 and autumn 1969. Typewritten publications of the time did not have the character of samizdat, as state censorship was either not applied or was completely inoperative. Typewritten copies from 1968–69 were either "manuscripts" or products of "free", "independent" publishing and could be accorded the status of a samizdat publication only *post-factum*, that is, at the beginning of the following "normalization" period.

(e) Early samizdat period, 1970–85. Samizdat production then reached *für sich* status, and the term *samizdat* started to be used; well-known series of samizdat editions were founded.

(f) Late samizdat period, 1986–89, the Mikhail Gorbachev years. Here samizdat publishing in Czechoslovakia reached its peak, more and more series of editions and samizdat periodicals were founded, and larger and larger numbers of "grey zone" readers had access to samizdat publications.[39]

(g) Postsamizdat period, 1989 to this day. Characterized by occasional nostalgic revivals of samizdat publishing. Some authors and editors, now equipped with personal computer printers, occasionally "publish" texts in a very limited number of copies to be used by themselves and a handful of friends but nevertheless give them the shape of a regular publication. Such "samizdat", however, is to be understood as a product of bibliophilism.

39) See Footnote 21.

VII. According to the type of technology used in samizdat production

The variety of technologies has already been outlined above. Let me just stress here again that, for most Czech and Slovak samizdat editors and distributors of 1948–89, a simple typewriter was the only working tool. Vrba 2001 (Footnote 3, 2, 10) in his useful essay suggests the same disproportion.

VIII. According to a variety of other criteria

Vrba (2001) also tried to categorize samizdat materials according to various ways of financing their production and distribution and according to whether they were sold or distributed for free. He also suggested sorting them according to the number of copies and print runs (from one copy to several hundred, rarely more than three to four hundred copies) and according to the type of typewriter used. Moreover, apart from Vrba's suggestions, it would be possible to classify them according to the type of readers, for example, the Charter 77 circle,[40] the circle of the underground community (the circle of the Plastic People of the Universe, the *Vokno* [Window] circle, the *Revolver Revue* circle, etc.),[41] the Jazzová sekce (Jazz Section)

40) Concerning Charter 77 samizdats, they were especially the so-called INFOCHs, i.e., *Informace o Chartě 77*; see its bibliography in GRUNTORÁD, Jiří (ed.), *Informace o Chartě 77 1978-1990. Článková bibliografie*, Brno (Czech Republic): Doplněk, 1998. The two most prominent Czech samizdat series of editions - Vaculík's Edice Petlice and Havel's Edice Expedice - were mostly distributed among the Charter 77 signatories; see their bibliographies in PREČAN, Vilém, "Edice Petlice 1973-1987" [Padlock Editions 1973-1987], *ACTA* 1, no. 3-4 (1987), pp. 35-91; GRUNTORÁD, Jiří, "Edice Expedice. Část 1. - 'Černá řada'" [Dispatch Editions. Part 1 - 'Black Series'], *Kritický sborník* 14, no. 3 (1994), pp. 66-78; GRUNTORÁD, Jiří, "Edice Expedice. Část 2. - 'Světlá řada'" [Dispatch Editions. Part 2 - 'Light Series'], in *Kritický sborník* 14, no. 4 (1994), pp. 71-80; see also ROMANOVÁ, Gabriela, *Příběh Edice Expedice* [The Story of the Dispatch Editions], Praha: Knihovna Václava Havla, 2014.

41) Concerning "underground samizdats", i.e., those produced by the members of the community of rock fans, poets, and artists who gathered at the beginning of the 1970s around the band The Plastic People of the Universe, it was mostly various samizdat anthologies - *sborníks* - of poetry (see the bibliography in MACHOVEC, Martin (ed.), *Pohledy zevnitř. Česká undergroundová kultura ve svědectvích, dokumentech a interpretacích* [Views from the Inside: Czech Underground Culture in Testimonies, Documents, and Interpretations], Praha: Pistorius and Olšanská, 2008,

community,[42] the various religious communities,[43] and the various regional circles.[44] One could even try to trace the degree of isolation as against openness of the various circles, but such a subgrouping would probably be too tentative and vague.

pp. 167-168; see also a more detailed bibliography on the website of ÚSTR: MACHO-VEC, Martin, *Nejvýznamnější samizdatové sborníky undergroundové literatury (1975-1989)*, Ústav pro studium totalitních režimů, http://www.ustrcr.cz/data/pdf/projekty/underground/underground-samizdat-sborniky.pdf (accessed in June 2019). Then, starting in 1979 and 1985, respectively, there were two major underground samizdat journals, *Vokno* and *Revolver Revue*; see their bibliographies in RŮŽKOVÁ, Jana - GRUNTORÁD, Jiří, "Samizdatový časopis Vokno" [The Samizdat Magazine Vokno], *Kritický sborník* 19 (1999-2000), pp. 193-231; JEŽEK, Vlastimil, "Bibliografie Revolver Revue (Jednou nohou) 1-13" [Bibliography of Revolver Revue (One Foot In) 1-13], *Kritický sborník* 11, no. 3 (1991) pp. 63-79 + JEŽEK, Vlastimil, "Bibliografie Revolver Revue (Jednou nohou) 1-13", *Kritický sborník* 11, no. 4. (1991), pp. 67-75.

42) Concerning Jazzová sekce's samizdats (or semilegal prints), see KOUŘIL, Vladimír, *Jazzová sekce v čase a nečase 1971-1987* [The Jazz Section in the Course of Good and Bad Times 1971-1987], Praha: Torst, 1999.

43) Besides the religious community of Jehovah's Witnesses (see Footnotes 9 and 38), it was especially in Slovakia that religious (in this case, Catholic) samizdat flourished. Part 12 of the Czech television documentary series *Samizdat*, mentioned in Footnote 4, was devoted to Slovak religious samizdat. From it we learn about the influence of the "secret Catholic Church" in Slovakia and about various Catholic periodicals, mostly produced with the help of offset printing machines kept in cellars; starting in 1973 and reaching print runs of as many as fifteen hundred copies in the 1980s, various periodicals came out in samizdat, e.g., František Mikloško's *Náboženstvo a súčasnosť* [Religion and Today], Vladimír Jukl's *Katolícky mesačník* (Catholic Monthly), Vladimír Durkovič's *Rodinné spoločenstvo* [Family Communion], and Ivan Polanský's *Historický zápisník* [History Notebook], whose only two issues (1986, 1987) dealt with the two prominent figures of Slovak clerical fascism, Jozef Tiso and Andrej Hlinka.

44) Concerning "regional samizdats", see POSSET, Johanna, Česká samizdatová periodika 1968-1989, Brno (Czechoslovakia): Továrna na sítotisk a společnost R&T, 1991; PETR, Pavel, "Moravský samizdat" [Moravian Samizdat], *Box*, no. 6 (1996), pp. 44-71; PETROVÁ, Jana, *Zapomenutá generace osmdesátých let 20. století. Nezávislé aktivity a samizdat na Plzeňsku Plzeňsku* [The Forgotten Generation of the 1980s. Independent Activities and Samizdat in the Plzeň Region], Plzeň (Czech Republic): Jana Petrová, 2009; MACHOVEC 2008 (Footnote 41), pp. 134-135; PŘIBÁŇ, Michal (ed.), *Český literární samizdat 1949-1989. Edice - časopisy - sborníky*, Praha: Academia - Ústav pro českou literaturu AV ČR, 2018; see also Footnote 43.

The definition of samizdat publishing as proposed above both widens and narrows the notion of it. On the one hand, samizdat publishing can exist only in totalitarian political systems or regimes and should not be confused with other "free", "independent", "alternative", "underground" publishing anywhere or at any time; on the other hand, what may be considered samizdat material exceeds by far the typewritten documents of a nation's conscience, the texts by prominent representatives of dissidence.

EGON BONDY AND THE SAMIZDAT PUBLICATION OF HIS WORKS

To test the applicability of the typology of samizdat outlined above, we will consider the samizdat publication of one of the best-known contemporary Czech writers, now a rather ill-famed ex-guru of Czech underground culture, the poet, prose writer, and philosopher Egon Bondy (born in Prague, Czechoslovakia, in 1930; died in Bratislava, Slovakia, in 2007).[45] Bondy's critics and opponents can hardly deny at least one thing: his incessant, continuous samizdat production, which extended over four decades, from 1948 until 1989. The three purely philosophical works published in Czechoslovakia in state-controlled publishing houses in the late 1960s under the author's real name (Zbyněk Fišer) represent an exception proving the rule: the creative writing was left to the author's *alter ego*, Egon Bondy, and found its place only on the thousands of typewritten pages of samizdat publications. Bondy's bibliography, published on the website of Libri Prohibiti,[46] includes for the years 1948–89 approximately sixty samizdat collections of poems (classified for our purpose as "first samizdat editions"); nearly thirty-two samizdat titles of prose (novels, novellas, short stories); ten samizdat philosophical essays and treatises; thirteen separate issues of the thir-

---

45) For work in English on and by Bondy, see PAGE, Benjamin B., "Translator's Introduction (2000)", in BONDY, Egon, *The Consolation of Ontology: On the Substantial and Nonsubstantial Models*, Lanham, MD: Lexington Books, 2001; MACHOVEC, Martin (ed.), *Views from the Inside: Czech Underground Literature and Culture (1948-1989)*, Praha: Department of Czech Literature and Literary Criticism, Faculty of Philosophy and Arts, Charles University, 2006; 2nd, augmented edition: Praha: Karolinum Press, 2018; RIEDEL, Jaroslav (ed.), *The Plastic People of the Universe*, Praha: Maťa, 1999.
46) *Bibliografie Egona Bondyho*: See Footnote 26.

teen-volume *Poznámky k dějinám filosofie* [Remarks on the History of Philosophy], published in samizdat between the years 1977 and 1987; three separate issues of political, Marxist analyses of the Soviet, the Central and Eastern European, and the Chinese models of Communism, published in samizdat in 1950, 1969, and 1985; thirteen separate issues of theater sketches (from the years 1968-70); and finally, three samizdat issues of Bondy's translations into Czech of texts by various foreign authors. While altogether approximately 135 separate issues of the author's own first samizdats came out during the four decades of totalitarianism in Czechoslovakia, samizdat reissues of his work would probably make the number three or four times higher.

Bondy's samizdat exists mostly in typewritten editions and copies. At the beginning of the 1950s Bondy, together with his friend, the poet Ivo Vodsed'álek, founded one of the first Czech samizdat series of editions, called Edice Půlnoc [Midnight Editions].[47] Each of this series's issues bore the pseudonyms or initials of the authors (in the case of their own texts, these were identical with the pseudonyms or initials of the editors of the issues) and included most of the features in Vrba's characterization of "established samizdat" editions (mostly format A5, the title page bearing the name of the edition, pagination, imprint, sometimes even a list of "books in print" or "coming out soon", the author's autograph, etc). From 1951 to 1955 almost fifty typewritten issues of works by Bondy, Vodsed'álek, Krejcarová, Pavel Svoboda, Hrabal, and several others came out in the Midnight Editions. One rare exception to his typewritten samizdat is a marginal collection of poems (Bondy's *Krajina a nemravnost* [Landscape and Immorality]), dated 1953, which appeared only in one calligraphic copy. After the mid-1950s

---

47) See MACHOVEC, Martin, "Několik poznámek k podzemní ediční řadě Půlnoc", *Kritický sborník* 13, no. 3 (1993), pp. 71-78; ZAND, Gertraude, *Totaler Realismus und Peinliche Poesie. Tschechische Untergrund-Literatur 1948-1953*, Wien: Peter Lang, 1998; ibidem, *Totální realismus a trapná poezie. Česká neoficiální literatura 1948-1953*, Brno (Czech Republic): Host, 2002; MACHOVEC, Martin, "Od avantgardy přes podzemí do undergroundu. Skupina edice Půlnoc 1949-1955 a undergroundový okruh Plastic People 1969-1989", in ALAN 2001 (Footnote 2), pp. 154-199, also in *Pohledy zevnitř* (Footnote 41), pp. 97-149; PŘIBÁŇ, Michal (ed.), 2018 – see Footnote 44; KUŽEL, Petr (ed.), *Myšlení a tvorba Egona Bondyho*, Praha: Filosofia, 2018.

Bondy's samizdat publications show almost no attempt to keep to the standard of "established samizdat", and they become more modest, simple typewritten copies, hardly distinguishable from the author's typewritten manuscripts. And in the late 1980s some of Bondy's works were published immediately upon completion in as many as three hundred copies in cyclostyle by the author's samizdat colleagues – mostly the editors of the underground magazine *Vokno*.

As far as motivation is concerned, Bondy's works reflect his "inner need" (Ia), but in the 1970s and 1980s they occasionally became a product of a "refined kind of graphomania" as defined in (If2): they suffer at parts from the author's overproduction and haste, which can be understood as a defense reaction to police intimidation and the impossibility of regular, legal publishing.[48]

Bondy's original texts prevail in his samizdat publishing (IIa, IIb), both those of fiction and of nonfiction (political, philosophical texts, occasional literary and art criticism, and review writing). His creativity and fertility are breathtaking. If Bondy's samizdat issues were to be classified according to the types of printed material (III), they would range over all subgroups from (a) to (f). As far as the anthologies and periodical volumes are concerned, Bondy's role was usually that of a contributor or a coeditor.

Bondy always carefully dated not only each of his samizdat issues but often also individual poems or texts in prose (IVa). Some of his samizdat is hardly distinguishable from diary entries, spatial-temporal segments, reflections of the author's own life and work. In numerous cases, "wild samizdat" reissues of his works antedated them (IVc). Thus, for example, a collection of poems written in 1951 (and accurately dated by its author with the same year) but retyped, say, in 1972 or 1985 still bore the date 1951.

---

48) Bondy's overproduction of literary texts, especially poetry, was criticized for instance by Jiří Kolář (KOLÁŘ, Jiří, *Dílo Jiřího Koláře VIII* [Works of Jiří Kolář VIII], Praha: Paseka, 2000, pp. 88–89) and Milan Knížák (KNÍŽÁK, Milan, *Bez důvodu* [Without Reason], Praha: Litera, 1996, p. 122. However, his poetry as a whole has not been adequately analysed yet, perhaps because of its enormous bulk; see BONDY, Egon, *Básnické dílo Egona Bondyho I-IX* [The Collected Poems of Egon Bondy I-IX], 9 vols., Praha: Pražská imaginace, 1990-1993; BONDY, Egon, *Básnické spisy I-III* [Collected Poetic Works I-III], 3 vols., Praha: Argo, 2014-2016.

This classification of Czech/Czechoslovak samizdat publishing in general and its application to Bondy's works is intended to elucidate samizdat for historiographers and to place samizdat writing in its social, political, and psychological contexts. It can hardly serve or replace literary interpretation, and so literary historians who claim that it is best to forget about all samizdat frameworks and instead concentrate on the interpretation of the works as literature may not be completely wrong.

Prague - Philadelphia - Durham, NC
2006, 2009

8. THREE EXAMPLES OF A VARIETY OF RELATIONS BETWEEN CZECH SAMIZDAT AND "TAMIZDAT" BOOK PRODUCTION OF THE 1970S AND 1980S[1]

Quoting a bit of a worn-out Latin motto, "*Habent sua fata libelli*", at the beginning of this survey may be excused. Certainly even books have their ups and downs, their moments of glory and moments of decay when they fall into oblivion – perhaps with some chance to have something to say again one day again. The reasons for which can sometimes be quite irrational and unpredictable as they definitely are not directly dependent on the literary value of each individual book alone.

If this is true for book production anywhere, anytime, it is probably even more conspicuous in the case of samizdat book production because of one reason: the very essence of samizdat book production lies more in an extra-literary sphere than in a purely literary one. In other words, what samizdat books contained was less important than the very fact of their existence which in itself was evidence of cultural and political resistance in times of totalitarian regimes.

The whole of this introduction is to say that we have to be extremely cautious when trying to measure the success – to say nothing about the quality – of a particular samizdat book according to its relatively high print runs or according to to how many times it had been published in samizdat. By the way, it is a well-known fact, that the highest print-runs of Czechoslovak samizdat in the 1970s and 1980s were achieved by the Jehovah Witnesses, though their output mostly consisted of poor translations of religious texts into Czech.

The following schema brings forth some of the typical, usual factors that might have made some samizdat editions more attractive than others – which can further elucidate the variety of relations between **samizdat publishers** on the one hand and the book pro-

1) This text was written for a panel discussion on samizdat held in Czech Center, New York City, November 2011; slightly altered, under the title "On Czech Samizdat and Tamizdat: Banned Books of 1970s and 1980s", it was published on the website of *Fair Observer*, 2014, https://www.fairobserver.com/region/europe/czech-samizdat-tamizdat-banned-books-1970s-1980s/.

duction of **exiled Czechoslovak publishers or foreign publishing houses** on the other hand. It may be worth noting that the literary quality of books is only one of these factors – and perhaps not always the most decisive one.

The book:
type of literature: factual books vs. fiction, imaginative literature;
theme of the book: topical, current Czechoslovak themes vs. perennial, timeless themes;
language of the book: Czech / Slovak originals vs. translated books.

The author:
his / her reputation at home: a well-known author before 1968/69 vs. an unknown one who started publishing only in samizdat;
his / her reputation abroad: ditto.

The target group of readers:
in Czechoslovakia: a particular group of readers at a certain period of time vs. dissident readership vs. general reading public in the country / in the whole world;
abroad: a particular group of readers in a particular country vs. a general reading public in the whole world.

The function / purpose of the book: entertainment vs. education vs. current (political) information.

The literary quality of the book: always disputable.

The origin of the book: original Czech / Slovak samizdats vs. samizdat editions of a banned book that had already been published before by regular printing presses vs. samizdat editions of a book written and published before in Czechoslovak exile abroad.

Only if we take into account all the above-mentioned factors in their mutual relations, and perhaps some more criteria of a more or less **extra-literary character**, could we try to estimate why and where and when a particular samizdat edition **may or may not** have been successful. Nevertheless, at least one fact can be taken for granted right away: i.e., **the success of a samizdat edition *alone* could not guarantee any other success of a respective book anywhere else, any time later** – and vice versa – the failure of an original samizdat book abroad did not have to explain its failure or success at home.

The three following examples are based on **three successful samizdat editions** which, with one exemption, roused little or no attention on the side of Czech exiled publishers, and, with another exemption, little or no attention on the side of foreign, especially Anglo-American publishers.

I.

Egon Bondy's novel *Invalidní sourozenci* [The Disabled Siblings] was written in 1974 by a little known author who never published any of his poetry and fiction before 1968 and in the "normalization" decades was utterly dependent on samizdat book production. The novel was inspired by the author's life in the Czech underground community of rock musicians, poets and artists and in it the author addressed the same community. The book worked as a sort of an apology or even an apotheosis of the "merry ghetto" of this community.

Now there are, incredibly, **14 different type-written editions** of the book found in Prague-based Libri prohibiti library which, together with **3 more different editions** found in the author's personal archives, probably represent **the absolute top record in Czech samizdat book production – 17 different type-written editions** of the discussed book.

The keen interest in the book, especially on the side of the above-mentioned Czech underground community, has always been in sharp discrepancy with little or no interest on the side of prominent Czech dissidents and dissident samizdat publishers, so had it not been for one edition in Václav Havel's Edice Expedice publishers – of Pavel Tigrid's interest that resulted in his publishing an extract of the book in Paris-based Czech exiled journal *Svědectví* (1980) – and later of Josef Škvorecký's interest that generated the first printed publication of the book in 68 Publishers (1981), the book would probably be only known and successful within a limited and somewhat isolated circle of readers at home.

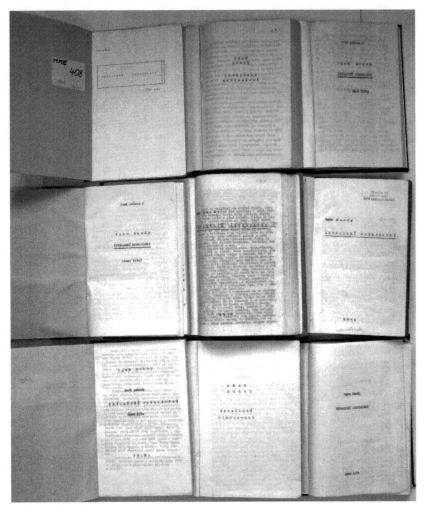

Different samizdat editions of Bondy's *Invalidní sourozenci*

Nevertheless, the tremendous success of the book among a section of Czech samizdat readers provoked **one more** edition abroad:
I have in mind Josef "Baghýra" Jelínek's (1927–2015) miniature piracy
reprints. Mr. Jelínek used to make the miniature reprints of Czech
books published in exile in his office in Erlangen, Germany, pursuing
only one aim: to make smuggling back to Czechoslovakia easier.

Bondy's book *Invalidní sourozenci* was published in Erlangen in
1983 and, according to the data given by Jiří Gruntorád, head of Libri

Invalidní sourozenci, Sixty-Eight Publishers, Toronto 1981
(the front cover brings a reprint of a picture by Rudolf Plaček, the back cover brings a photo of the author)

prohibiti library, some time later Josef Jelínek even made one more reprint of the book: maybe several hundred of the miniature copies of *Invalidní sourozenci* were successfully smuggled into Czechoslovakia in those years: so insatiable was the Czech readers' thirst for this book that the demand probably lasted until the late 1980s!

Of course, the book was published by regular printing presses in Czechoslovakia soon after 1989 – first in 1991, next in 2001, and in 2012 for the third time. It was even published in three translations, in Italian, German, and Slovenian (some parts of the book also in Polish and Hungarian)[2] but everywhere and every time met with only little success: its time is probably gone now. The target group

2) Egon Bondy's *Invalidní sourozenci* in translations: in Italian as *Fratelli invalidi*, Milano: Eleuthera, 1993; in German as *Die Invaliden Geschwister*, Heidelberg: Elfenbein, 1999; in Slovenian as *Invalidna sorojenca*, Vnanje Gorice: Police Dubove, 2017.

A miniature reprint of Toronto edition of *Invalidní sourozenci*, Erlangen, 1983

of its devoted readers has begun dying out, and the role of the book has been fulfilled.

II.

This following one is an example of a very different samizdat publication. Milan Machovec's (1925–2003) monograph on Jesus was originally written in 1969 to fit the demands of Prague based Orbis / Svoboda publishers' series of books called PORTRÉTY that consisted of brief, concise monographs always titled only with the name of a respective historic figure.

Since the author was a well-known person both at home and abroad, being one of the founders of Christian-Marxist dialogue[3] that took place both in the East and the West in the 1960s, it was

---

3) On Christian-Marxist dialogues of 1960s and on M.M.'s role in them see for instance: STÖHR, Martin (ed.), *Disputation zwischen Christen und Marxisten*, München: Kaiser Verlag, 1966; KELLNER, Erich (ed.), *Schöpfertum und Freiheit in einer humanen Gesellschaft. Marienbader Protokolle*, Wien – Frankfurt – Zürich: Europa Verlag, 1969; OESTEREICHER, Paul (ed.), *The Christian Marxist Dialogue. An International Symposium*, London: The Macmillan Comp., 1969; MOJZES, Paul, *Christian-Marxist Dialogue in Eastern Europe*, Minneapolis: Augsburg Publishing House, 1981; JINDROVÁ, Kamila – TACHECÍ, Pavel – ŽDÁRSKÝ, Pavel (eds.), *Mistr dialogu Milan Machovec. Sborník k nedožitým osmdesátinám českého filosofa*, Praha: Akropolis, 2006; LANDA, Ivan – MERVART, Jan (eds.), *Proměny marxisticko-křesťanského dialogu v Československu*, Praha: Filosofia, 2017.

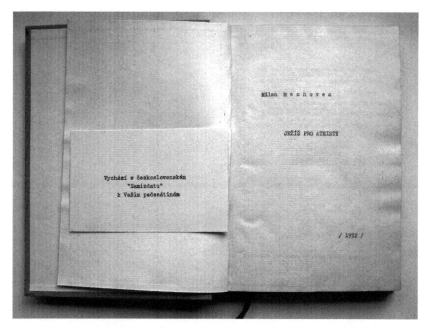

One of the samizdat editions of *Ježíš pro ateisty*, anonymous, but probably belonging to Vaculík's Edice Petlice circle

not difficult to rouse the interest of foreign publishers in Western Europe and even in more remote parts of the world.

The **9 samizdat editions** of the book *Ježíš pro ateisty* [Jesus for Atheists; in English translation published under the title *A Marxist Looks at Jesus*][4] found in the Libri prohibiti library (including exemplars from Vaculík's Edice petlice and Havel's Edice Expedice) are, as we are told, the average number, nevertheless the print runs of such typewritten editions were usually limited: it was a factual book, a serious treatise that could hardly compete with more attractive books of fiction, a fact, which makes the incredibly keen interest in the book on the side of foreign publishers in the 1970s and 1980s even more unbelievable: the book was published **6 times** only in Germany [under the title *Jesus für Atheisten*] and later on in **10 more languages** in **11 more countries** – including Japan and South Korea.

4) The English translation: MACHOVEC, Milan, *A Marxist Looks at Jesus*, London: Darton, Longmann & Todd, 1976 / Philadelphia: Fortress Press, 1976.

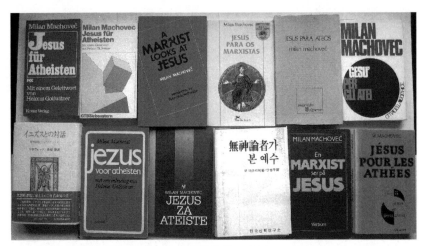

A German, English, Portuguese, Spanish, Italian, Japanese, Dutch, Slovenian, Corean, Swedish, and French edition of *Ježíš pro ateisty*

On the other hand the book had never been published in its Czech original by any exiled Czech publishing house. Here we are, of course, faced with a different kind of an appeal: as it is hard to believe that there would not be enough interesting books on Jesus Christ published in the West, it was probably **the author himself** who made the book attractive. Or, better said, what the author was supposed to be: a banned Marxist in a reportedly socialist country who wanted to make Christianity interesting even in the eyes of the so-called atheists. Such a hypothesis could also explain the lack of interest in the book on the side of Czech exiled publishers. They were mostly forced into exile because they could not cope with atheistic Marxists and Communists ruling their home country: why should they publish a book written by one of them, though one who later got in trouble with party bosses?

Back in Czechoslovakia at the beginning of 1990s, the book also met with little interest. It was published as early as 1990 under a less provocative title of *Ježíš pro moderního člověka* [Jesus for a Present-Day Man] and in a large print run that could not sell and had few if any reviews. The second edition of 2003[5] got to print only some months after the author's death. It was a small print

5) MACHOVEC, Milan, *Ježíš pro moderního člověka*, 2nd edition, Praha: Akropolis, 2003.

run that hardly paid. Nowadays, the book is on its way to oblivion, having fulfilled its temporary role both at home and abroad relatively well.

III.

The third example is the so-called *"Hnědá kniha" o procesech s českým undergroundem* ["Brown Book" on the Trials of the Czech Underground], published for the first time in samizdat in 1976 (edited by Jaroslav Kořán and Václav Vendelín Komeda), again in 1977 or 1978 (unknown editors), and then again, enlarged, in 1980 (edited by Jaroslav Suk). It is a publication whose way to readers was extraordinarily unusual. As an anthology of the most different texts – documents, testimonies, literary texts, essays, song lyrics, etc. – it was completed as a source of true, factual information, that was to face the massive official propaganda launched by the the totalitarian regime during the trial of the members of the underground rock band, The Plastic People of the Universe. As we know from the recent history of Czechoslovakia, this trial was one of the most important factors that led to the establishment of Charter 77 by the end of the same year – and the so-called *"Brown Book"* undoubtedly served as one of the eye-openers of the day. By the way: the name of the volume is purely incidental: its first edition had no name and was bound in a brown-coloured cardboard folder – because this was reportedly the only cardboard colour available at the time. The second edition already had the name of the so-called *"Brown Book"*, the title found in quotes, of course.[6]

Since the extra-literary function and the topical, up to date purpose of a such publication is more than obvious it should not surprise us to find out that the*"Brown Book"* had never been published abroad or again in samizdat after 1980 – and it was only 35 years after the day of the nameless samizdat started circulating, that a critical, annotated edition came out.[7] Such books can probably only function as a "mediator" of information, some of which may only be of ephemeral value. Some of the texts found in the *"Brown*

6) See detailed comments in the printed book: MACHOVEC, M. – NAVRÁTIL, P. – STÁREK, F. Č. (eds.), *"Hnědá kniha" o procesech s českým undergroundem*, Praha: ÚSTR, 2012, esp. pp. 446–454.
7) See the previous Footnote.

„HNĚDÁ KNIHA"

o procesech
s českým
undergroundem

The cover of the commented printed edition of "*Brown
Book*" (2012) respected the colour of the cover of
the original nameless samizdat although its choice was
quite incidental, random

Book" were published prior to it, some others later, some were translated into foreign languages but **as a whole** the "*Brown Book*" was of no interest on the side of Czech exiled publishers. And there was no need to be sorry too much because the anthology had fulfilled its extra-literary function almost immediately.

And yet there was a response to the "*Brown Book*" among the Czechoslovak exiles, though bearing an absolutely different title. We have in mind the first LP of The Plastic People of the Universe, called *Egon Bondy's Happy Hearts Club Banned*, released in the UK

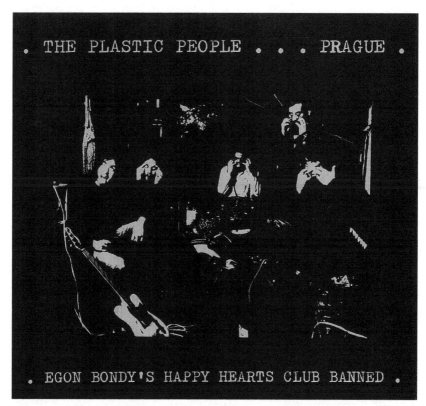

The original sleeve of the first LP of the Plastic People of the Universe (1978)

and France in 1978 together with a voluminous catalogue either in English (*The Merry Ghetto*) or in French (*Le ghetto joyeux*)[8] which incorporated a number of texts found only in the *"Brown Book"* before.

The editors of the 1978 LP and of both the catalogues – the Canadian Paul Wilson, the London-based Czech exile Ivan Hartel, and the Frenchman Jacques Pasquier – never even mentioned the *"Brown Book"* as an invaluable source of information, but again, we do not have to blame them for it: instead they managed to create their own

8) *The Plastic People... Prague. Egon Bondy's Happy Hearts Club Banned*, London – Paris: Boží Mlýn & SCOPA Invisible Production; see detailed comments on this release with catalogues mentioned in *"Hnědá kniha"*, 2012 (Footnote 6), esp. pp. 395–408, 450, 493–495; see also RIEDEL, Jaroslav, *Plastic People a český underground*, Praha: Galén, 2016, pp. 240–258.

The LP released in Britain was accompanied by the English catalogue and the one released in France had a French catalogue (the print run of French mutations were probably very limited and thus they soon became a collector's item)

version of the original samizdat which functioned as the proverbial first snowball that set an avalanche into movement.

The Plastic People of the Universe were not to be forgotten, more and more records with their music were released in the West before 1989, and all their music was published on a number of CDs after that year in their home country – and they themselves became a living legend whereas the *"Brown Book"* having served its extra-literary purpose became a collection of documents highly appreciated by archivists and historians up to these days.

There is no doubt we could find many more examples of the once successful Czech samizdat books that either "made it" abroad or met there with little on no interest because of the suggested or other reasons. All of these examples, however, could be taken as a proof of a very specific, unparalleled function of the phenomenon called *samizdat*.

Prague – New York
November 2011 [Fair Observer 2014]

9. MY ITINERARY HAS BEEN MONOTONOUS FOR QUITE A WHILE:[1] MAGOR'S SWAN SONGS

To this day, Ivan Martin Jirous (23rd September 1944 – 9th November 2011), a.k.a. Magor – a nickname he took up as his literary pseudonym (loosely translated as "The Loony") – is known in Czech society primarily for being a dissident, political prisoner (he was in prison five times for a total of nine years during the 1970s and 1980s), an extravagant freak and a troublemaker. In the eyes of some so-called upstanding and decent members of Czech consumer society, he actually largely deserved his repeated imprisonment prior to 1989. This judgement does not come as a surprise when we consider that Jirous literally dedicated his entire life to independent, autonomous culture, non commercial art and the free, liberal arts in general, something that often goes hand in hand with an unconventional lifestyle. All of this runs counter to the pseudo-values of mainstream consumer culture which as we can see a quarter of a century after the fall of the totalitarian regime in Czechoslovakia – are not much different to those espoused by the socialist masses before 1989.

1) The title of this text and also of the book of selected poems by Jirous to which the text was originally an epilogue (London: Divus, 2017) is a quotation of an incipit of one of poems in *Magor's Swan Songs*: "Monotónní můj itinerář posledních let. / Jako bych už jen s eskortami / měl Čechy uvidět. / V Klášterci nad Ohří na římse / spatřil jsem Pannu v elipse / paprsků zářivých. / Nepomodlit se byl by hřích. / Z chomutovského jel jsem soudu. / Poslední léta rodnou hroudu / vidím jen na eskortách. / Ach. / Však kdybych přistál třeba v Orly, / ta záře světla od mandorly / navždycky by mě minula. / A úsměv taky neviděl bych, / který na duši Jirka Tichý / hodil mi jako horké cíchy. / Nepomodlit se byl by hřích." In Marek Tomin's translation (the book cited, p. 19): "My itinerary has been monotonous for quite a while / As if it was my lot to regard / Bohemia in the company of an armed guard. / On the way from Chomutov after a trial / In an aureole of radiant light / The Holy Virgin I chanced to see / On a ledge, in Klášterec nad Ohří. / Not to have said a prayer would have been a sin. / Of late I only glimpse my native lands / In an armed officer's hands. / Woe is me. / Maybe if I landed in some place like Orly / The mandorla's radiant light / Would never have passed my sight, / Nor would I have seen the comforting grin / That Jirka Tichý threw my way / As if to wrap my soul in a warm duvet. / To have not said a prayer would have been a sin." See the Czech original as a part of the collection *Magorovy labutí písně* in *Magorova summa*, 3rd edition, vol. I, Praha: Torst 2015, p. 319.

In spite of this, a minority exists in contemporary Czech society that appreciates the work of Jirous and positively values his civic courage under totalitarianism, his uncompromising attitude toward the political establishment during the so-called "normalization", as well as his broad intellectual scope and the breadth of subjects that he has written about. However, only few recognize him as a theoretician of the Czech underground, an independent cultural movement that was, *de facto*, forced into illegality. In terms of the mainstream, fewer still value Jirous as a poet. But then again, poetry has always only been read by a negligible percentage of the people, a fact not likely to change in the future. In this respect, it is not only Jirous who is currently neglected in the Czech Republic, but also poets of far greater renown.

Jirous' life and work are, in fact, an excellent reflection of the social and political developments in Czechoslovakia during the four decades of the totalitarian regime – from the initial hard, Soviet-style Stalinism of the first half of the 1950s, through the period of the thaw after 1956, all the way to the difficult and progressive battle for greater intellectual and creative freedom in the 1960s. The early 1960s were Jirous' adolescent and university years, while during the second half of the decade he was already working as an art historian, journalist and zealous promoter of some of the most groundbreaking trends in art, such as pop art, new figuration, action painting, conceptual art and happenings.

In order to adequately understand Jirous' role in Czech culture during the 1970s and 1980s, we need to recall that by the late 1960s the Stalinist totalitarian regime had practically collapsed in Czechoslovakia and for a short period – in 1968 – the country emerged as an island of freedom within the Soviet bloc where tolerance, plurality and information flow were practically unrestricted. It is one of the paradoxes of 20th century European history, now being forgotten, that although highly significant, these rare attempts to wrench free of the grip of Big Brother in the Kremlin also had severe and long-lasting consequences for small Central European nations.

The Czechoslovak Prague Spring certainly did not materialise out of thin air; instead its groundwork had been laid throughout the 1960s, as freedom of speech grew incrementally, year on year. Previously banned books were starting to get published; it was easier to travel across the border to the West; 1950s political prisoners were being rehabilitated; the dogmatic version of Marxism gradually stopped being the only accepted and permitted ideology – all of that formally still under the so-called working-class government, or its vanguard, the Communist party (with its would-be Marxist ideology). In addition, various Christian denominations suddenly found increasing space for their activities, and some Marxists were even willing to have discussions with their representatives, thus admitting the fallibility of their own ideology. In the midst of this increasingly dynamic social and cultural milieu, Jirous was studying art history at Charles University in Prague (he completed his master's thesis on visual poetry, specifically the works of Jiří Kolář and Henri Michaux, in 1970, at the last possible minute, just as the pro-Soviet regime imposed after the occupation of Czechoslovakia by the Warsaw Pact military forces in August 1968 had started to strengthen its grip on the country). He started to have his work published in 1965 in various art journals, which, while still marginal, were now legal to publish, such as the magazine *Výtvarná práce* [Creative Work], From the mid-1960s, Jirous also started to actively participate in Czech cultural life, primarily in various art events. He became a member of the unofficial association of artists known as *Křižovnická škola čistého humoru bez vtipu* [the Crusaders' School of Pure Humour Without Jokes, or: the Order of Crusaders for Pure Humour Without Banter], which included Karel Nepraš, Naďa Plíšková, Olaf Hanel, Eugen Brikcius, Otakar Slavík and Zbyšek Sion, all of whom are seen today as key figures of Czech art in the second half of the 20th century, fully utilising the relative freedom of those years, as well as making his own personal contribution to cultural freedom. Jirous was not only engaged in the visual arts, but also in literature (he was always a passionate reader and his later literary work illustrates his high level of erudition) and contemporary music, including rock, which would eventually have fateful consequences.

Today it is difficult even for people in the Czech Republic to imagine the shock people felt as the renewal of pluralist democracy in Czechoslovakia was crushed by the Soviet-led military invasion, the only upside being that it led to the definitive unmasking of the Soviet Union, allegedly its ally and guarantor of peaceful coexistence in the Eastern Bloc, as a totalitarian, albeit post-Stalinist, state. It is not necessary to mention here the countless personal dramas comprising the tragedy of an entire nation: everything has already been well documented, depicted and published. Within roughly a year after the invasion, the Soviet occupiers were able to start re-establishing an oppressive one-party state, this time uncompromisingly pro-Soviet, with a *de facto* puppet and collaborationist government. Tens of thousands of Czechoslovaks fled to the West to live in exile; those who stayed and disagreed with the political overthrow lost their jobs; all liberal, independent information media were banned from the beginning of the 1970s; books by opponents of the regime were withdrawn from sale and taken out of public libraries; and political trials commenced once again in 1970. Although these trials did not result in death sentences like in the 1950s, the pro-Kremlin Communist Party once again held power tightly in its hands.

And as could have been expected, the art journals to which Jirous had contributed in the 1960s were shut down, and Jirous himself – together with thousands of others considered "unadaptable" – was deprived of the possibility to publish, and his artist friends were no longer allowed to exhibit or perform music in public.

And so began his "journey into the underground", the unofficial sphere, the final retreat for those unwilling to give up their artistic ambitions, and who refused to compromise not only their artistic, but also their civic honour by conforming to the new circumstances.

Jirous' activities during that time are well known. He described them himself in his *Zpráva o třetím českém hudebním obrození* [Report on the Third Czech Musical Revival], 1975,[2] a programmatic

---

2) In the English translation by Paul Wilson, this text was published under the title *Report on the Third Czech Musical Revival* in the catalogue *The Merry Ghetto*, which was a supplement to the LP *Plastic People... Egon Bandy's Happy Hearts Club Banned* (London – Paris 1978); this translation was published a second time in the anthology *Views from the Inside. Czech Underground Literature and Culture (1948-1989)*, ed. MACHOVEC, Martin, Praha: Karolinum Press, 2018; an abridged version of *Zpráva*, but under the same English title (translation: Eric Dluhosch) was also published in the anthology HOPTMAN, Laura – POSPISZYL, Tomáš (eds.), *Primary Documents. A Sourcebook for Eastern and Central European Art since the 1950s*, New York: The Museum of Modern Art, 2002. Reprint of the catalogue *The Merry Ghetto* was published on DVD by Martin Machovec: *The Merry Ghetto / Le ghetto joyeux*, Praha: 2012.

manifesto published several times in samizdat and already translated into a number of different languages by the 1970s. Jirous played an indisputable role in the fact that The Plastic People of the Universe, one of many 1960s Czech rock groups, later became one of the most significant symbols of Czech cultural resistance. It is a well-known and historically recognised fact that the decimation of the underground community around the Plastics in 1976 and the subsequent political trials and imprisonment of its representatives, Jirous foremost among them, inspired leading Czech dissidents – intellectuals and artists known abroad – to found the civic initiative Charter 77 a year later.

This is how in a matter of a few years Jirous had gone from an art historian, critic and journalist, to being the main organiser of unofficial art events, theoretician of the Czech underground and soon after a dissident and political prisoner. Needless to say, Jirous never had any intention to build such a "career". After 1989, he recalled more than once that at the end of the 1960s he and his friends were solely concerned with defending the minimal space of freedom, which the totalitarian regime was soon to take away from them anyway. It was never their intention to create a specific counter-culture, let alone one that would manifest itself in an ostentatious manner. They were driven to it by the intolerance of the totalitarian regime.

No more needs to be said about the socio-political context Jirous was embroiled in as the 1960s came to an end, and the 1970s began, which led him to act in ways he had not foreseen, or intended. At that time, however, he was still practically unknown as a poet. But before we outline his role in Czech poetry, let's take a brief look at his theoretical writings and other texts in which he addressed the cultural underground, as these are also important for understanding his work as a poet. Probably the most valuable literary text of this kind is *Pravdivý příběh Plastic People* [The True Story of The Plastic People], 1983–1987,[3] Jirous' account of the key historical

---

3) This work was published in Czech at the beginning of 1990 in instalments in the periodical *Studentské listy*. The most important book edition is still the extensive anthology of Jirous' essays and journalism *Magorův zápisník* [Magor's Notebook], Michael Špirit (ed.), Praha: Torst, 1997, that included both *The True Story*, as well as *The Report on the Third Czech Musical Revival*. Both texts were published again later in Czech in various publications.

events leading to his "descent into the underground" and his life and work in the unofficial sphere, an existence which was soon to become illegal (i.e., punishable by law). It is an unparalleled story due to the specifics of its time and place, exquisitely delivered by one of its most competent witnesses.

However, it was another of Jirous' texts on a similar topic that captured the imagination of critics. The *Report on the Third Czech Musical Revival* was written not only as a factual account, but also as a sort of apologetics for a certain lifestyle, a kind of manifesto in which Jirous elucidated the need to form a "second culture" a sphere that would become as independent as possible of the state-regimented and controlled official culture, which in Jirous' interpretation was a pseudo-culture. While this idea is certainly contentious, a less well-known fact is that Jirous drew on various postulates proposed by theoreticians of 1960s Western counter-culture (in the text he quoted Jeff Nuttall and Ralf-Rainer Rygulla,[4] for example, as well as mentioning Timothy Leary, and later on, *ex post facto*, he also noted that he had already known about Jerry Rubin and Theodore Roszak at the end of the 1960s). However, more than through theories, Jirous was influenced by the liberal-mindedness of artists themselves – whether it was the Beat Generation poets, or pop art's ironic relationship with consumerism, as embodied by his beloved Andy Warhol, as well as by the highly charged and subversive non commercial culture of the original 1960s underground rock scene (The Velvet Underground, The Fugs, Captain Beefheart, David Peel, The Grateful Dead, as well as those who were later exploited by show business – Morrison's Doors, Zappa's Mothers of Invention, Jimi Hendrix, Janis Joplin and some others). In this sense, Jirous' *Report* can be read as just one of many belated responses to the unofficial Western culture of the 1960s, albeit a very interesting and specific one, originating where no one would expect it, but still no more than a response. Nevertheless, what came out of the Czech underground community within Charter 77 was considerably different from the career paths of most representatives of the Western

4) See NUTTALL, Jeff, *Bomb Culture*, New York: Delacorte Press, 1968; RYGULLA, Ralf-Rainer (ed.), *Fuck you (!) Underground-Gedichte*, Darmstadt: Josef Melzer Verlag, 1968 (bilingual English and German anthology of American poets with an extensive epilogue by Rygulla in German).

underground who were either devoured by commercialism, or destroyed by drug addiction; ruined by their own success or marginalised by the mainstream to a nullifying extent. In that sense, we can paradoxically thank the totalitarian regime in Czechoslovakia for its intolerance – the oppression of its dissident artists actually contributed to their social importance.

As a promoter and historian of modern art, as well as a theoretician of the cultural underground, regardless of whether one calls it the counter-culture or alternative culture, Jirous had an indisputably unique significance in the context of Czech culture. Keeping in mind, however, that when viewed from an international cultural perspective, he is simply one of many.

Let us now take a look at Jirous the poet. Initially, however, it should be mentioned that as regards poetry, any kind of theorizing in institutions, whether social, scientific or cultural, at least since the 19th century, has always been related to earlier ideas, thus making it somewhat groundless to argue about poetry's originality – a poet worthy of the name either is one, or not. One cannot be a poet only "to some extent". In the case of Jirous, whose poetry is brimming with various paraphrases, appropriations, various literary metatexts and dedications to the living or dead, including notorious figures, the question of originality acquires a special meaning.

Jirous is the author of 21 collections of poetry, one consisting of poetry and prose for children (he wrote these in prison, sending them in letters to his two young daughters) with the last three compiled after his death from his literary estate.[5] His first book of poetry *Magorův ranní zpěv* [Magor's Morning Song] – is from 1975; neither this book, nor the four subsequent ones from 1979–1981, brought Jirous much acclaim, not even from the underground community. As yet, he was not making much effort to promote his own poetry, perhaps due to his excessive self-criticism; none of his first collections

---

5) In addition to individual publications of Jirous' various poetry collections (prior to 1989 only by samizdat or exile publishers), Jirous' poetry was organised in several collections, out of which the most extensive one is *Magorova summa* [Magor's Sum]; ed. Martin Machovec; 1st edition 1998, 2nd supplemented edition 2007, 3rd supplemented edition 2015: this last edition in three volumes contains Jirous' entire poetry œuvre including the collections from his literary estate.

were included in the series of samizdat anthologies of underground poets he edited. His first two poetry collections – *Magorův ranní zpěv* and *Magorova krabička* [Magor's Morning Song; Magor's Box] (1975; 1979), consist primarily of very short texts with frequent wordplay, linguistic experiments, comments referring to specific people or situations, real or imagined fragments of conversations with friends, and combinations of different languages. It is a sort of literary and artistic freak show of experiments, which is evidently one of the aesthetic expressions of the already mentioned *Crusader School*, and as his work progresses we can also observe the influence of the poetics of Egon Bondy's totální realismus [total realism] or trapná poesie [poetry of awkwardness or poetry of embarrassment] (and also by extension the similar poetry of Ivo Vodseďálek). This is only one perspective, however. In a completely different way, these texts are related to the experimental new-Latin poetry of Jirous' friend and fellow prisoner, Eugen Brikcius or the nonsense "*zaum*" poetry of Andrej Stankovič, another important underground poet.

Today, after all his poetry work has already been published, there is no doubt that the height of his work is the collection *Magorovy labutí písně* [Magor's Swan Songs], which he wrote in prison between 1981 and 1984 and which, when it was published for the first time in samizdat in 1985, immediately won considerable fame for the author, at least within Czech dissident and underground circles.[6]

6) Until now only a few small anthologies of Jirous' poetry have been published in English translation, primarily from the collection *Magor's Swan Songs*. See: 1/ The magazine *Yazzyk*, 3, 1994, Praha, translations by Anne Bryson and Jana Klepetářová; 2/ The special issue of *New Orleans Review*, vol. 26, no. 1-2: *Ten Years After the Velvet Revolution. Voices from the Czech Republic*, STONE, Sophia (ed.), New Orleans, USA, 2000 (translations by Jiří Flajšar and Robert Hýsek); 3/ The bilingual anthology VOLKOVÁ, Bronislava – CLOUTIER, Clarice (eds.), *Up the Devil's Back – Po hřbetě ďábla*, 2008, Boomington, IN, USA, translations by both editors; 4/ The journal *Word & Sense*, 9-10, 2008, Praha, translations by Kirsten Lodge; 5/ Worth mentioning is the anthology from the collection *Okuje* (2008) translated to English by Bernie Higgins, Toby Litt and Tomáš Míka: released with the CD *Magor & Postcommodity*, undated [2010]; 6/ The magazine *Inkshed*, no. 23 (Spring/Summer 1992), London, pp. 25-27, brought four poems by Jirous from collections *Magorova mystická růže* [Magor's Mystical Rose] and *Magorovi ptáci* [Magor's Birds] in Toby Litt's and Tomáš Míka's translation. With the exception of item 6/ all of these translations, as well as translations to other languages, are recorded in the 3rd edition of *Magorova Summa* [Magor's Sum] (2015).

A number of other samizdat publications followed, as well as two publications by Czech exile publishers in the West, and after 1989 several independent, as well as collected publications at home.[7] *Magor's Swan Songs* also earned Jirous the Tom Stoppard Prize in 1985, awarded by the Czech community in exile. Thirteen years later, after Jirous' collected poetic works were first published under the title *Magorova summa* [Magor's Sum] (1998), the book came in number one in the "Book of the Year" category of the readers' survey in one of the Czech Republic's leading daily newspapers *Lidové noviny*. Then, in 2006, his letters from prison, *Magorovy dopisy* [Magor's Letters], 2005, again came in first in the same survey. In that same year, Jirous also became the laureate of the prestigious Jaroslav Seifert Prize, awarded primarily for his work as a poet. So, in the end "the troublemaker" became Poet Laureate. This changed absolutely nothing in the life of the poet, but these official awards were noticed by at least part of mainstream Czech society and Jirous became a kind of celebrity, at least in the last few years of his life.

At the end of the day, it does not matter much under what circumstances a particular text was written – whether the author's suffering resulted from hard labour in a concentration camp, starvation in the village of their birth or alcohol or drug addiction, or whether they had lived happily and peacefully in prosperous times and were able to adequately depict both the dark and the bright sides of life thanks to their own imagination. Nonetheless, to completely ignore possible connections between a poet's life and work is also incorrect, especially when such connections are obvious. This is unequivocally the case of Jirous' collection *Magor's Swan Songs,* a book that enriched Czech prison literature. The assertion can certainly be made that in prison Jirous truly became a poet (specifically while serving his fourth, three-and-half-year sentence in the harshest Czechoslovak prison). Since Jirous was not allowed to write anything but letters home while in jail, he had to memorize his poems, waiting for an opportune moment to secretly write them down on a scrap of paper that would later be smuggled out. It was also this fact that influenced the form of the poems, specifically their

---

7) The most current bibliographic details can be found in the 3rd edition of *Magorova Summa* [Magor's Sum].

prevalent regular rhythm and rhyme schemes, which made them easier for the author to remember.

Perhaps the most distinct attribute of the collection is the strange tension between fragility, tenderness and precision of the poetic form, and the hardly imaginable brutality of the prison world, which we get a glimpse of through his verse. But neither does Jirous avoid giving us specific "messages", often aided by vulgarity. One can also regard the collection in its entirety as a form of testimony, testimony of several years of life in a harsh Czechoslovak prison: 1981–1985 A.D. The indication *Anno Domini* is not merely a formality here. Although Jirous grew up in a Roman Catholic family, he did not find a path to God – a truly deep, authentic religious spirituality – until he was in prison. Numerous texts in the collection are written in the manner of biblical psalms or prayers. The abyss of a "reprobate" assumes the specific image here of a "shit-hole", where a prisoner is held in a country allegedly run by a humane, socialist regime. All of Jirous' convictions were for "disturbance of the peace", but in reality he was only "guilty" of co-creating a free space for Czech dissent; needless to say, he never committed a criminal offence. A number of the other texts in the book are like inner monologues, replacing dialogues he might have had with absent friends, forced into exile at the beginning of the 1980s, and whom the poet now perceived "as if they were no longer alive" – there wasn't even a faint hope that he would ever see them again. But there are not only recollections of friends who were unlikely to ever return; there are also prayers to God and the Virgin Mary, prayers for saints to intercede, some of whom the poet was able to see daily (the prison in Valdice near Jičín, Eastern Bohemia, is located in a formerly Carthusian, Baroque monastery and several statues including Saint Hugh of Lincoln adorned the façade of the church, which at the time served as the prisoners' workplace. This saint's attribute – a white swan – became the emblem of *Magor's Swan Songs,* but there are also references to figures not exactly compatible with catholic orthodoxy – Master Jan Hus, T. G. Masaryk or George Orwell, for instance). There is not only the real prison world including murderers, violent homosexuals or brutal prison wardens, but also the world of dreams and the imagination – depressive as well as hopeful, tragic, as well as depicted with mocking self-irony, humour that actually makes us shudder.

The horizontal plane of earthly finiteness and suffering is perfectly balanced here with the vertical plane of entirely authentic, albeit unorthodox piousness.

Of course, even in the *Swan Songs* Jirous cannot deny his level of erudition. It is clear from numerous poems in the collection that he is *Poeta Doctus*; some of his texts abound in so many literary appropriations and allusions that they would be worthy of commentary comparable to that added by T. S. Eliot to his publication of *The Waste Land* (for that matter, Jirous acknowledges Eliot in his poetry several times). And this creates yet more tension in these texts: between intellectual refinement, bordering on artfulness, and the predominantly simple, yet always elaborate, poetic form. Expressions of an intellectual's ambitions are immediately confronted by the banal and commonplace. The authenticity of this intellectual world examines the effort to somehow wait out one's time in prison, to survive, to live to see the day when one will be released from prison into the free world, even though in the case of Czechoslovakia in the 1980s, this freedom was still limited – it was freedom behind barbed wire, behind the Iron Curtain.

The collection *Magor's Swan Songs* was soon noticed by critics – some of the first reviews were published by the Parisian exile journal *Svědectví - Temoinage* written by Eugen Brikcius in 1986 and Sylvie Richterová in 1987, to name two. Today there is extensive literature about the *Swan Songs,* as there is about Jirous' poetry as a whole, though it is only available in Czech. The literary critic Jiří Trávníček wrote specifically about the *Swan Songs* in his study *Běsy a stesky kajícníkovy* [The Penitent's Demons and Sorrows],[8] as follows:

> The source of energy in Jirous' writing is contact. The poet's verses constantly need to be directed at someone, related to people, cultural figures, saints, and to God. This is related to the great inner dialogue of the collection, the incessant addressing of some recipient, inviting them into the poem through a memory... [...] The truth of life and the truth of the text melt together here. From another angle: it is as if the authenticity of the text needed to be verified by the authenticity of a life's stance.

8) In TRÁVNÍČEK, Jiří, *Poezie poslední možnosti* [Poetry of the Last Opportunity], Praha: Torst, 1996, pp. 185-198.

Only a prisoner can warrant the prisoner's lines, no one else. It is not in the words, but in what is behind them. [...] There is something perhaps childishly innocent in it, how Jirous unburdens himself before us of his losses and failures - often through prayers and appeals to God or the Virgin Mary. It brings to mind the prison oppressions and pleas, which another prisoner and Jirous' predecessor, François Villon, had confessed. [...] Similarly to Mácha's Vilém from the poem *Máj* [May], who comes to realize only during his last night and under the pressure of the silence of the prison cell, the makeshift of the earthly code, by which he is condemned, and he submits himself to the all governing cycle of nature, the same environment also changes Jirous - a prisoner turns into a monk. [...] The same torment, however, is simultaneously the reverse side of the feeling of unchaining, of freedom: [...] in Jirous' case it is the knowledge that the true judge of our acts is not in the camouflaged shadow-plays of socialist paragraphs, but in the one and only eternal Truth.

After Jirous was released from Valdice, his fourth stint in prison, he continued to be engaged in various civil initiatives. After 1989 he was even politically active, but it was always only in marginal groups. As an author, he practically stopped writing any theoretical texts, or journalism, only continuing to write poetry. He put together more and more collections, some of which contain new literary gems. But he never surpassed the collection *Magor's Swan Songs* as a whole. He even lived to see official recognition as a poet in his own country, although quite late in his life. Internationally, however, hardly anyone knows anything about Jirous the poet, Jirous the civic initiator and defender of Czech underground culture or Jirous the essayist and art critic - yet.

Prague - London
September 2017
Translated by Vanda Krutsky, Marek Tomin and Kip Bauersfeld

10. REPORT ON THE THIRD CZECH MUSICAL REVIVAL BY IVAN MARTIN JIROUS - ITS ORIGINS, STRUCTURE AND FUNCTION

Much has already been written about Jirous's *Report on the Third Czech Musical Revival*, although attention has focused chiefly on the manner of its publication, and on the pragmatic value of the text; for example, the function it acquired *ex post facto*, and its ideological influence and impact at home and abroad (i.e., within the Czech dissent, among Czech exiles, and abroad in general, prior to 1989).

Jirous's *Report* was judged to be a kind of "manifesto" of 1970s Czech underground culture, and at various periods it was received and read either positively – in an unequivocal and even reverent fashion (such as by Egon Bondy,[1] Zdeněk "Londýn" Vokatý,[2] František Stárek

---

1) Although Bondy made no specific reference to the text anywhere, there are a number of texts in the collection of poems *Trhací kalendář* [Tear-off Calendar] that he compiled towards the end of 1975 that indicate that Jirous's arguments and the terminology employed in the *Report* have a close affinity, such as, for instance: "(...) But we have reached a historical phase / when this division is starting to be too sharply defined / and those of us who have no interest in the Establishment / are completely excluded from society for precisely that reason // Thus a second culture is emerging / that doesn't care about so-called people / And this second culture is strong because it is initially weak / and the culture of the Establishment is weak because it is so powerful / and roars at it" (Czech original in E. B.: *Básnické spisy II*, Praha: Argo, 2015, pp. 743–744).

2) See VOKATÝ, Zdeněk, "Sen o kole", in *O svobodě a moci*, Köln – Roma: Index – Listy, 1980, pp. 343–350 [text dated 28th February 1979]. Vokatý talks here about how Jirous's views on life in the underground are perceived and what they might give rise to: "We have rejected the Establishment and everything it has to offer. And we know why. We've even rejected the Establishment's destruction. And we also know why. Now what? We've decided to create a second culture and release those who want to join it from their despondency and resignation. But can we really see the world and the people in it with fresh eyes? Setting off into the desert like this is something fantastic [...]" (p. 350).

Čuňas,[3] Ivan Hartel[4] at al.), with reservations (e.g., Svatopluk Karásek[5] and Pavel Zajíček[6]), or negatively (e.g., Milan Knížák,[7] Jan Ságl,[8]

3) STÁREK, František Čuňas in Czech TV's documentary serial *The Underground Phenomenon* (2012; part 10, called "Magor is the Greatest Czech"): "Magor's merit was in actually framing the Czech Underground as a parallel structure. He framed it as a human factor, in other words as a community, and also framed its main postulates."

4) Hartel included Jirous's *Report* as the most significant text in the catalogues *The Merry Ghetto* and *Le ghetto joyeux*, i.e. the English and French versions of the booklet that accompanied the Plastic People's first LP, *Egon Bondy's Happy Hearts Club Banned* (London - Paris 1978).

5) KARÁSEK, Sváťa - HÁJEK, Štěpán - PLZÁK, Michal, *Víno tvé výborné* [The Good Wine of Yours], Praha: Kalich, 1998, pp. 106-107. Karásek states there: "When he was writing the 'Report on the Third Czech Musical Revival' I went into a greenhouse where he happened to be writing it. He read me what he wrote about me, and I said to him: 'Why are you writing it. What do you intend to do with it?' And he said: 'We'll give it to people, of course!' And I said: 'Well that's tantamount to denunciation. You describe here what we do and the police will immediately get hold of it and will be better informed. Is it worth it?' [...]" Karásek goes on to recall how Jirous subsequently convinced him of the usefulness of the *Report*, but in retrospect it is clear that his fears at the time were justified.

6) ZAJÍČEK, Pavel: "A kámen ideálu skřípe mezi zuby" (interview with Ondřej Štindl), *Lidové noviny, Orientace* supplement, 20th December 1997: "LN: In his *Report* Ivan Martin Jirous described you as chiliast. Do you agree with that? PZ: No. He dreamt that up when he was writing that text of his in an elated state somewhere in a greenhouse. Possibly my texts from the seventies affected people in that way. The text that is closest to a 'chiliastic' mood is Purification."

7) KNÍŽÁK, Milan, "Ivane, Martine, Magore, (Ivanu Jirousovi, 1975)", in *Bez důvodu*, Praha: Litera, 1996, pp. 120-123. Knížák states in his letter: "You have created an artificial aureola of avant-garde about the Plastics who have never been anything but a bunch of sound guys who wanted to play beat music and you forced on them and infected them with ideas which are alien to them and which they've never understood, so the result was always just an embarrassing copy or paraphrase of what had already been invented long ago [...]" (p. 122).

8) SÁGL, Jan, *Tanec na dvojitém ledě / Dancing on the Double Ice*, Praha: KANT, 2013, pp. 30-31. Ságl does not specifically refer to the *Report* here, but voices his reservations about IMJ in general, which can be applied to the *Report* also, as Ságl's chief objection was to publication of underground acitivities.

Václav Černý,[9] Petr Fidelius[10] and Vladimír Merta[11]). It should be added straight away that this assessment could only occur within the dissent in the wider sense: i.e., the **unofficial** and **intellectual scene** prior to November 1989, and its heirs after that year; before then, elsewhere in society Jirous's *Report* had to be deplored - or what was more typical - totally ignored, like everything else that was not controlled by Czechoslovak official circles, and the police in particular. In the seventies and eighties the *Report* also inspired further reflection among dissidents, which is dealt with below.[12] It is only in recent years that literary historians and researchers in the social sciences field in general have started to pay serious attention to this

9) It concerns two studies by ČERNÝ from 1979 and 1980: "Nad verši Věry Jirousové a o kulturním stanovisku našeho undergroundu" (in *Tvorba a osobnost I*, Praha: Odeon, 1992) and "O všem možném, dokonce i o 'hippies' a 'novém románu'" (in *Tvorba a osobnost II*, Praha: Odeon, 1993). Jirous replied to Černý in the article "Nikdy nebyla v troskách" (1980), in *Magorův zápisník* (1997) on pp. 402–418. Černý does not specifically take issue with Jirous and the *Report*, but simply - somewhat one-sidedly - attempts to interpret the underground culture phenomenon. In terms of specifics, Jirous's response is more interesting.

10) FIDELIUS, Petr [PALEK, Karel], "K Jirousově koncepci undergroundu" [Jirous's Concept of the Underground], written in 1981, *Souvislosti* 4, no. 1 (1993); also in FIDELIUS, Petr, *Kritické eseje*, Praha: Torst, 2000 (ibidem: *Kultura oficiální a neoficiální* [1981]).

11) MERTA, Vladimír, "Čtvrté hudební obrození. Příspěvek k typologii jednoho nemyšlení" [The Fourth Musical Revival. A Contribution to the Typology of Non-Cogitation], in ELŠÍKOVÁ, Monika (ed.), *Aby radost nezmizela. Pocta Magorovi*, Praha: Monika Vadasová-Elšíková [sic!], 2011 (see Footnote 25).

12) There is no evidence that the *Report* was read with any great interest either in 1975, or even particularly appreciated by the the musicians of The Plastic People, DG 307, Umělá hmota or their fans in the underground community. The fact that the *Report* was not regarded as particularly significant, let alone a breakthrough cultural achievement, is indicated by the total absence of any reference to it in two handwritten *Chronicles of the Plastic People* (one edited by Pavel Prokeš, the other by Josef Vondruška) covering 1975. In an interview with Jan Pelc (*Bez ohňů je underground*, Praha: BFS, 1992) Milan Hlavsa says (p. 105): "Magor had just completed The Report on the Third Czech Musical Revival, and started to engage in further education of adults. He organised talks in various towns, reading from the Report and playing our recordings. He was really successful with that." But Hlavsa says nothing about the *Report*'s contents.

text, including Jonathan Bolton,[13] Veronika Tuckerová[14] and Martin Valenta.[15]

Almost no attention has yet been paid to the circumstances of the text's creation, and particularly to its structure (i.e., it has not been subjected to more detailed textual criticism).

I. The genesis of the text

Jirous dated his *Report* February 1975, so it was written during the fairly brief period of underground culture's boom, when it was holding public events without official permission, which were not illegal in the narrow sense but were held on various pretexts, most frequently as wedding celebrations. Of particular significance in this respect was the so-called "First Festival of the Second Culture" (as it was dubbed retrospectively in line with the title used in Jirous's *Report*), which took place on 1st September 1974 at Postupice near Benešov as a celebration of the wedding of Arnošt and Jarka Hanibal. It was there "for the first time in the history of the Czech Underground" that several bands (not only rock bands) took part, as well as two solo singers (who were not rock-oriented).

One non-musical event worth mentioning took place on 4th and 5th November 1974 at the Na Zavadilce pub at Klukovice near Prague, when Bondy read from the manuscript of his book *Disabled Siblings*, a text that had a considerable influence on the formation of the un-

---

13) BOLTON, Jonathan, *Worlds of Dissent. Charter 77, The Plastic People of the Universe, and Czech Culture under Communism*, Cambridge and London: Harvard University Press, 2012; in Czech translation: *Světy disentu. Charta 77, Plastic People a česká kultura za komunismu*, Praha: Academia, 2015.

14) TUCKEROVÁ, Veronika, "Jirousova Zpráva o třetím českém hudebním obrození: úvaha o formě a kulturní kontinuitě" [Jirous's Report on the Third Czech Musical Revival: a reflection on its form and cultural continuity], in ONUFEROVÁ, Edita – POKORNÁ, Terezie (eds.), *Magorova konference (k dílu I. M. Jirouse)*, Praha: Revolver Revue, 2014. I have particularly drawn on that study for the present text.

15) STÁREK, František Čuňas – VALENTA, Martin, *Podzemní symfonie Plastic People* [The Plastic People's Underground Symphony], Praha: Argo, 2018, the chapter entitled "Jirous a jeho Zpráva" [Jirous and his Report], pp. 54–60. There is no indication which sections of the book are by which author, but it may be assumed that Valenta probably wrote this particular chapter.

derground community's "ideology", and which was also dealt with by Jirous in the *Report*. Towards the end of 1974, The Plastic People made some so-called "studio" recordings of their compositions in the chapel at Houska Castle, which were subsequently issued on their first LP in 1978 (*Egon Bondy's Happy Hearts Club Banned*, released abroad, of course). These were the first recordings of Czech underground music of relatively high quality. By then Jirous had already served his first prison term (1973-74) and the underground community had already suffered harsh police harassment: on 30th March 1974 the audience at a concert at Rudolfov near České Budějovice was brutally dispersed and several of them were prosecuted. These facts are now familiar, but it necessary to view the writing of the *Report* in the light of them because they were an undoubted influence.

Now to some less well-known facts:

After spending October 1974 in a psychiatric clinic at Horní Beřkovice, Jirous took a job towards the end of that year as a labourer working on the renovation of the park at Měšice Chateau near Prague, where his friend, the musician and landscape gardener Vratislav Brabenec, was in charge of the project. At that time Jirous was living, among other places, at a nearby farm at Zlatý Kopec, where one of the first underground communities was established, but he also slept over in the greenhouse at Měšice,[16] where he wrote

16) Marie Benetková testifies to this in her text "Zlatý kopec - dějiny české undergroundové komuny" [Goldberg - history of a Czech Underground Commune], in STÁREK, František Čuňas - KOSTÚR, Jiří (eds.), *Baráky. Souostroví svobody*, Praha: Pulchra, 2010: "Ivan built a bed for himself in the greenhouse: an old door supported by two sawing horses. On top he placed a mattress, of which there were always lots of discarded ones outside the hospital, and some blankets. Ivan made a writing desk out of two other sawing horses and a big sheet of reinforced glass. Once he'd added a reading lamp he had a ready-made office and bedroom. He would then sleep and spend his nights in the greenhouse when he wanted to escape from the lures of Prague: the only person to tempt him out to the pub was old Láďa but Ivan was mostly able to resist him. We used to find Ivan in the morning sleepy and still in bed complimenting himself on his house of glass. On the occasions he actually did go the pub and stayed out late he was less complimentary about his doss house, and

the *Report*. Evidence for this is contained in his still unpublished correspondence with Juliana Stritzková,[17] whom he married on 9th January 1976 (the church wedding was at Hostim near Moravské Budějovice on 17th January 76 and one of the celebrations of their marriage was the so-called 2nd Festival of the Second Culture on 21st February 1976 at Bojanovice). Jirous would seem to have worked at Měšice until the end of February 1975; letters from March were sent from Horní Počernice and Prague, and a letter from September 1975 already bears the Prague address Pod Zvonařkou, where he later lived with Juliana at No. 6.

Jirous's letters to Juliana from December 1974 to February 1975 contain many useful facts, including details about the circumstances surrounding the writing of the *Report*.

In a letter from Zlatý Kopec from 3rd December 1974: "As well as that I'm giving a lecture about the underground to doctors at Beřkovice on Monday of next week and have to cobble it together somehow."

In a letter from 14th December 1974:

I'm writing that lecture on the underground, and now I'm half-way through I keep up thinking of excuses for how to get out of it [...] You'd be amazed at where I'm now staying; it's not possible to work at Zlatý Kopec either – bad light plus Vráťa and Marie [Vratislav Brabenec and his wife Marie Benetková], and I'm obliged to chat. So I've moved into the greenhouse in the chateau park (Charlie [Karel "Charlie" Soukup] lived here before me). On top of two sawing horses I've got a sheet of glass with wire mesh inside – it's used for windows. Above it I've got a light bulb in a tin lamp and in front of me cucumber plants are sprouting. All around is an unobtrusive sort of mess and there is an open door

would say he felt hoodwinked by the Surrealists, whom he'd blame for the fact he had only a glass house and a hangover" (p. 63).

17) All the available Jirous correspondence (i.e. published and unpublished) is digitised for internal purposes at the Institute for Czech Literature of the Academy of Sciences. I am grateful to Daniela Iwashita for making this correspondence available to me and allowing me to quote from it.

to another part of the building [...] Through the glass above me and all around I can see darkness. Quite simply it is an ideal underground and I have ideal scope for concentration. Unfortunately it's a bit cold here, but maybe that's better for reflection.[18]

The following from a letter of 3rd February 1975 from Zlatý Kopec:

Tomorrow I'll try to put together at least the first part of the Report on the Third Czech Musical Revival at last. As I wrote to you, this is supposed to be a time of supreme intellectual and other activity, but apparently there are eruptions on the sun until 5th February – so it strikes me that one's situation is always uncertain, but I can't afford to go on blaming my scholarly inactivity on something else.

Of crucial significance is a letter from Měšice dated 11th February 75:

[...] so I'm sitting here in the greenhouse at Měšice [...] I'm diligently writing the Report on the Third Czech Musical Revival until I run out of sensible ideas [...] It's ages since I've been able to write like this, in fact it's the first time since I got back from j[ail]; it's grown into a whole book: i.e., it will have over 20 pages excluding notes, and there'll also be a collection of texts – old texts of the Plastics that you don't even know, of Aktuáls, Umělá hmota, Bondy's things set to music, Zajíček, Charlie [Soukup] and Sváťa [Karásek]; Zorka [Ságlová] will do the layout and there'll be lots of photos from Ságl (as well as Helena [Wilsonová] and [Petr or Pavel] Prokeš); it'll come it in five copies probably. I'm bringing together in it all my theoretical blather about this music and the second culture, that I otherwise hawk around the pubs, so that in my old age I don't have to tire myself and will be able simply to tell people to read it in the Report.

That "lecture on the underground" for psychiatrists at Horní Beřkovice psychiatric institution probably wasn't the beginning of his work on the *Report,* but there would definitely seem to be

18) Marek ŠVEHLA quotes from this letter in his book *Magor a jeho doba* [Magor and his Times], Praha: Torst, 2017, p. 279, without acknowledging the source.

a connection. Jirous wrote most of the *Report* in the Měšice green-house probably in the first half of February 75, when he was thinking of including it in a collection of texts by underground authors, although in the end he did not achieve it in the form he described. (The first samizdat underground collection edited by Jirous – *Egonu Bondymu k 45. narozeninám invalidní sourozenci* [To Egon Bondy on his 45th Birthday from Disabled Siblings] – is dated January 1975, when it was presented in the pub at Klukovice at Bondy's birthday party. Jirous had been definitely compiling it over the previous few months. A sort of residuum of the collection which he was considering at Měšice in February of 1975 could be regarded in the second of these anthologies – namely *Ing. Petru Lamplovi k 45. narozeninám* [To Ing. Petr Lampl on his 45th Birthday] – dated December 1975. But that collection has never been linked with the *Report* and its contents only partly correspond to Jirous's plan).

Finally some better known facts: The manuscript of the *Report* has not survived and carbon copies of the author's original samizdat of 1975 are now extremely rare.[19] During that year IMJ read the text of the *Report* at various venues, where he also distributed carbon copies of that typescript, the best known of those readings being at the SSM Club at Přeštice on 13th December 1975.[20] The Libri Prohibiti has a copy of the first publication of the *Report* in an established samizdat series of editions, namely Havel's Edice Expedice (described in the imprint as "Volume 6: Copied by *Václav Havel* in 1976 for himself and his friends").

A number of probable motivations for writing the *Report* have been mentioned earlier, and one could speculate about others, albeit the danger of such speculations is obvious. One could easily identify or confuse those motivations with its function, role, and purpose, and with its literary and extra-literary impact and influence; i.e.,

19) One of them is in the private archive of Jozef Furman in Košice, Slovakia (see Footnote 21). Another (with two carbon copies) was attached to the prosecution's indictment before the trial of Stárek, Havelka and Skalický as an "exhibit"; a copy of that indictment is in the private archive of František Stárek.
20) See ŠVEHLA, Marek, *Magor a jeho doba*, Praha: Torst, 2017, Chapter 15, particularly p. 308.

everything that the *Report* gave rise to as a result of its being read and interpreted, and also, of course, in the light of the events that happened soon after it started to circulate as samizdat. One cannot even be sure who was most likely Jirous's intended readership of the *Report*, who was his "target group", but the recollections of Karásek and Hlavsa, cited above, are evidence that, unlike Bondy's *Disabled Siblings,* the *Report* was not written *a priori* for the people who were its subject, i.e. *pro foro interno* (which would anyway be fairly odd, and indeed might give rise to the suspicion that the author had a tendency towards a kind of "sectarianism"), but was actually intended for a much broader public, for the purposes of education and "enlightenment". So it would appear that at the beginning of 1975, Jirous believed that by distributing the *Report* he could gain more supporters for the underground community, as well as for its lifestyle and cultural resistance **from among the young,**[21] and probably did not expect it would receive any response from intellectuals in various other circles of the broader "parallel polis" that was gradually coming into being, although that was where it would eventually find the greatest number of readers (including critics and opponents).

Thus the *Report* was read by the dissent within the country, as well as by exiles, as a sort of quintessence of the underground's "ideology", as an expression of the aspirations of one specific section of

---

21) The reservations that Jirous's closest friends from the underground community had regarding the distribution of the *Report* is fairly understandable, but the *Report* would seem to have been read avidly by communities of young people in the countryside who shared the outlook of Jirous's circle and the Plastic People but often had no close contact with it or personal connections. Eloquent testimony of this is provided by Jozef Furman from the Košice circle of Marcel Strýko (ČT serial *Fenomén underground,* part 30, "Divoký východ" [The Wild East], directed by Břetislav Rychlík, 2014). In it Furman recalls being at Přeštice in December of 1975, where Jirous read the *Report* and he received a typescript of the text which he took back to Košice and gave it to friends, thereby "changing their lives", particularly in the sense that they realized it was possible to work on something and do things their own way. (However in subsequent private correspondence Furman recalled that he received a carbon copy of the author's original samizdat edition of the *Report* from Jirous earlier "in a flat in Prague [probably at the Němecs' in the Ječná Street flat] where Magor read his *Report*", and not at Přeštice, where he also was later, although Jirous probably did not hand out the text of the *Report* there.)

the unofficial cultural scene of the first half of the 1970s, one that evaded supervision by the authorities, and which was allegedly made up essentially of rock musicians and their fans. Neither interpretation was quite right, but a simplification current at the time.

The fact is that the "ideological section" at the end of the *Report* is the most problematic and contradictory part of the entire text, and, as we shall show when analysing it, it is only partly Jirous's *ipsissima verba*, "own words" - his own ideas. The reason why the *Report* was interpreted as a kind of calling card of solely the unofficial **musical** scene was partly because of the author's choice of its rather confusing and poetical title, which he immediately proceeds to call into question in the introduction: Was there actually any "first musical revival" in the Czech lands? And the author then admits that the theory of the "second musical revival" that was supposed to precede the third of the revivals was based on some slogan or witticism of his friend Karel Voják. Clearly the *Report* deals with far much more than music. The *Report* is anything but a musicological treatise.[22] Moreover the *Report* documents the musical activity of underground bands mostly in terms of social, psychological, historical, and "art historical" analysis, or in relation to song texts, rather than analysis of music as such.

II. The structure of the text of the *Report*. Its literary genre[23]

A. The actual text of the *Report*
In her study on the *Report* (pp. 137-139, 141-143 op. cit. in Footnote 14), Veronika Tuckerová reflects on whether the *Report* is actually "a report" and seems to conclude that the prevailing factuality, informativeness and striving for objective description of the phenonema

22) The only possible attempt at musicology in the *Report* are the comments on Knížák's music for the Aktual band (in chapter 6).

23) Reference will be made here to the version of the *Report* published in the book *Magorův zápisník* [Magor's Notebook, hereafter MN] (ed. Michael Špirit, Praha: Torst, 1997), albeit that version is not free of errors. The most recent publication to date, which also includes fairly extensive notes, forms part of the *"Brown Book" on the Trials of Czech Underground* published by the Institute for the Study of Totalitarian Regimes (ÚSTR), Prague 2012.

studied, which are evident in Jirous's text, mean that the *Report* need not be read as an "essay", as it is classified in Špirit's bibliography in *Magor's Notebook*,[24] but it can be seen more as journalism. (In its German translation "Report" is "Bericht", the French translation by Petr Král has a modified, abridged title, but in the text the term "zpráva" is translated as "rapport".) However, Tuckerová concludes that "Jirous's *Report* is and isn't a report" (p. 141 op. cit.), with which one can only agree. Nevertheless we need to assess to what extent the *Report* is true to its name, because if the *Report on the Third Czech Musical Revival* was simply a "report", a "Bericht" in its most humdrum sense, it would probably be far less inspirational, and it would not have provoked as much passionate polemic and harsh condemnation, one example of which was actually written immediately after Jirous's death, as if its author was waiting for that moment.[25]

24) Tuckerová also points out that this is the second text in Jirous's œuvre to be entitled "Zpráva" [Report], the first being his *Zpráva o činnosti Křižovnické školy* [Report on the Activity of the Crusaders School], written in 1972, (pp. 125-133 of MN). But there are also other texts by Jirous, which do not have that description in their titles, but are very similar to both "Reports" in terms of content and style. One is the "článek" [article]: *Český underground - geneze a přítomnost hnutí* [The Czech Underground - its Genesis and Present State], which was published in 1988 in issue no. 6 of *Informace o Chartě* [Information about Charter 77], and subsequently in print in 2012 in Viktor Karlík's catalogue, *Podzemní práce / Underground Work*, the other is the text *Česká literatura 70. a 80 let* [On Czech Underground Literature of the 70s and 80s], which was written for the conference about Czech literature held in New York in March 1990. That text first came out in magazine form in *Vokno*, no. 18, 1990, and then in book form in the volume *Pohledy zevnitř*, 2008 (English translation, *Views from the Inside*, 2018). But Tuckerová also notes that in common with the the the "Reports", the text entitled *Pravdivý příběh Plastic People* [The True Story of the Plastic People] also includes in its title an indication of genre, and which also suggests factuality, and where possible an objective description of the topic in question.

25) I refer to the text of Vladimír Merta mentioned earlier which states *inter alia* regarding the *Report*: "I found a badly written pamphlet: provocative theories offset by a passionate personal defence of several bands. But in no way was it a theoretically erudite perspective, of the kind we might lack at the present time" (pp. 104–105 op. cit. in Footnote 11). It is truly a bit strange that this text of Merta's was published in a book with the subtitle "Tribute to Magor". Karel Kocour Havelka responded to Merta with his text "Kecy. Otevřený dopis adresovaný písničkáři Vladimíru Mertovi a nakladatelce Monice Elšíkové" [Bullshit. An Open Letter to the Songster V.M. and the publisher M.E.], *MFD, Víkendová příloha Dnes*, 24th - 25th November 2012.

The *Report* is a fairly short text divided into thirteen chapters, 2 to 12 of which more or less chronologically describe the actual events during and because of which the "psychedelic band", The Plastic People of the Universe, which, from 1968, under the influence of Ivan Martin Jirous, began to perceive "the underground" not in terms of another rock music genre but in the sense of "a spiritual standpoint", [26] became the centre of a wider community of rock and non-rock musicians, artists, photographers, film-makers, writers, poets, and intellectuals, who made music, created art, and wrote solely within the framework of the notional underground "merry ghetto" into which they had been confined by the established "normalised", and essentially totalitarian regime. The exception to the chronological approach are the first chapter, in which the reader is placed *in medias res* (describing how a concert by Umělá hmota and The Plastic People of the Universe at Líšnice near Prague was arbitrarily banned by a local Communist bigwig – Jirous compares him here to "servants of the Anti-Christ" – at the end 1974), part of the fifth chapter and chapter thirteen which are not only a summary of the earlier chapters but also an apologia for the underground community as it appeared in the mid-1970s, as well as an outline of its "ideology" (dealt with in greater detail below).

First a summary of the contents of chapters two to twelve:

II. The profuseness and vibrancy of the rock scene in Czechoslovakia towards the end of the 1960s, and why the events depicted are described as the "third musical revival", the beginning of which the author dates to 1973.

Merta's errors were pointed out by Martin Machovec in an interview with Miroslav Balaštík, "Žij a pracuj vskrytu", *Host* 27, no. 2 (2012).

26) This is well illustrated by the story recalled by Hlavsa in the book *Bez ohňů je underground* (on p. 69 of the first edition from 1992): "This is also related to the memorable debate on this topic in the U Bubeníčků pub sometime in sixty-nine when Magor tried to explain the difference between a psychedelic sound and the underground. Until then we had regarded the underground as a musicial orientation. After a lengthy lecture about how psychedelic was a musical orientation whereas the underground was an attitude to life, Přemek [Jiří "Přemysl" Števich] closed the debate with the words: 'So psychedelic is with fires and if there are no fires it's underground!'"

III. The Primitives Group, which introduced the Czech audience to the music of the American underground rock scene (e.g., Jimi Hendrix, The Grateful Dead, The Doors, The Fugs and Frank Zappa's Mothers of Invention); the so-called psychedelic sound as interpreted by The Primitives: achieving a state of liberation, a change of mind-set by various different effects; its affinity with happenings.

IV. The beginnings of The Plastic People of the Universe in 1968, and the band's original "emotional perception" of the concept of the underground as "a mythological world with a different mentality" (which was allegedly the origin of the reference to the "Universe" in the band's name); how The Plastic People drew inspiration from The Primitives, and in addition to The Fugs and Zappa were the first on the Czech rock scene to introduce compositions by the New York band The Velvet Underground.

V. The change in the concept of "the underground" at the beginning of the 1970s; how The Plastic People were deprived of the status of a professional band at the beginning of the "normalization era", which did not deter them from continuing their activity, unlike other rock bands. Here Jirous writes for the first time not just as a historian but also as a passionate defender of that resistance, and even as a judge; he makes claims (ethical as well as aesthetic) about the music of The Plastic People, as about any other art form, and after the first chapter again makes use of religious analogies:

It is better not to play at all than to play music that does not flow from one's own convictions. It is better not to play at all than to play what the establishment demands. And even this statement appears too mild. It is not better; it is absolutely essential. This stand must be taken right at the beginning.

For as soon as the first compromise is made, whether it is accompanied by hypocritical excuses or it springs from an honest belief that it doesn't really matter, everything is lost. As soon as the devil (who today speaks through the mouth of the establishment) lays down the first condition: cut your hair, just a little, and you'll be able to play – you must say no. As soon as the devil (who today speaks through the mouth of the establishment) says – change your name and you'll be able to continue playing what you've been playing – you must say no, we will not play at all.

What is also more striking about this chapter than elsewhere is that no specific mention is made of the Husák regime, the establishment of a collaborationist puppet government, and that government's project for "normalising" society (the term "normalization" does not appear even once in the *Report*!). Instead the author repeatedly uses the English term "Establishment", which was both vague and extremely uncommon in Czech at that time, and the term is sometimes used as a metaphor for the devil: i.e., a religious concept of evil. (Jirous's concept of the "Establishment" will be dealt with further when interpreting the final chapter of the *Report*.)

VI. Knížák and his band Aktual; Jirous speaks highly of Knížák's contribution to the underground music scene, pointing out that in the case of Aktual it was not rock music but "techniques of aleatoric music and serial composition"; he regards Knížák as a creator of "happenings, environments and events", and also values his lyrics in Czech. Jirous writes here as an art historian who perceives the rock music phenomenon as simply one of many forms of artistic expression.

VII. The origins of The Plastic People's musical and artistic experiments; for example, their second creative phase, which was by then entirely "underground": i.e., it occurred away from the official music scene. Jirous points out that apart from their own lyrics they soon started to set to music actual poems, citing William Blake, Edmund Spenser and Jiří Kolář (although he fails to mention that it was he himself who suggested these poems to the band), but Jirous stresses that the major turning point for The Plastic People was the discovery of Egon Bondy's verse, and even attempts a brief characterisation of Bondy's poetry – probably the first such ever written – in which connection he cites Jeff Nuttall's statement about "the Pauline lie", without attributing its author.[27] Jirous mentions the experimental

---

27) Nuttall is mentioned by Jirous at the end of the fourth chapter alongside Sanders, Ginsberg and Leary as one of the pioneers of the underground – in a sociological and cultural sense – "in the early sixties". The passage used by Jirous in characterising Bondy's poetry comes from Nuttall's book *Bomb Culture* (New York: Delacorte Press, 1968, p. 264): "To eradicate utterly and forever the Pauline lie implicit in Christian convention, that people neither shit, piss, nor fuck." It is part of a list of aspirations that Nuttall introduces with the words: "Four years ago the underground was anxious to bring about the following developments on a larger scale." The reference

happenings in relation to The Plastic People's first attempt to put a text by Ladislav Klíma to music (the song *Jak bude po smrti* [How It Will Be After Death] played at a concert at Klukovice in June 1973), and the concert at Veleň in December 1973, at which the one of the outstanding underground poets Pavel Zajíček first drew attention to himself.[28]

VIII. Here Jirous explains why he considers 1973 as the beginning of the new "musical revival", recalling that it was the year when two new underground bands were formed: the Midsummer Night's Dream Band and DG 307 (both of which represented for him "different musicial orientations" than rock music). However for him that year was above all a moment of a certain psychological turning point: "It was a time when we all began to realize that the situation we were living in was not temporary, that it would last for a long time, probably forever. It was definitively a rather dead period as far as our collective activities were concerned; a time of muteness and hangover as far as the official cultural situation was concerned, at least compared to how it seemed at the beginning of the 1970s." Jirous ends this chapter with words that are actually a paraphrase of the Milton quote that heads the final chapter: "We must learn to live in the existing world in a way that is both joyful and dignified." (Regarding the Milton quote see *infra*.)

IX. In this and the next chapter Jirous continues his factual description of the diversified underground scene of 1973–74. Here he focuses on the Midsummer Night's Dream Band, which comprised solely artists from the unofficial circle around the so-called Crusaders' School of Pure Humour without Jokes: i.e., non-musicians, and how it managed to introduce music into a broader art context – happenings, "neo Dadaist" events.

X. Pavel Zajíček's band DG 307, which Jirous once more praises highly not only for its experimental musical expression, but also for Zajíček's "chiliastic" lyrics: "DG is the desperate cry of normal people who are incapable of adjusting to the world presented to

of "four years ago" thus relates to 1964, since Nuttall's book was first published in 1968, which explains Jirous's dating of Nuttall's statement (and his own early role in the U.S. underground movement).

28) See the Plastic People's CD, *Do lesíčka na čekanou 1. 12. 1973*, Guerilla Records, Louny 2006.

them by contemporary consumer society." The chapter is testimony to the genesis of one of the most significant artistic projects of the Czech musical and literary underground.

XI. Jirous cites Lautréamont's statement that "*Someday everyone will make art,*" in defence of the right of untrained, non-professional musicians and artists to liberate their creative potential, mentioning as an instance of this the band Umělá hmota of Josef Vondruška and Milan "Dino" Vopálka (who are not named in the chapter). He recalls the connection with urban folklore, but in fact it was an implicit protest against the absurd demands of the "normalisers" that rock musicians should meet certain musical standards, which were actually a way of censoring them. It was an attempt to rehabilitate live rock music as played in the West and Czechoslovakia in the 1960s, and defend spontaneously created space for free creative, however "artless", "primitive" or "naïve".

XII. Concerning the solo underground musicians Svatopluk Karásek and Karel "Charlie" Soukup, whom Jirous viewed as an example of the diversity of the underground scene. Jirous stresses that Soukup's lyrics are not mawkish like so-called protest songs. "there is not one sacred issue connected to consumer society that he leaves in peace". In the case of the protestant pastor Karásek he stresses the religious themes that resonate with his own *cri de coeur* ("Say no to the Devil, say no"), but he also detects these themes not only in the texts of the "chiliastic preacher" Pavel Zajíček (he does so in chapters X. and XII.), but also as at the level of philosophical utopia in Bondy's prose work *Disabled Siblings*, whose visions might already have been realized in the "First Music Festival of the Second Culture" at Postupice.

So much then for the majority of the *Report*'s content, which needed to be summarised in greater detail because it helps make clear that the passages that have given rise to polemic and criticism consist of just part of the opening chapter and a few paragraphs of the final chapter.

In the first chapter, which is written in the form of reportage, as already noted, there is emphasis on the peace-loving "passive resistance" aspect of the underground community and Jirous twice draws a parallel with religious thinking, according to which those who wish to live in truth confront the "servants of the Anti-Christ", whom he identifies with the Establishment of A. D. 1974. It must be acknowledged that this initial uncompromising approach and the first instance of analogy with the world of religious radicals might come as a surprise to some readers.

The thirteenth and final chapter is headed by a quotation by John Milton: "We must act with reason in this world of evil, the place in which God has irrevocably placed us," (the epigraphs are dealt with in detail in the next section of this study). In it Jirous explains what he means by the terms "underground" and "second culture", what is and isn't the goal of the underground, and the difference between underground activities in the West and Czechoslovakia:[29]

> The underground is a mental attitude of intellectuals and artists who consciously and critically determine their own stance towards the world in which they live. It is **the declaration of a struggle against the Establishment**, the regime. It is a movement that works chiefly through the various art forms but whose representatives are aware that art is not and ought not to be the final aim of an artist's efforts. The underground is created by people who have understood that **within the bounds of legality nothing can be changed, and who no longer even attempt to function within those bounds**. <u>Ed Sanders of The Fugs put it very clearly when he declared a total 'attack on culture'</u> **This attack can be carried out only by people who stand outside that culture.** <u>Briefly put, the underground is the activity of artists and intellectuals whose work is unacceptable to the Establishment and who, in this state of unacceptability, do not remain passive,</u> **but attempt through their work and attitudes to destroy the Establishment**. Two absolutely necessary characteristics of those who have chosen the underground as their spiritual home are rage and humility.

---

29) The emphasis in **bold** and the <u>underlining</u> in the following extensive quotations is mine, MM. All the English citations from the *Report* come from the 2nd edition of *Views from the Inside*, Praha: Karolinum Press, 2018, pp. 7–36 (Paul Wilson's translation). The Czech original text is in MN as mentioned above.

Further:

It is a sad and frequent phenomenon in the West, where, in the early 1960s, the idea of the underground was theoretically formulated and established as a movement, that some of those who gained recognition and fame in the underground came into contact with official culture (for our purposes, we call it the first culture), which enthusiastically accepted them and swallowed them up as it accepts and swallows up new cars, new fashions or anything else. In Bohemia, **the situation is essentially different, and far better than in the West,** because we live in an atmosphere of absolute agreement: the first culture doesn't want us and we don't want anything to do with the first culture.

And finally:

For things are not in order. There has never existed a period in human history which could be considered an exclusively happy one; and genuine artists have always been those who have drawn attention to the fact that things are not in order. This is why **one of the highest aims of art has always been the creation of unrest. The aim of the underground in the West is the destruction of the establishment. The aim of the underground here in Bohemia is the creation of a second culture:** a culture that will not be dependent on official channels of communication, social recognition, and the hierarchy of values laid down by the establishment; **a culture which cannot have the destruction of the establishment as its aim because in doing so, it would drive itself into the establishment's embrace;** a culture which helps those who wish to join it to rid themselves of the scepticism which says that nothing can be done and shows them that much can be done when those who make the culture desire little for themselves and much for others.

Jirous came in for a lot of criticism for these somewhat contradictory and rather confused statements. What was meant by the frequent references to "the Establishment"? A society founded on consumerism? What the Trotskyists called "political and economic management" in the USSR? The ruling group or class in a totalitarian regime? Or a combination of them all?[30] So those artists who had "declared a struggle" against the Establishment were intent on destroying it, or not? Did a "first culture" and "second culture" exist, and can there be a "third" and more cultures? Isn't there rather a single culture which takes an "authentic" form or a (political or commercial) "conformist" form? What is more understandable is Jirous's at first sight absurd statement that "the situation in Bohemia [i.e. in the Czech lands, or in Czechoslovakia as a whole] is essentially different, and far better than in the West", which is immediately specified and explained: "the desire for recognition, success, the winning of prizes and titles" is eliminated in a totalitarian regime, unless the artist was willing to collaborate with it.

In the final chapter of the text the author apparently realized the contradiction between the need "to destroy the Establishment" and the striving to create something independent of it, which is why he tried to differentiate the "aims" of underground culture on either side of the Iron Curtain. This contradiction is easier to clarify if one realizes that these "confrontational appeals" did not originate with Jirous, but with Sanders, who is mentioned in the text, and Ralf-Rainer Rygulla, who is not. The passages underlined in Jirous's *Report* are simply a loose translation of a text by that German theorist of Western "counter-culture" from the end of the 1960s, which is why it seems

30) In her above-mentioned study Tuckerová writes very pertinently: "The condemnation of consumerism is the [Report's] closest link with movements in the West. Evidence of Jirous's British or American inspiration is the use of the word 'Establishment', which occurs at least sixteen times in the text [...] And it is precisely the use of the expression Establishment – first used in this sense in 1955 by a journalist of the British Spectator magazine – that lends Jirous's text a wider validity. It distances it from the specific situation of 'normalization', so that it does not refer solely to the existing Husák regime, but criticizes it within a broader and also more allegorical and metaphorical context" (p. 135). It should it be added that the use of the expression "establishment" in a political and religious sense (and likewise "disestablishment" or even "anti-establishment" – the established church = the state church) has a long tradition in Anglo-Saxon culture reaching back to the 16th century, which is common knowledge, although the expression has not yet taken root in Czech. Modern re-interpretation of the term "Establishment" within the Anglo-American culture is usually attributed to the American sociologist C. Wright Mills and his theory of "power elites". See his book *The Power Elite*, Oxford: Oxford University Press, 1956.

incongruous here: "Der von Ed Sanders geforderte 'totale Angriff auf die Kultur' kann nicht durch systemimmanente Kritik erfolgen, sondern durch Kritik von aussen, d.h. von Kriminellen, Süchtlingen und Farbigen. [...] Die Leute vom Underground haben erkannt, dass innerhalb der Legalität nichts mehr verändert werden kann."[31]

Thus one cannot deny a certain degree of ideological and intellectual confusion in the final chapter of the *Report*, and the author can also be criticised for excessively polarized standpoints, but 1) if critics of Jirous's alleged theories of the underground took the trouble they would find in his earlier texts more precise and more conciliatory formulation of the same ideas; 2) one cannot ignore the entirely unequivocal conclusion of the entire *Report*: Jirous gives hope to those in the totalitarian regimes who have fallen prey to scepticism by showing that it is possible to create an independent and free culture even under the most unfavourable conditions; he also makes an appeal for the preservation of the ethical dimension of culture in general and seeks a space in which it is possible to preserve one's human dignity.

B. The quotations used to head the chapters of the *Report* as an attempt to provide a historical context

We are paying particular attention to these epigraphs not only because there are so many of them, but because they convey a specific message. Although we concede that Jirous's *Report* is essentially a factual account and only to a very limited extent proposes a would-be "ideology of the underground" or "second culture" which, *nota bene* as we have pointed out earlier does not entirely consist of Jirous's own thinking, we cannot ignore the fact that the very existence of some kind of "underground" in Czechoslovakia in the mid-1970s, and the attempt to create an "independent culture" was something quite unusual, which lead some to suspect a tendency towards

---

31) From Rygulla's afterword to an anthology of American underground poetry (RYGULLA, R.-R., ed., *Fuck you! Underground Gedichte*, 1. Aufl., Darmstadt: Josef Melzer Verlag, 1968). Jirous doesn't mention Rygulla in the *Report*, but he does in his text *Sedmá generace romantiků* [The seventh Generation of Romantics] of 1969, where he criticises his (but originally Sanders') concept of "total assault on culture", the key passage of which is on p. 693 of MN).

something truly chiliastic, some kind of sectarianism divorced from reality. This did not necessarily relate to the musical, literary and other artistic activities developed in the underground community described by Jirous, but rather the way he interpreted them. But he himself seems to have been aware of that danger, which is why he used the various epigraphs to provide historical parallels to the facts described, and thus show that the **Czech underground was simply a new expression of age-old artistic and spiritual ambitions, striving for something new, unconventional, more free** (perhaps "anti-systemic", to use today's "suspect" political jargon). And he did all this in an awareness of the specific nature of the existing conditions, which provided no scope for "other opinions" – and which the intrinsically intolerant totalitarian political system was neither able nor permitted to provide.

One might also speculate that by incorporating "cultural references" in the form of epigraphs, Jirous also bore in mind the possibility that the readers of the *Report* would, after all, include some of those intellectuals, whom he could hardly hope to "enlist" into the underground, but he could at least try to gain their sympathy for "the cause". And as we know, he did achieve that to a certain extent.

There are seven manifest epigraphs in the *Report*, but the parallel in the introduction between the trip to Líšnice and "the pilgrimages of the first Hussites into the mountains" may also be regarded as an epigraph of sorts, and the same could apply to the closing quotation from Martin Húska, or the Duchamp quotation at the end of the fifth chapter. This makes **a total of ten analogies between the world of underground culture and the cultural heritage of the past.** Of those ten "anchorings", five are obviously of a religious character. Apart from the opening comment and the closing quotation, which suggest a parallel between the Czech underground and the Hussite millenarians of the 15th century,[32] there is also a telling quotation from

---

32) Regarding the supposed quotation of Martin "Loquis" Húska, this was a misapprehension on Jirous's part. The words are attributed to the priest Jan Němec of Žatec (Johannes von Tepl), Húska's colleague. On pp. 262-309 of his his book *Ktož jsú boží bojovníci* (Praha: Melantrich, 1951) Josef Macek quotes from a tract *Ze života kněží táborských* [From the Lives of Taborite Priests] by Jan of Příbram, namely Příbram's critique of the Taborite millenarians including Martin Húska and Jan Němec (Johannes von Tepl). According to Příbram on p. 297, Jan Němec states

St Matthew's gospel.[33] However, without context the quotation from Milton could be ambiguous: "We must act with reason in this world of evil, the place in which God has irrevocably placed us." (It is more categorical in Jirous's paraphrase at the end of chapter 8, mentioned earlier).[34] The first epigraph in the *Report* (discounting the opening one), but one which is least markedly religious, is the quotation from a text by the American underground band The Fugs: "When the mode of the music changes / When the mode of the music changes / The walls of the city shake," which has overtones of the biblical story of Joshua's conquest of Jericho (Joshua 6:20).[35]

in a dispute over the meaning of holy communion: "A faithful man is worthier than the sacrament." On page 456 of his book *Husitská ideologie* [Hussite ideology] (Praha: Academia, 1961) Robert Kalivoda writes: "Elements of Húska's arguments are evident particularly in a tract by Jan Němec of Žatec (if Christ was present in the host he could be eaten by mice and flies; a good man is worthier than the sacrament, Christ is more perfect in a good man than in the sacrament). The tract is entitled 'Cum spiritus veritatis' printed by Sedlák, loc. cit." Earlier R. K. refers to the book by J. Sedlák, *Táborské traktáty eucharistické*, Brno (Austria-Hungary): 1918. Here on p. 22 of the actual text the following passage appears: "Secondly, a believer is much worthier than the sacrament..." and on p. 17 of the appendix as part of the tract "Joannis de Zacs" [i.e. Johannes / Jan of Žatec / of Zacs / von Tepl] beginning with the words "Cum spiritus veritatis...", it states in Latin: "Secundo notet fidelis, quod homo fidelis est multum dignior quam sacramentum..." It has not been possible to locate the newer source from which Jirous apparently quotes.

33) Again, the devil took him to a very high mountain and showed him all the kingdoms of the world and their splendour. "All this I will give you," he said, "if you will bow down and worship me." (Matthew 4:8-9).

34) The quotation is from Milton's *Areopagitica*: "To sequester out of the world into Atlantick and Eutopian polities, which never can be drawn into use, [we] will not mend our condition; but to ordain wisely as in this world of evill, in the midd'st whereof God hath plac'd us unavoidably" (Areopagitica – A speech of Mr. John Milton for the Liberty of Unlicensed Printing, to the Parliament of England, London 1644). Milton is not advising people to "sensibly adapt to prevailing evil" but to be realistic and not retreat into utopias and dreams, but try to confront the world of evil.

35) Ed Sanders used the original English text (a composition entitled *When the Mode of the Music Changes* that first came out on the The Fugs' LP *It Crawled Into my Hands, Honest* in 1968) as an epigraph for his book *FUG YOU* (Philadelphia: Da Capo Press, 2011, p. ix) and gave the following explanation of its source: "When the mode of the music changes the walls of the city shake. – Tuli Kupferberg adapted (and considerably improved) from Damon of Athens, ca. 460 B.C."

Three of the epigraphs are purely literary: the first, by Comte de Lautréamont mentioned earlier;[36] the second, a Czech translation of one of Kafka's aphorisms – "From a certain point on, there is no more turning back. That is the point that must be reached." – which eloquently supports the author's argument, while also creating a link between the "merry ghetto" of the Czech underground and the thousand-year ghetto of European Jewry;[37] and finally, a quotation from Duchamp, a classic of modern art: "The great artist of tomorrow will go underground," which is already somewhat profaned and its meaning is not entirely clear in the Czech translation used.[38]

The remaining two epigraphs may be regarded as references to voices "calling for freedom" or seeking a better world: The text of

A passage in Book 4 of Plato's *Republic* reads (in Paul Shorey's translation): "'To put it briefly, then,' said I, 'it is to this that the overseers of our state must cleave and be watchful against its insensible corruption. They must throughout be watchful against innovations in music and gymnastics counter to the established order, and to the best of their power guard against them, fearing when anyone says that «That song is most regarded among men which hovers newest on the singer's lips», lest haply it be supposed that the poet means not new songs but a new way of song and is commending this. But we must not praise that sort of thing nor conceive it to be the poet's meaning. For a change to a new type of music is something to beware of as a hazard of all our fortunes. **For the modes of music are never disturbed without unsettling of the most fundamental political and social conventions,** as Damon affirms and as I am convinced.'" Kupferberg is obviously combining Plato's quote from Damon with the story of Joshua destroying the walls of Jericho with a blast from the ram's horn.

36) A quotation from Lautréamont's *Poésies II*: "La poésie doit etre faite par tous, non par un."

37) Jirous probably used the Czech translation by Rio Preisner (Kafka, *Aforismy*, Praha: Československý spisovatel, 1968, p. 7): "Jistým bodem počínaje není již návratu. Toho bodu je třeba dosáhnout."

38) This statement by Duchamp from 1961 has already been commented on in detail in the book *Views from the Inside* (2018, p. 18), so suffice it to recall that the main source would seem to be an interview Duchamp gave to Jean Neyens in 1965, at the end of which Duchamp says: "Une table ronde qu'on avait faite à Philadelphie, on m'avait demandé «Où allons-nous?». Moi j'ai simplement dit: «Le grand bonhomme de demain se cachera. Ira sous terre.» En anglais c'est mieux qu'en français – «Will go underground.» Il faudra qu'il meure avant d'être connu. Moi, c'est mon avis, s'il y a un bonhomme important d'ici un siècle ou deux – eh bien! il se sera caché toute sa vie pour échapper à l'emprise du marché… complètement mercantile (rire) si j'ose dire."

Vesmírná symfonie [The Universe symphony] ("Krásný je svět, / ale plas-tičtí lidé to nevidí…" [The world is beautiful / but plastic people don't see it]) is Jirous's translation of the words of a text written in English by Michal Jernek *The Universe Symphony and Melody about Plastic Doctor* from 1969, which The Plastic People set to music, and which Jirous also comments on at the beginning of the fourth chapter of the *Report*.[39] So it is actually the only self-referential epigraph in the *Report*, which would seem to be a way of indicating the gulf between the spiritual world of the underground in the mid-1970s and its beginnings.

Finally there is the epigraph at the very beginning, allegedly by Mao Tse-Tung, the only epigraph from the *Report* that literary historians and editors have noted so far:

> In the great cultural revolutions there is only one way for the people – to free themselves by their own efforts. Nothing must be used that would do it for them. Believe in people, rely on them and respect their initiative. Cast away fear! Don't be afraid of commotion. Let people educate themselves in the great revolutionary movement.

This is not necessarily a verbatim quotation of Mao as is clear from the broader context in which the unknown author invokes Mao himself. It is part of a proclamation by the Central Committee of the Chinese Communist Party from 1966, the original English text of which is in the footnote.[40] Of themselves, the words of the quotation would not give cause for irritation were their author not named Mao Tse-Tung.

---

39) See RIEDEL, Jaroslav (ed.), *The Plastic People of the Universe, Texty*, 2nd edition, pp. 36–40, the passage quoted is on pp. 37–38.
40) *Peking Review*, vol. 9, no. 33 (12th August 1966), pp. 6–11. "Decision of the Central Committee of Chinese Communist Party Concerning the Great Proletarian Cultural Revolution 4. [...] In the Great Proletarian Cultural Revolution, the only method is for the masses to liberate themselves, and any method of doing things in their stead must not be used. Trust the masses, rely on them and respect their initiative. Cast out fear. Don't be afraid of disturbances. Chairman Mao has often told us that revolution cannot be so very refined, so gentle, so temperate, kind, courteous, restrained and magnanimous. Let the masses educate themselves in this great revolutionary movement and learn to distinguish between right and wrong and between correct and incorrect ways of doing things."

A poignant example of how even decades later Jirous's *Report* was capable of annoying even his fans and admirers are the comments on this epigraph from the pen of Jirous's biographer Marek Švehla:

Jirous placed at the beginning a paradox that one would hardly expect from a thoughtful and educated person, who had such a distrust of Communism – he opened his essay on freedom with a quotation from of its worst enemies, the Chinese Communist leader Mao Tse-Tung. Undoubtedly it was under the influence of Egon Bondy, a fervent admirer of Mao. At the time Jirous himself knew little about Mao and had no information about the crimes he was committing in China, and how he was utterly opposed to free-thinking people. He simply borrowed Mao's 'thoughts' and he was taken by the appealing but totally vapid theses about people's ability to free themselves by means of their own activity, which also applied to the Czech situation.[41]

In one of the *Report's* first appearances in print, namely in Tigrid's Paris-based *Svědectví*,[42] where it appeared under the pseudonym of Jan Kabala with the altered title of *Report from the Czech Musical Underground*, the "Mao quotation" was omitted. In *Magor's Notebook* it is printed without comment.

Regarding the Christian parallels, it is not fortuitous that the author chose as analogies of the Czech underground of the 1970s so-called fringe or even "heretical" figures, whose mission was to invoke the original meaning of God's word in opposition to a secularised church, and to the world of the powerful and rulers, as well as a biblical text opposing the world of pharisees and hypocrites, who had gained the world but lost their souls (Matthew 16:26).

III. The purpose served by the *Report*
It is a well-known fact that the immediate and very specific usefulness (but also exploitability) of the *Report* as a basic source of information about what the Czech underground was or was not, was confirmed the year after Jirous wrote it, i.e. 1976, a year of

41) ŠVEHLA, Marek, *Magor a jeho doba*, Praha: Torst, 2017, chap. 14, pp. 283–284.
42) *Svědectví* 13, no. 51 (1976), pp. 571–586.

persecution and political trials of leading figures of the Czech underground culture headed by Jirous. The fundamental significance of the *Report* was proved by the *"Hnědá kniha" o procesech s českým undergroundem* ["Brown Book" on the Trials of the Czech Underground], which initially appeared in samizdat and naturally also included Jirous's *Report*.[43]

Evidence that many key theoretical texts on the form of Czechoslovak dissent were influenced to a certain extent by Jirous's *Report* was provided quite recently by Martin Valenta (*Podzemní symfonie Plastic People*, Argo, Praha, 2018), so I shall only briefly allude to them here. On pages 98–99 and 101–103 op. cit. Valenta quotes the aforementioned anthology *O svobodě a moci* (Köln – Roma: Index – Listy, 1980) – which comprised *inter alia* texts by Václav Havel (*Moc bezmocných* [The Power of the Powerless]), Václav Benda (*Paralelní polis* [The Parallel Polis]), Jiří Němec (*Nové šance svobody* [New Opportunities for Freedom]), and Zdeněk Vokatý (*Sen o kole* [Dream about a Wheel]) – while indicating to what extent these authors came to terms with the phenomenon of underground culture, knowledge of which they would have had difficulty acquiring (apart from the last named, who was one of its protagonists), except via Jirous's *Report*. There were several other texts that could be mentioned in this respect, of course (such as many of Egon Bondy's reflections from the 1980s, which would scarcely have arisen without Jirous's *Report*),[44] and there is also scope for closer investigation of echoes of Jirous's text in the works of his successors. Just a few at random: the phrase "living in truth" used by Jirous in the *Report* (and in the same year 1976 also by Bondy in the prose *Šaman*) and the way that postulate is transformed in the writing of Václav Havel;[45] Jirous's concept of the independence

43) See *"Hnědá kniha" o procesech s českým undergroundem*, its first printed, enlarged and commented edition, Praha: ÚSTR, 2012.
44) See MACHOVEC, Martin, "Egon Bondy – apologeta a teoretik českého undergroundu?", in KUDRNA, Ladislav (ed.), *Reflexe undergroundu*, Praha: ÚSTR, 2016, pp. 210–226.
45) See BOLTON, Jonathan, "Šaman, zelinář a 'život v pravdě'" [The Shaman, The Greengrocer, and 'Living in Truth'], in SUK, Jiří – ANDĚLOVÁ, Kristina (eds.), *Jednoho dne se v našem zelináři cosi vzbouří. Eseje o Moci bezmocných*, Praha: ÚSD AV ČR, 2016, pp. 27–33. In English: J.B.,"The Shaman, the Greengrocer, and 'Living in Truth'", *East European Politics, Societies, and Cultures* 32, no. 2 (May 2018), pp. 255–265.

of the "second culture" and Benda's concept of the "parallel polis"; Jirous's emphasis on mutual respect and tolerance, and on culture as opposed to politics in the sense of its traditional paradigm, and Havel's concept of "apolitical politics". But let the above list suffice, as these topics merit much more extensive independent study.

Concerning the critics of Jirous's ideological concepts in the *Report*, Veronika Tuckerová, in her study, which has been mentioned several times already (in *Magorova konference (k dílu I. M. Jirouse)*, Praha: Revolver Revue), focuses chiefly on Petr Fidelius (p. 140 op. cit.), acknowleding the consistency of his text *K Jirousově koncepci undergroundu* [Jirous's Concept of the Underground] while highlighting shortcomings in Fidelius's "critical methods of textual and linguistic analysis which take the text 'at its word'". Nevertheless Fidelius's critique of the *Report* is clearly the most serious of the various criticisms of the text and is free of the emotiveness of Knížák's or Ságl's response (not to mention Merta's latterday hate-filled reaction).

Any future assessment of the significance of Jirous's *Report on the Third Czech Musical Revival* will certainly have to take into account Fidelius's criticisms. However, in conclusion, the point should be made once more that these and similar criticisms actually only concern certain ambiguities in the "ideological component" of the *Report*, which is limited almost entirely to the thirteenth chapter and is only marginal elsewhere in the text.

In our view the *Report* remains a very valuable source text not only in respect of facts about this part of Czech cultural history, but also as a plea for artistic creation to have an ethical dimension, and last but not least, it is a visionary warning against the irreparable disruption of human culture if totalitarian regimes were to become "established" worldwide.

Prague, September 2018
Translated by Gerald Turner

(Bondy's prose *Šaman*, which is discussed by Bolton with regards to Havel's concept of "living in truth", was written in March 1976, i.e. practically the same time as Jirous's *Report*.) See E.B., *Šaman*, Praha: Akropolis, 2006.

Underground literature and culture - Czech dissidence with regards to Czech underground culture - Samizdat book/periodical production (English, Czech, German titles)

The bibliography does not contain the titles of all the books and articles mentioned in the text and the footnotes since some of them refer only indirectly to the main topic of this volume. On the other hand, the titles of some books and articles (especially the English ones) not mentioned in the text are included here because of their seminal importance for the themes discussed.

Adamy, Herbert, *Byl jsem manažerem ilegální továrny* [I Was a Manager of an Illegal Factory], Praha: Ostrov, 1999.

Alan, Josef (ed.), *Alternativní kultura. Příběh české společnosti 1945–1989* [Alternative Culture: The Story of Czech Society, 1945–1989], [Contributions: Josef Alan, Tomáš Bitrich, Michal Bregant, Martin Čihák, Stanislav Dvorský, Jiří Gruntorád, Lenka Jungmannová, Vladimír Just, Marie Klimešová, Martin Machovec, Josef Moucha, Alice Růžičková, Josef Vlček, Tomáš Vrba], Praha: Nakladatelství Lidové noviny, 2001.

Beale, Lewis, "The Rockers Who Started a Revolution", *Herald Tribune*, 16th January 2002.

Benda, Václav, "Paralelní polis" [The Parallel Polis], in *O svobodě a moci* [On Freedom and Power], Köln – Roma: Index – Listy, 1980, pp. 101–110.

Benetková, Marie, "Zlatý kopec – dějiny české undergroundové komuny" [Goldberg – History of a Czech Underground Commune], in *Baráky. Souostroví svobody* [Shanties. The Archipelagos of Freedom], Stárek, František Čuňas – Kostúr, Jiří (eds.), Praha: Pulchra, 2010, pp. 30–73.

Blažek, Petr – Pažout, Jaroslav (eds.), *Nejcitlivější místo režimu. Výbor na obranu nespravedlivě stíhaných očima svých členů. Diskusní setkání 19. října 2007* [The Most Irritable Spot of the Regime: Committee for the Defense of the Unjustly Persecuted as Seen through the Eyes of Its Members. A Discussion Meeting of October 19, 2007], Praha: Pulchra, 2008.

Blažek, Petr – Schovánek, Radek (eds.), *VONS.cz, Webové stránky o dějinách Výboru na obranu nespravedlivě stíhaných (1978–1989)* [VONS.cz, Website on the History of the Committee for the Defense of the Unjustly Persecuted (1978–1989)], www.vons.cz, esp. www.vons.cz/ informace-o--charte-77, 2007.

Blažek, Petr (ed.), *Opozice a odpor proti komunistickému režimu v Československu 1968-1989* [Opposition and the Resistance against the Communist Regime in Czechoslovakia 1968-1989], Praha: Dokořán, 2005.

Bock, Ivo – Hänsgen, Sabine – Schlott, Wolfgang, "Kultur jenseits der Zensur" [The Culture beyond Censorship], in Eichwede 2000, pp. 64-77.

Bock, Ivo, "Der literarische Samizdat nach 1968" [The Literary Samizdat after 1968], in Eichwede 2000, pp. 86-93.

Bolton, Jonathan, "The Shaman, the Greengrocer, and 'Living in Truth'", *East European Politics, Societies, and Cultures* 32, no. 2 (May 2018), pp. 255-265.

Bolton, Jonathan, *Worlds of Dissent. Charter 77, The Plastic People of the Universe, and Czech Culture under Communism*, Cambridge and London: Harvard University Press, 2012.

Bondy, Egon, "Berta" [Běta] (part 3, section XXII – an excerpt from a novella), *Yazzyk Magazine* 4, (1995), pp. 64-69.

Bondy, Egon, "Cellar Work" [Sklepní práce] (an excerpt from a novella), *Yazzyk Magazine* 1, (1992), pp. 23-26.

Bondy, Egon, *Básnické dílo Egona Bondyho* [The Collected Poems of Egon Bondy], 9 vols., Praha: Pražská imaginace, 1990-1993.

Bondy, Egon, *Básnické spisy* [Poetic Works], 3 vols., Praha: Argo, 2014-2016.

Bondy, Egon, *Bezejmenná* [Nameless], 2nd edition, Praha: Akropolis, 2019.

Bondy, Egon, *The Consolation of Ontology: On the Substantial and Nonsubstantial Models*, translated by Benjamin B. Page, Lanham – Boulder – New York – Oxford: Lexington Books, 2001 [On Egon Bondy, see: "Translator's Introduction (2000)"].

Bondy, Egon, *Filosofické dílo I-IV* [Philosophical Works I-IV], 4 vols., Praha: DharmaGaia, 2007-2013.

Bondy, Egon, *Invalidní sourozenci* [The Disabled Siblings], 4th edition, Praha: Akropolis, 2012.

Bondy, Egon, "Kořeny českého literárního undergroundu v letech 1949-1953" [The Roots of the Czech Literary Underground, 1949-1953], *Haňťa Press* 2, no. 8 (1990), pp. 5-9; commented in *Pohledy zevnitř*, 2008.

Bondy, Egon, *Poznámky k dějinám filosofie* [Notes on the History of Philosophy], 6 vols., Praha: Vokno, 1992-1997.

Bondy, Egon, *Prvních deset let* [The First Ten Years], Praha: Maťa, 2002.

Borecký, Vladimír, *Odvrácená tvář humoru (Ke komice absurdity)* [The Reverse Side of Humour (On the Comicality of the Absurd], Liberec – Praha: Dauphin, 1996.

Boudník, Vladimír, *Dopisy Vladimíra Boudníka Mikuláši Medkovi* [Letters of Vladimír Boudník to Mikuláš Medek], Praha: Jan Placák – Ztichlá klika, 2012.

Boudník, Vladimír, *Dopisy Vladimíra Boudníka přátelům 1949-1953* [Letters of Vladimír Boudník to Friends 1949-1953], Praha: Jan Placák - Ztichlá klika, 2015.

Boudník, Vladimír, *Z korespondence I (1949-1956)* [From the Correspondence I], Praha: Pražská imaginace, 1994.

Boudník, Vladimír, *Z korespondence II (1957-1968)* [From the Correspondence II], Praha: Pražská imaginace, 1994.

Boudník, Vladimír, *Z literární pozůstalosti* [From the Literary Papers], Praha: Pražská imaginace, 1993.

Brabec, Jiří - Gruša, Jiří - Hájek, Igor - Kabeš, Petr - Lopatka, Jan, *Slovník českých spisovatelů* [Dictionary of Czech Writers], Toronto: Sixty-Eight Publishers, 1982.

Brabenec, Vratislav - Kalenská, Renata, *Evangelium podle Brabence. Rozhovor Renaty Kalenské* [The Gospel according to Brabenec. Talks with Renata Kalenská], Praha: Torst, 2010.

Brabenec, Vratislav, *Sebedudy a jiné texty z let 1966-1987* [Self-Bagpipes and Other Texts from 1966-1987], Praha: Kalich, 2010.

Brikcius, Eugen, *A tělo se stalo slovem* [And the Flesh Became Word], Radim Kopáč (ed.), Brno, Czech Republic: Větrné mlýny, 2013.

Brikcius, Zuzana (ed.), *Charta Story - Příběh Charty 77 / The Story of Charter 77*, Praha: Národní galerie, 2017.

Brukwicki, Jerzy, "'Neuer Himmel, neue Erde.' Die Symbolik der Solidarność 1980 bis 1989" ['New Heaven, New Earth': The Symbology of Solidarność, 1980-1989], in Eichwede 2000, pp. 124-128.

Bučilová, Lenka, *Zorka Ságlová. Úplný přehled díla* [Zorka Ságlová. A Complete Survey of her Work], Praha: KANT, 2009.

Burian, Václav - Galík, Josef - Machala, Lubomír - Podivínský, Martin - Schneider, Jan, *Česká a slovenská literatura v exilu a samizdatu. Informatorium pro učitele, studenty i laiky* [Czech and Slovak Literature in Exile and in Samizdat. An Informatory for Teachers, Students, and Laics], Olomouc, Czechoslovakia: Hanácké noviny, 1991.

Černá [Krejcarová], Jana, *Adresát Milena Jesenská* [To: Milena Jesenská], 3rd edition, Praha: Torst, 2014.

Černý, Václav, "Nad verši Věry Jirousové a o kulturním stanovisku našeho undergroundu" [On Věra Jirousová's Poetry; also on the Cultural Standpoint of our Underground], in Černý, Václav, *Tvorba a osobnost* [Creation and Personality], Kabíček, Jaroslav - Šulc, Jan (eds.), Praha: Odeon, 1992, pp. 900-908.

Černý, Václav, "O všem možném, dokonce i o 'hippies' a 'novém románu'" [Miscellanea, even on "Hippies" and "The Nouveau Roman"], in Černý,

Václav, *Tvorba a osobnost II* [Creation and Personality II], Kabíček, Jaroslav – Šulc, Jan (eds.), Praha: Odeon, 1993, pp. 553–562.

Černý, Václav, *O povaze naší kultury* [On the Nature of our Culture], Brno, Czechoslovakia: Atlantis, 1991.

Císařovská, Blanka – Prečan, Vilém (eds.), *Charta 77. Dokumenty 1977–1989* [Charter 77: Documentary 1977–1989], 3 vols., Praha: Ústav pro soudobé dějiny AV ČR, 2007.

Daniel, Aleksandr, "Wie freie Menschen" [As Free People], in Eichwede 2000, pp. 38–50.

Day, Barbara, *The Velvet Philosophers*, London: The Claridge Press, 1999.

Denčevová, Ivana – Stárek, František Čuňas – Stehlík, Michal, *Tváře undergroundu* [The Faces of the Underground], Praha: Radioservis, 2012.

Devátá, Markéta – Suk, Jiří – Tůma, Oldřich (eds.), *Charta 77. Od obhajoby lidských práv k demokratické revoluci 1977–1989. Sborník z konference k 30. výročí Charty 77. Praha, 21.–23. března 2007. Charter 77: From the Assertion of Human Rights to a Democratic Revolution, 1977–1989. The proceedings of the conference to mark the 30th anniversary of Charter 77. Prague, 21–23 March 2007*, Praha: ÚSD AV ČR, 2007.

Dočekal, Jaroslav, "Smršťovače – hořké dávky. Z dopisů Jaroslavu Rotbauerovi" [Shrinkers – Bitter Doses. From Letters to Jaroslav Rotbauer], *Revolver Revue*, no. 29 (1995), pp. 129–160.

Dočekal, Jaroslav, *Dopisy Jaroslava Dočekala Vladimíru Boudníkovi I–II* [Letters of Jaroslav Dočekal to Vladimír Boudník I–II], Praha: Jan Placák – Ztichlá klika, 2017.

Drda, Adam, "Ti, kteří nepodepsali (O lidech v opozici, ne-signatářích Charty 77)" [Those Who Did Not Sign (On Oppositionists, Non-Signatories of Charter 77)], *Revolver Revue*, no. 33 (1997), pp. 215–224.

Drubek, Natascha, "Sich (k)einen Namen machen: Die Židovská jména der Honza K." [How to Become (un)known: The Jewish Names of Honza K.], *Slovo a smysl / Word & Sense* 14, no. 28 (2017), pp. [51]–73.

Dvorský, Stanislav, "Židovská jména – bájení a skutečnost" [The Jewish Names – Myths and Reality], *Souvislosti* 28, no. 3 (2017), pp. 48–62.

Eichwede, Wolfgang (ed.), *Samizdat. Alternative Kultur in Zentral- und Osteuropa: Die 60er bis 80er Jahre. Dokumentationen zur Kultur und Gesellschaft im östlichen Europa* [Samizdat: Alternative Culture in Central and Eastern Europe: From the 1960s to the 1980s. Documentary of Culture and Social Life in Eastern Europe], Edition Temmen, vol. 8, Bremen: Forschungsstelle Osteuropa an der Universität Bremen, 2000.

Eichwede, Wolfgang, "Archipel Samizdat" [Archipelago Samizdat], in Eichwede 2000, pp. 8–19.

Eichwede, Wolfgang, "The Conception of the Exhibition," in Hamersky 2002, pp. 15–19.

Elšíková, Monika (ed.), *Aby radost nezmizela. Pocta Magorovi* [Let Joy not Disappear. A Tribute to Magor], [Contributions: Zbyněk Petráček, Jan Macháček, Petr Placák, Pavel Zajíček, Vratislav Brabenec, Sváťa Karásek, Jan Steklík, Jiří Gruntorád, Juliána Jirousová, František Lízna, Františka Jirousová, Marta Veselá Jirousová, Daniel Degtěv, Vladimír Zavadil, Miroslav Skalák Skalický, Vladimír Lábus Drápal, Eva Štolbová, Zuzana Brejcha, Eva Turnová, Anna Irmanovová, Vladimír Merta, Ilona Franckоvá, Nadia Rovderová Láďa Heryán, Václav Havel, Jana Hradilková, Eva Tomková, Oldřich Navrátil, Dáša Vokatá, Karel Schwarzenberg, Monika Elšíková], Praha: Monika Vadasová-Elšíková, 2011.

Falk, Barbara J., *The Dilemmas of Dissidence in East-Central Europe: Citizen Intellectuals and Philosopher Kings*, New York – Budapest: Central European University Press, 2003 (see Chapter 3 – "Czechoslovakia: From Interrupted to Velvet Revolution", Part "The Underground Music Scene and the Trial of the PPU").

Fidelius, Petr [Palek, Karel], "K Jirousově koncepci undergroundu" [Jirous's Concept of the Underground], *Souvislosti* 4, no. 1 (1993), pp. 33–46.

Fidelius, Petr [Palek, Karel], *Kritické eseje* [Critical Essays], Praha: Torst, 2000.

Glanc, Tomáš (ed.), *Samizdat Past & Present* [Contributions: Tomáš Glanc, Miroslav Červenka, Josef Jedlička, František Kautmann, Petr Fidelius, Jiří Gruša, Tomáš Vrba, Jiří Gruntorád, Martin Machovec, Alena Přibáňová, Michal Přibáň, Petr Šámal, Weronika Parfianowicz-Vertun], Praha: Institute of Czech Literature – Karolinum Press, 2018.

Goetz-Stankiewicz, Marketa (ed.), *Good-bye, Samizdat. Twenty Years of Czechoslovak Underground Writing*. With a Foreword by Timothy Garton Ash, with an Introduction "Samizdat Literature: An Introduction" by Igor Hájek [Contributions: Igor Hájek, Alexander Kliment, Ivan Klíma, Pavel Kohout, Jan Trefulka, Jiří Gruša, Dominik Tatarka, Karel Pecka, Lenka Procházková, Eda Kriseová, Egon Bondy, Milan Uhde, Ludvík Vaculík, Bohumil Hrabal, Paul Wilson, Jan Patočka, Milan Jungmann, Miroslav Kusý, Zdeněk Urbánek, Jan Lopatka, Eva Kantůrková, Jiřina Šiklová, Petr Fidelius, Václav Havel, Erazim Kohák, Ivan M. Havel (Sakateka), Zdeněk Neubauer (Sidonius), Milan Šimečka, Ladislav Hejdánek, Martin Palouš, Radim Palouš, Tomáš Halík, Zdeněk Kratochvíl], Evanston: Northwestern University Press, 1992.

Gruntorád, Jiří (ed.), *Informace o Chartě 77, 1978–1990. Článková bibliografie* [Information on Charter 77, 1978–1990. Bibliography of Articles], Brno, Czech Republic: Doplněk, 1998.

Gruntorád, Jiří, "Edice Expedice. Část 1. - 'Černá řada'" [Dispatch Editions. Part 1 - "Black Series"], *Kritický sborník* 14, no. 3 (1994), pp. 66–78.

Gruntorád, Jiří, "Edice Expedice. Část 2. - 'Světlá řada'" [Dispatch Editions. Part 2 - "Light Series"], *Kritický sborník* 14, no. 4 (1994), pp. 71–80.

Gruntorád, Jiří, "Samizdatová literatura v Československu sedmdesátých a osmdesátých let" [Samizdat Literature in Czechoslovakia of the 1970s and 1980s], in Alan 2001, pp. 493–507.

Hamersky, Heidrun (ed.), *Samizdat: Alternative Culture in Central and Eastern Europe from the 1960s to the 1980s* [Contributions: Václav Havel, György Konrád, Vilém Prečan, László Rajk, Wolfgang Eichwede], Bremen: Research Centre for East European Studies at the University of Bremen, 2002.

Hanáková, Jitka, *Edice českého samizdatu 1972-1991* [The Editions of Czech Samizdat 1972–1991], Praha: Národní knihovna České republiky, 1997.

Havel, Václav, "Český úděl?" [The Czech Deal?], in Havel, Václav, *Eseje a jiné texty z let 1953-1969 (Spisy 3)* [Essays and Other Texts 1953–1969. Works, vol. 3], Praha: Torst 1999, pp. 888–897.

Havel, Václav, "Hovězí porážka" [Beef-slaughter], in Havel, Václav, *Eseje a jiné texty z let 1970-1989 / Dálkový výslech (Spisy 4)* [Essays and Other Texts 1970–1989 / A Long-Distance Interrogation. Works, vol. 4], Praha: Torst, 1999 (written in 1984), pp. 446–452.

Havel, Václav, "Moc bezmocných" [The Power of the Powerless], in Havel, Václav, *Eseje a jiné texty z let 1970-1989 / Dálkový výslech. Spisy 4* [Essays and Other Texts 1970–1989 / A Long-Distance Interrogation. Works, vol. 4], Praha: Torst, 1999, pp. 224–330.

Havel, Václav, "The Power of the Powerless", in *The Power of the Powerless: Citizens against the State in Central-Eastern Europe*, John Keane (ed.), Armonk: M. E. Sharpe, 1990.

Havel, Václav, "The Power of the Powerless", in *Václav Havel, or, Living in Truth. Twenty-two Essays Published on the Occasion of the Award of the Erasmus Prize to Václav Havel*, Jan Vladislav (ed.), London: Faber and Faber, 1986, pp. 36–122.

Havel, Václav, *Disturbing the Peace. A Conversation with Karel Hvížďala* [Dálkový výslech], transl. by Paul Wilson; New York: Knopf & Vintage Books, 1990.

Havel, Václav, *Open Letters: Selected Writings, 1965-1990*, Paul Wilson (ed.), New York: Vintage Books, 1990 [See the text "The Trial"].

Hlavsa, Milan - Pelc, Jan, *Bez ohňů je underground* [No Fires, Thats the Underground], 3rd edition, Praha: Maťa - BSF, 2016.

Hoptman, Laura - Pospiszyl, Tomáš (eds.), *Primary Documents. A Sourcebook for Eastern and Central European Art since the 1950s*; Foreword by Ilya Kabakov, New York: The Museum of Modern Art, 2002.

Hrabal, Bohumil, *Too Loud a Solitude* [Příliš hlučná samota], transl. by Michael Henry Heim, San Diego – New York – London: Harcourt Brace Jovanovich Publishers, 1990.

Hrabal, Bohumil, "Co je poezie?" [What is Poetry?], in *Jarmilka. Sebrané spisy Bohumila Hrabala 3* [Collected Works of Bohumil Hrabal 3, Jarmilka], Praha: Pražská imaginace, 1992, pp. 50–55.

Hrabal, Bohumil, "Něžný barbar" [Tender Barbarian], in *Obrazy v hlubině času. Sebrané spisy Bohumila Hrabala 6* [Collected Works of Bohumil Hrabal 6, Images in the Depth of Time], Praha: Pražská imaginace, 1992, pp. 197–280.

Hrabal, Bohumil, "Příliš hlučná samota" [Too Loud a Solitude], in *Sebrané spisy Bohumila Hrabala 9 – Hlučná samota* [Collected Works of Bohumil Hrabal 9, Loud Solitude], Praha: Pražská imaginace, 1994, pp. 7–78.

Hrabal, Bohumil, "Taneční hodiny pro starší a pokročilé" [Dancing Lessons for the Advanced in Age], in *Sebrané spisy Bohumila Hrabala 5 – Kafkárna* [Collected Works of Bohumil Hrabal 5, Kafkaesque World], Praha: Pražská imaginace, 1994, pp. 7–56.

Hrabal, Bohumil, *Bambino di Praga – Barvotisky – Krásná Poldi* [Jesus Baby of Prague – Colour-prints – Lovely Poldi], Praha: Československý spisovatel, 1990.

Hrabal, Bohumil, *Dancing Lessons for the Advanced in Age* [Taneční hodiny pro starší a pokročilé], transl. by Michael Henry Heim, New York – San Diego – London: Harcourt Brace & Comp., 1995.

Hrdlička, František – Bratršovská, Zdena (eds.), *Jak chutná nezávislost. 33 životních ohlédnutí* [The Taste of Independence. Looking back at 33 Lives], Praha – Olomouc, Czech Republic: Votobia, 1998.

Hynek, Karel, *S vyloučením veřejnosti* [With the Exclusion of the Public], Praha: Torst, 1998.

Jelínek, Oldřich, "Jak to všechno začalo..." [How it All Began], *Haňťa Press* 5, no. 14 (1993), pp. 10–15.

Ježek, Vlastimil, "Bibliografie Revolver Revue (Jednou nohou) 1–13" [Bibliography of Revolver Revue (One Foot In) 1–13], *Kritický sborník* 11, no. 3, 1991, pp. 63–79.

Ježek, Vlastimil, "Bibliografie Revolver Revue (Jednou nohou) 1–13" [Bibliography of Revolver Revue (One Foot In) 1–13], *Kritický sborník* 11, no. 4 (1991), pp. 67–75.

Jirous, Ivan Martin, "A hudebníky ve větvích nebylo vidět" (1981) [And the Musicians Couldn't Be Seen among the Branches], in *Magorův zápisník*, Praha: Torst, 1997, pp. 199–202.

Jirous, Ivan Martin, "Jsou to divný kluci" (1981) [They're Strange Guys], in *Magorův zápisník*, Praha: Torst, 1997, pp. 212–217.

Jirous, Ivan Martin, "Kundy rty ústa tváře masky" (1980) [Cunts Lips Mouths Faces Masks], in *Magorův zápisník*, Praha: Torst, 1997, pp. 208-211.

Jirous, Ivan Martin, "Pravdivý příběh Plastic People" [The True Story of The Plastic People], in *Magorův zápisník*, Praha: Torst, 1997, pp. 255-256.

Jirous, Ivan Martin, "Report on the third Czech Musical Revival", in *Views from the Inside. Czech Underground Literature and Culture (1948-1989)*, Martin Machovec (ed.), 2nd, amended edition, Praha: Karolinum Press, 2018, pp. 7-36.

Jirous, Ivan Martin, *Magorova summa* [Magor's Sum], Martin Machovec (ed.), 3rd, complete edition, Praha: Torst, 2015.

Jirous, Ivan Martin, *Magorův zápisník* [Magor's Notebook], Michael Špirit (ed.), Praha: Torst, 1997.

Jirous, Ivan Martin, *My itinerary has been monotonous for quite a while. Selected prison poems translated from Czech by Marek Tomin / with an afterword by Martin Machovec*, London: Divus, 2017.

Jirous, Ivan Martin, "Zpráva o třetím českém hudebním obrození" (1975) [Report on the third Czech Musical Revival], in *Magorův zápisník*, Praha: Torst, 1997, pp. 171-198.

Jirousová, Věra (ed.), *K.Š. - Křižovnická škola čistého humoru bez vtipu* [The Crusaders' School of Pure Humour without Jokes] (Art Catalogue), Hradec Králové - Praha: Galerie moderního umění Hradec Králové - Středočeská galerie Praha, 1991.

Jirousová, Věra, "Koncert Plastic People na počest Ladislava Klímy" [Concert of The Plastic People in Honour of Ladislav Klíma], *Svědectví* 16, no. 62 (1981), pp. 230-233.

Jungmannová, Lenka, "Podzemní kultura prizmatem sepětí moci a ideologie" [Underground Culture Clasped between Power and Ideology], in ACTA UNIVERSITATIS PALACKIANAE OLOMOUCENSIS. FACULTAS PHILOSO-PHICA. STUDIA MORAVICA 4. Symposiana. Sborník příspěvků přednesených na prvním mezioborovém sympoziu Česká kultura a umění ve 20. století, Petr Komenda (ed.), Olomouc, Czech Republic: UP v Olomouci, 2006, pp. 211-214.

Karásek, Sváťa - Hájek, Štěpán - Plzák, Michal, *Víno tvé výborné* [The Good Wine of Yours], Praha: Kalich, 1998.

Karásek, Svatopluk, *Protestor znamená vyznávám* [Protestor Means: I Confess], Praha - Žďár n. Sázavou: EKK - Kalich, 1993.

Karásek, Svatopluk, *Say No to the Devil* (the booklet added to the record with Karásek's texts in Czech original and in English translation by Paul Wilson), Uppsala: Šafrán 78 & Boží Mlýn, 1979.

Karásek, Svatopluk, *V nebi je trůn* [There is a Throne in Heaven], Praha: Maťa, 1999.

Karlík, Viktor, *Podzemní práce (Zpětný deník) / Underground Work (Retroactive Diary)*, Praha: Revolver Revue, 2012.

Kenney, Padraic, *A Carnival of Revolution: Central Europe 1989*, Princeton, NJ: Princeton University Press, 2003.

Kissel, Wolfgang S., "Samizdat als kulturelles Gedächtnis. Terror und GULag in der russischen Erinnerungsliteratur der sechziger Jahre" [Samizdat as Cultural Memory: Terror and GULag in Russian Memoirs Written in the 1960s], in Eichwede 2000, pp. 94-104.

Klaniczay, Gábor – Trencsényi, Balázs (eds.), *Mapping the Merry Ghetto: Musical Countercultures in East Central Europe, 1960-1989, East Central Europe*, 38, 2011, Leiden, the Netherlands: Brill, 2011.

Klíma, Ivan, "The Unexpected Merits of Oppression", in *Law & Literature, 2, Issue 1: The Writer and The State* (Berkeley, CA: University of California Press), 1990, pp. 37-42.

Knížák, Milan – Pokorný, Marek – Valoch, Jiří, *Zorka Ságlová*, Praha: Národní galerie, 2006.

Knížák, Milan, *AKTUAL: Děti bolševizmu / Kids of Bolshevism* (a CD), Louny: Guerilla Records, 2005 (the booklet added to the record with some of Milan Knížák's lyrics written for the band Aktual, both in Czech original and in English translation).

Knížák, Milan, *Bez důvodu* [Without Reason], Praha: Litera, 1996.

Knížák, Milan, *Nový ráj* [A New Paradise], Praha: Galerie Mánes – Uměleckoprůmyslové museum, 1996.

Knížák, Milan, *Písně kapely Aktual* [The Songs of the Band Aktual], Machovec, Martin – Riedel, Jaroslav (eds.), Praha: Maťa, 2003.

Knížák, Milan, *Unvollständige Dokumentation / Some Documentary. 1961-1979* (with Jindřich Chalupecký's essay in German and English translation: "Die Geschichte von Milan Knížák / The Story of Milan Knížák"), Berlin [West]: Edition Ars Viva!, 1980.

Kolář, Jiří, *Dílo Jiřího Koláře VIII* [Works of Jiří Kolář VIII], Praha: Paseka, 2000.

Konrád, György, "Looking Back at Samizdat", in Hamersky 2002, pp. 7-10.

Kotek, Josef, "UNDERGROUND MUSIC a její sociální otazníky" [The Social Issues of Underground Music], *Melodie* 7, no. 2 (1969), pp. 37-40.

Kotyk, Petr – Kotyková, Světlana – Pavlíček, Tomáš (eds.), *Hlučná samota. Sto let Bohumila Hrabala 1914-2014* [Loud Solitude. The Centenary of Bohumil Hrabal 1914-2014], Praha: Mladá fronta – Památník národního písemnictví, 2014.

Kouřil, Vladimír, *Jazzová sekce v čase a nečase 1971-1987* [The Jazz Section in the Course of Good and Bad Times 1971-1987], Praha: Torst, 1999.

Kožmín, Zdeněk - Trávníček, Jiří, *Na tvrdém loži z psího vína. Česká poezie od 40. let do současnosti* [The Hard Bed of Wild Wine: Czech Poetry from the 1940s to the Present Time], Brno, Czech Republic: Books, 1998.

[Krchovský], J. H., *Mladost - radost...* [To be Young is Heaven], Brno, Czech Republic: Větrné mlýny, 2005.

Krchovský, J. H., "If I Want to Vanish Without a Trace and Other Poems", transl. by O. T. Chalkstone, in *Anthology of Slavic Poetry*, Piotr Kasjas (ed.), [London, UK]: Kasjas Publishing, 2016, pp. 120-123.

Krchovský, J. H., "Seven Poems (Translated from the Czech by Justin Quinn)", *METRE* [Magazine of international poetry], vol. 10, Hull - Praha - Dublin, (Autum 2001), pp. 62-64.

Krchovský, J. H., *Básně* [Poems], Brno, Czech Republic: Host, 1998.

Krchovský, J. H., *Líně s tebou spím / Lazy Love. The Plastic People of the Universe, in Memoriam Milan Hlavsa* (a CD), Praha: Globus Music, 2001 (the booklet added to the record contains some poems by J.H.K. in Marek Tomin's translation).

Krejcarová, Jana, "A Letter" [Dopis Egonu Bondymu], with "An introduction to her life and work" by A. G. Brain [Gerald Turner]; *Yazzyk Magazine*, no. 2 (1993), pp. 64-67.

Krejcarová-Černá, Jana, *Tohle je skutečnost (Básně, prózy, dopisy)* [This is Reality (poems, prose, letters)], Praha: Torst, 2016.

Kubínová, Pavlína (ed.), *Tschechische Schriftsteller / Czech Writers*, Praha: Ministry of Culture of the Czech Republic, 2001.

Kudrna, Ladislav (ed.), *Podhoubí undergroundu* [Hotbed of the Underground], [Contributions: Jáchym Topol, Michal Stehlík, Zdeněk Nebřenský, Josef Rauvolf, Ladislav Kudrna, Martin Tharp, Martin Valenta, Jan Cholínský, Barbara Bothová, Jan Blüml], Praha: Ústav pro studium totalitních režimů, 2018.

Kudrna, Ladislav (ed.), *Reflexe undergroundu* [Essays on the Underground] [Contributions: Josef Rauvolf, Vladimír 518, František Stárek Čuňas, Jan Cholínský, Prokop Tomek, Petr Blažek, Martin Valenta, Barbara Bothová, Ladislav Kudrna, Markéta Brožová, Jáchym Topol, Martin Machovec, Petr Placák, Mirek Vodrážka], Praha: Ústav pro studium totalitních režimů, 2016.

Kužel, Petr (ed.), *Myšlení a tvorba Egona Bondyho* [Egon Bondy's Thoughts and Literary Activity], [Contributions: Petr Kužel, Petra Macháčková, Jan Černý, Vít Bartoš, Ladislav Hohoš, Jiří Holba, Peter Púčik, Olga Lomová, Marina Čarnogurská, Ľubomír Dunaj, Jan Mervart, Petr Rohel, Dirk Mathias Dalberg, Jaroslav Fiala, Martin Machovec, Gertraude Zandová, Oskar Mainx, Martin Pilař], Praha: Filosofia, 2018.

Lamarová, Milena (ed.), *Zorka Ságlová 1965-1995* (art catalogue), Praha – Litoměřice: Galerie výtvarného umění v Litoměřicích, 1995.

Libánský, Abbé Jaroslav, *My Underground. Rodinné fotoalbum – Family Album – Familienfotoalbum 1972/82*, Wien: Institut für culturresistante Güter, 2004.

Literature and Politics in Central Europe: Studies in Honour of Marketa Goetz- -Stankiewicz, Leslie Miller, Klaus Petersen, Peter Stenberg, Karl Zaenkel (eds.), (including the study by Vilém Prečan, "Independent Literature and Samizdat in Czechoslovakia"), Columbia, SC, USA: Camden House, 1993.

Lopatka, Jan, "Literatura v katakombách?" [Literature in the Catacombs?], in Lopatka, Jan, *Šifra lidské existence* [The Code of Human Existence], Praha: Torst, 1995, pp. 225-238.

Lopatka, Jan, "Mimořádný zájem o poezii" [An Extraordinary Interest in Poetry], in Lopatka, Jan, *Předpoklady tvorby* [Premises of Creative Work], Praha: Český spisovatel, 1991, pp. 139-145.

Machovec, Martin – Navrátil, Pavel – Stárek, František (eds.), *"Hnědá kniha" o procesech s českým undergroundem* ["Brown Book" on the Trials of the Czech Underground], [Contributions: František Stárek, Ivan Martin Jirous, Egon Bondy, Pavel Zajíček, Karel Soukup, Svatopluk Karásek, Přemysl Blažíček, Miroslav Červenka, Jan Lopatka, Jiří Černý, Jan Patočka, Jaroslav Suk, Dana Němcová, Věra Jirousová, Zdeněk Mlynář, Václav Havel, Jiří Němec, Vratislav Brabenec, Petr Uhl, Vendelín Komeda, Jaroslav Kořán, Helena Klímová, Pavel Navrátil, Ivan Hartel, Paul Wilson, etc.], Praha: Ústav pro studium totalitních režimů, 2012.

Machovec, Martin (ed.), *Pohledy zevnitř. Česká undergroundová kultura ve svědectvích, dokumentech a interpretacích* [Views from the Inside: Czech Underground Culture in Testimonies, Documents, and Interpretations], [Contributions: Ivan Martin Jirous, Paul Wilson, Egon Bondy, Jáchym Topol], Praha: Pistorius and Olšanská, 2008.

Machovec, Martin (ed.), *Views from the Inside: Czech Underground Literature and Culture (1948-1989)*, [Contributions: Ivan Martin Jirous, Paul Wilson, Egon Bondy, Jáchym Topol], Praha: Ústav české literatury a literární vědy FF UK, 2006.

Machovec, Martin (ed.), *Views from the Inside. Czech Underground Literature and Culture (1948-1989)*, [Contributions: Ivan Martin Jirous, Paul Wilson, Egon Bondy, Jáchym Topol], 2nd, amended edition, Praha: Karolinum Press, 2018.

Machovec, Martin (ed.), *Židovská jména 1949* [Jewish Names 1949], [Contributions: Egon Bondy, Sarah Silberstein, Isaak Kuhnert, Nathan Illinger, Gala Mallarmé, Benjamin Haas, Dina Š., Edmond Š., Herbert Taussig,

Pavel Ungar, Arnold Stern, Szatmar Neméthyová], Praha: Nakladatelství Lidové noviny, 1995.

Machovec, Martin, "Czech Underground Literature, 1969-1989: A Challenge to Textual Studies" in *Voice, Text, Hypertext: Emerging Practices in Textual Studies*, Raimonda Modiano, Leroy F. Searle, and Peter Schillingsburg (eds.), Seattle – London: University of Washington Press & Walter Chapin Simpson Center for the Humanities, 2004, pp. 345-357.

Machovec, Martin, "Několik poznámek k podzemní ediční řadě Půlnoc" [Several Remarks on the Underground Midnight Editions], *Kritický sborník* 13, no. 3 (1993), pp. 71-78.

Machovec, Martin, "Polopatická impertinence" [An Impertinence in a Down--to-Earth Manner], *Kritická příloha Revolver Revue* 17, no. 8 (1997), pp. 231-235.

Machovec, Martin, "Šestnáct autorů českého literárního podzemí" [Sixteen Authors of the Czech Literary Underground], *Literární archiv PNP*, no. 25 (1991), pp. 41-77.

Machovec, Martin, "Společenství a poetika undergroundu" + "Próza undergroundu, okruh Revolver Revue" [The Underground Community and its Poetry + the Prose of the Underground, the Revolver Revue Circle], in *Dějiny české literatury 1945-1989, IV, 1969-1989*, Pavel Janoušek (ed.) Praha: Academia, 2008, pp. 279-295, 455-460.

Machovec, Martin, "Židovská jména rediviva. Významný objev pro dějiny samizdatu" [The Jewish Names Revived. An Important Finding for the History of Samizdat], *A2* 3, no. 51-52 (2007), pp. 10-11.

Machovec, Martin, *A Brief Report on Present Knowledge of Czech Samizdat Phenomena 1948-1989*, Praha: Libri Prohibiti, 2004, libpro.cts.cuni.cz/clanky.htm.

Machovec, Martin, *Bibliografie Egona Bondyho (se soupisem rukopisné pozůstalosti a archivované korespondence)* [Bibliography of Egon Bondy with the Catalogue of Manuscript Estate and Archived Correspondence), Praha: Libri Prohibiti, http://www.libpro.cz/docs/bibliografie-egona--bondyho-2018_1530980541.pdf, 2006-2018.

Machovec, Martin, *Nejvýznamnější samizdatové sborníky undergroundové literatury (1975-1989)* [The Most Important Samizdat Anthologies of Underground Literature (1975-1989)], https://www.ustrcr.cz/data/pdf/projekty/underground/underground-samizdat-sborniky.pdf.

Mainx, Oskar, *Poezie jako mýtus, svědectví a hra. Kapitoly z básnické poetiky Egona Bondyho* [Poetry as Myth, Testimony and Game. Chapters from the Poetics of Egon Bondy], Ostrava: Protimluv, 2007.

Mandler, Emanuel (ed.), *Dvě desetiletí před listopadem 89* [Two Decades before November 89], Praha: Ústav pro soudobé dějiny AV ČR – Maxdorf, 1993.

Mandler, Emanuel, "O hrdinech a o těch druhých" [On Heroes and the Others], *Kritická příloha Revolver Revue* 17, no. 8 (1997), pp. 218-231.

Marysko, Karel, *Dílo Karla Maryska I-XII* [Karel Marysko, Works I-XII], 12 vols., Praha, Pražská imaginace, 1995-1996.

Mazal, Tomáš, *Spisovatel Bohumil Hrabal* [The Writer Bohumil Hrabal], Praha: Torst, 2004.

Medek, Mikuláš, *Texty* [Texts], Praha: Torst, 1995.

Merhaut, Vladislav, *Grafik Vladimír Boudník* [The Graphic Artist Vladimír Boudník], Praha: Torst, 2009.

Merhaut, Vladislav, *Zápisky o Vladimíru Boudníkovi* [Notes on Vladimír Boudník], Praha: Edice Revolver Revue, 1997.

Merta, Vladimír, "Čtvrté hudební obrození. Příspěvek k typologii jednoho ne-myšlení" [The Fourth Musical Revival. A Contribution to the Typology of Non-Cogitation], in *Aby radost nezmizela. Pocta Magorovi* [Let Joy not Disappear. A Tribute to Magor], Monika Elšíková (ed.), Praha: Monika Vadasová-Elšíková, 2011, pp. 100-118.

Militz, Anna, *Ani víru, ani ctnosti člověk nepotřebuje ke své spáse: příběh Jany Černé* [Neither Religion, nor Virtue are Necessary for one's Salvation: the Story of Jana Černá], Olomouc, Czech Republic: Burian a Tichák, 2015.

Morganová, Pavlína, *Czech Action Art. Happenings, Actions, Events, Land Art, Body Art and Performance Art Behind the Iron Curtain*, Praha: Karolinum Press, 2014.

Müller, Miloš – Cibulka, Petr, "'Přál bych si, aby tady moc byla pro občana.' Rozhovor s Petrem Cibulkou" ["I Would Like the Power to Be Granted to Citizens of This Country": An Interview with Petr Cibulka], *Sklepník* 7, no. 1 (1994), pp. 47-52.

Naughton, James D. (ed.), *Eastern & Central Europe. Traveller's Literary Companion*; Brighton: In Print Publishing Ltd, 1995.

Němec, Jiří, "Nové šance svobody" [New Opportunities for Freedom], in *O svobodě a moci* [On Freedom and Power], Köln – Roma: Index – Listy, 1980, pp. 257-268.

O svobodě a moci [On Freedom and Power], [Contributions: Václav Havel, Rudolf Battěk, Václav Benda, Václav Černý, Jiří Dienstbier, Jiří Hájek, Ladislav Hejdánek, Miroslav Kusý, Zdeněk Mlynář, Jiří Němec, Petr Pithart, Jiří Ruml, Jakub S. Trojan, Petr Uhl, Josef Vohryzek, Zdeněk Vokatý, Josef Zvěřina], Köln – Roma: Index – Listy, 1980.

O'Connor, Rory, "Jailhouse Rock: In the Eastern European Underground, Making Music Can Be Downright Dangerous" [An Interview with Karel Voják], *Mother Jones magazine*, May 1979, see: http://www.mediachannel.org/ news/reports/jailhouse.shtml/.

Onuferová, Edita – Pokorná, Terezie (eds.), *Magorova konference (k dílu I. M. Jirouse)* [Magor's Conference (On I. M. Jirous's Work)], [Contributions: Terezie Pokorná, Marek Vajchr, Viktor Šlajchrt, Petr Hruška, Martin Hybler, Mike Baugh, Justin Quinn, Paul Wilson, Jiří Gruntorád, František Stárek, Martin Machovec, Ondřej Němec, Dana Němcová, Luboš Merhaut, Pavla Pečinková, Petr Jindra, Magdalena Juříková, Robert Krumphanzl, Veronika Tuckerová, Nicolas Maslowski, David Bartoň, Miroslav Petříček, Michael Špirit, Michal Geisler, Adam Drda], Praha: Revolver Revue, 2014.

Otáhal, Milan, *Opoziční proudy v české společnosti 1969–1989* [Oppositional Currents in Czech Society 1969–1989], Praha: ÚSD AV ČR, 2011.

Page, Benjamin B., "Translator's Introduction (2000)", in Bondy, Egon, *The Consolation of Ontology: On the Substantial and Nonsubstantial Models*, Lanham – Boulder – New York – Oxford: Lexington Books, 2001, pp. ix–xv.

Pánek, Fanda, *Vita horribilis 1972–1985*, Praha: Kalich, 2007.

Patočka, Jan, *Heretical Essays on the Philosophy of History*, Chicago: Open Court, 1996.

Pauer, Jan, "Charta 77. Moralische Opposition unter den Bedingungen der Diktatur" [Charter 77: Moral Opposition under the Conditions of Dictatorship], in Eichwede 2000, pp. 52–63.

Pelc, Jan, *...a bude hůř* [...and it's Gonna Get Worse], Praha: Maťa, 2000.

Petr, Pavel, "Moravský samizdat" [Moravian Samizdat], Box, no. 6 (1996), pp. 44–71.

Petrová, Jana, *Zapomenutá generace osmdesátých let 20. století. Nezávislé aktivity a samizdat na Plzeňsku* [The Forgotten Generation of the 1980s. Independent Activities and Samizdat in the Plzeň Region], Plzeň, Czech Republic: Jana Petrová, 2009.

Pilař, Martin, *Underground*, Brno, Czech Republic: Host, 1999.

Placák, Petr, *Medorek*, 3rd edition, Praha: Plus, 2010.

Placák, Petr, *Obrovský zasněžený hřbitov* [A Huge Snow-Covered Graveyard], Praha: Torst, 1995.

Porter, Robert, *Comedies of Defiance. An Introduction to Twentieth-Century Czech Fiction*, Brighton – Portland: Sussex Academic Press, 2001.

Posset, Johanna, *Česká samizdatová periodika 1968–1989* [Czech Samizdat Periodicals 1968–1989], Brno, Czechoslovakia: Továrna na sítotisk a společnost R&T, 1991.

Posset, Johanna, *Tschechische Samizdat-Periodika 1968–1988* [Czech Samizdat Periodicals 1968–1988], Master's thesis, Wien: University of Vienna, 1990.

Prečan, Vilém (ed.), *Charta 77, 1977–1989*, Scheinfeld – Bratislava: Čs. středisko nezávislé kultury – Archa, 1990.

Prečan, Vilém (ed.), *Human Rights in Czechoslovakia: A Documentation*, Paris: International Committee for the Support of Charter 77, 1983.

Prečan, Vilém, "Bibliography of the Czechoslovak Samizdat: Samizdat Periodicals 1977–1988", *ACTA* 2, no. 5–8 (1988), pp. 64–82.

Prečan, Vilém, "Edice Petlice 1973–1987" [Padlock Editions 1973–1987], *ACTA* 1, no. 3–4 (1987), pp. 35–91.

Prečan, Vilém, "Independent Literature and Samizdat in Czechoslovakia", in *Literature and Politics in Central Europe: Studies in Honour of Markéta Goetz-Stankiewicz*, Leslie Miller et al. (ed.), Columbia, SC: Camden House, 1993, pp. 91–107.

Prečan, Vilém, "The World of Czech and Slovak Samizdat", in Hamersky 2002, pp. 11–13.

Prečan, Vilém, *Independent Literature and Samizdat in Czechoslovakia* (a catalogue to the exhibition V.Z.D.O.R. Výstava nezávislé literatury v samizdatu a exilu 1948–1989), Praha – Scheinfeld-Schwarzenberg, Germany: Památník národního písemnictví – Ústav pro soudobé dějiny ČSAV – Československé dokumentační středisko nezávislé literatury, 1992.

Prečan, Vilém, *Independent Literature and Samizdat in Czechoslovakia*, Praha: Památník národního písemnictví – Ústav pro soudobé dějiny ČSAV, 1992.

Prečan, Vilém, *Nezávislá literatura a samizdat v Československu 70. a 80. let* [Independent Literature and Samizdat in Czechoslovakia of the 1970s and 1980s], Praha: Ústav pro soudobé dějiny ČSAV, 1992.

Přibáň, Jiří, *Disidenti práva. O revolucích roku 1989, fikcích legality a soudobé verzi společenské smlouvy* [Dissidents of Law: On the 1989 Velvet Revolutions, Fictions of Legality, and Contemporary Version of the Social Contract], Praha: Sociologické nakladatelství, 2001.

Přibáň, Jiří, *Dissidents of Law: On the 1989 Velvet Revolutions, Legitimations, Fictions of Legality, and Contemporary Version of the Social Contract*, Aldershot, U.K.: Ashgate, 2002.

Přibáň, Michal (ed.), *Český literární samizdat 1949–1989. Edice – časopisy – sborníky* [Czech Literary Samizdat 1949–1989. Editions – Periodicals – Anthologies], Praha: Academia – Ústav pro českou literaturu AV ČR, 2018.

Putna, Martin C. – Zadražilová, Miluše, *Rusko mimo Rusko. Dějiny a kultura ruské emigrace 1917–1991* [Russia outside Russia: History and Culture of the Russian Exile 1917–1991], vol. 2, Brno, Czech Republic: Petrov, 1994.

Putna, Martin C. (ed.), *Měli jsme underground a máme prd. Podzemní básníci o Havlovi* [We Used to Have the Underground, Now We're in Deep Shit. The Underground Poets on Havel], Praha: Knihovna Václava Havla, 2009.

Putna, Martin C., "Mnoho zemí v podzemí" [Many Grounds in the Underground], *Souvislosti* 4, no. 1 (1993), pp. 14-32.

Putna, Martin C., *Česká katolická literatura 1945-1989* [Czech Catholic Literature 1945-1989], Praha: Torst, 2017 (see chapter "Underground", pp. 725-801).

Pytlík, Radko, *The Sad King of Czech Literature Bohumil Hrabal. His Life and Work* [translated by Kathleen Hayes], Praha: Emporius, 2000.

Riedel, Jaroslav (ed.), *The Plastic People of the Universe*, Praha: Globus Music & Maťa, 1999.

Riedel, Jaroslav (ed.), *The Plastic People Of The Universe: Texty*, 2nd edition, Praha: Maťa, 2001.

Riedel, Jaroslav, *Plastic People a český underground* [The Plastic People and the Czech Underground], Praha: Galén, 2016.

Romanová, Gabriela, *Příběh Edice Expedice* [The Story of the Dispatch Editions], Praha: Knihovna Václava Havla, 2014.

Rössler, Josef Bobeš, *Obraz doby aneb Chaotické vzpomínky na život v českém undergroundu 70. let* [The Way the Times Were, or: Chaotic Recollections of Life in the Czech Underground of 1970s], Praha: Pulchra, 2009.

Roth, Susanna, *Laute Einsamkeit und bitteres Glück. Zur poetischen Welt von Bohumil Hrabals Prosa* [Loud Solitude and Bitter Happiness: The Poetic World of Fiction by Bohumil Hrabal], Bern: Peter Lang, 1986.

Růžková, Jana – Gruntorád, Jiří, "Samizdatový časopis Vokno" [The Samizdat Magazine Vokno], *Kritický sborník* 19, (1999-2000), pp. 193-231.

Ságl, Jan, *Tanec na dvojitém ledě / Dancing on the Double Ice*, Praha: KANT, 2013.

Sanders, Edward, *A Visit to Praha. For the Praha Writers' Festival 2005*, Praha: Haštalská Hotel Josef, 2005.

Sedlackova Gibbs, Helena, *Moral Politics and Its Others: The Charter 77 Dissident Movement in Czechoslovakia (1977-1989)*, UMI Microform 3089390, New York: Department of Comparative Literature, New York University, 2003.

Serafin, Steven (ed.), *Twentieth-Century Eastern European Writers. Third Series*, Detroit - San Francisco - London - Boston - Woodbridge: Gale Group, 2001.

Ševčík, Jiří - Morganová, Pavlína - Dušková, Dagmar (eds.), *České umění 1938-1989 / programy / kritické texty / dokumenty* [Czech Art 1938-1989 / Programmes / Critical Texts / Documents], Praha: Academia, 2001.

Short, David (ed.), *Bohumil Hrabal (1914-1997). Papers from a Symposium*, London: SEES, University College, 2004.

Skilling, Gordon H., *Charter 77 and Human Rights in Czechoslovakia*, London: Allen and Unwin, 1981.

Skilling, Gordon H., *Samizdat and an Independent Society in Central and Eastern Europe*, Oxford: Macmillan Press, 1989; Columbus: Ohio State University Press, 1989 [See Part II, Chapter 4 - "Other Independent Currents"].

Škvorecký, Josef, "Bohemia of the Soul", *Daedalus. Journal of the American Academy of Arts and Sciences* 119, 1 (Winter 1990), "Eastern Europe... Central Europe... Europe", pp. 111–139.

Škvorecký, Josef, "Prague Winter", *The American Spectator*, vol. 16, no. 9 (1983), pp. 19–23.

Slavíková, Duňa (ed.), *Křižovnická škola čistého humoru bez vtipu* [The Crusaders' School of Pure Humour without Jokes], (Art Catalogue), Roudnice nad Labem, Czech Republic: Galerie moderního umění v Roudnici nad Labem, 2015.

Smetana, Vladimír Hendrix, *Od dospívání k dozpívání. Vzpomínky na život v českém undergroundu* [When the Singing Had to Stop. Remembrance of Life in the Czech Underground], Praha: Pulchra, 2015.

Stankovič, Andrej, *Knihy básní I- II*, Praha: Triáda, 2017.

Stárek, František Čuňas - Kostúr, Jiří (eds.), *Baráky. Souostroví svobody* [Shanties. The Archipelagos of Freedom], Praha: Pulchra, 2010.

Stárek, František Čuňas - Valenta, Martin, *Podzemní symfonie Plastic People* [The Underground Symphony of The Plastic People], Praha: Argo, 2018.

Steiner, Peter, *The Deserts of Bohemia. Czech Fiction and Its Social Context*, Ithaca - London: Cornell University Press, 2000.

Suk, Jiří - Andělová, Kristina (eds.), *Jednoho dne se v našem zelináři cosi vzbouří. Eseje o Moci bezmocných* [One Day Something in the Greengrocer Snaps. Essays on The Power of the Powerless], [Contributions: Jiří Suk, Kristina Andělová, Steven Lukes, Jonathan Bolton, Roger Scruton, Barbara J. Falk, Aleksander Kaczorowski, James Krapfl, Karel Hrubý, Petr Hlaváček, Jan Pauer, Delia Popescu, James F. Pontuso, Lenka Karfíková, Kacper Szulecki, Marci Shore, Jiří Přibáň, Miloš Havelka, Bohumil Doležal, Petr Pithart, Jiří Hanuš, Václav Bělohradský, Martin Škabraha, Roman Kanda, Robert B. Pynsent, Miroslav Kusý, Barbara Day, Kieran Williams, Lenka Jungmannová, Petr Sedlák, David D. Danaher, Stanislav Komárek], Praha: ÚSD AV ČR, 2016.

Suk, Jiří, "Podrobná zpráva o paralelní polis. Nad korespondencí Václava Havla a Františka Janoucha" [The Detailed Report on the Parallel Polis: The Correspondence between Václav Havel and František Janouch], in *Havel, Václav - Janouch, František, Korespondence 1978-2001*, Praha: Akropolis, 2007, pp. 9–29.

Švandrlík, Miloslav, *Černí baroni aneb Válčili jsme za Čepičky* [The Black Barons, or As We Soldiered under Comrade Čepička], Praha: Mladá fronta, 1990.

Švehla, Marek, *Magor a jeho doba* [Magor and his Times], Praha: Torst, 2017.

Svoboda, Vladislav [Smetana, Vladimír] Hendrix, "Od dospívání k dozpívání / When the Singing Had to Stop", in *Pope Smoked Dope / Papež kouřil trávu. Rocková hudba a alternativní vizuální kultura 60. let / Rock music and the alternative visual culture of the 1960s* [a catalogue to an exhibition], Praha: KANT, 2005, pp. 74–89.

Szaruga, Leszek, "Untergrundpresse in Polen. Ein Beschreibungsversuch" [The Underground Press in Poland: A Modest Description], in Eichwede 2000, pp. 130–134.

The Merry Ghetto [A booklet/catalogue added to the record *The Plastic People... Praha. Egon Bondy's Happy Hearts Club Banned*], [Lyrics and texts by Egon Bondy, Pavel Zajíček, Josef Vondruška, Svatopluk Karásek, Milan Koch, Miroslav Skalický, František Vaněček, Václav Havel, Ivan Hartel, Jan Patočka, Ivan M. Jirous, Paul Wilson; edited anonymously by Ivan Hartel, Paul Wilson, Jacques Pasquier], London – Paris: Boží Mlýn & SCOPA Invisible Production © and The Plastic People Defense Fund, 1978.

Topol, Jáchym – Weiss, Tomáš, *Nemůžu se zastavit* [I Can't Stop Myself], Praha: Portál, 2000.

Topol, Jáchym, "Game Park" [Obora] (a poem translated by A. G. Brain [Gerald Turner]), *Yazzyk Magazine*, 4, Praha, 1995.

Topol, Jáchym, *Miluju tě k zbláznění* [I Love You Like Mad], Brno, Czechoslovakia: Atlantis, 1990.

Trávníček, Jiří, "Běsy a stesky kajícníkovy" [The Demons and Complaints of a Penitent], in Trávníček, Jiří, *Poezie poslední možnosti* [Poetry of the Last Opportunity], Praha: Torst, 1996, pp. 185–198.

Trávníček, Jiří, "Tři generace českého undergroundu" [Three Generations of Czech Underground], in Kožmín – Trávníček, 1998, pp. 236–244.

Troup, Zdeněk, "Poezie totality" [Poetry of Totality], *Rozeta* 1, no. 1 (1991), pp. 16–18.

Tucker, Aviezer, *The Philosophy and Politics of Czech Dissidence from Patočka to Havel*, Pittsburgh: University of Pittsburgh Press, 2000.

Tuckerová, Veronika, "Jirousova Zpráva o třetím českém hudebním obrození: úvaha o formě a kulturní kontinuitě" [Jirous's Report on the Third Czech Musical Revival: a reflection on its form and cultural continuity], in *Magorova konference (k dílu I. M. Jirouse)*, eds. Onuferová, Edita – Pokorná, Terezie, Praha: Revolver Revue, 2014, pp. 134–144.

Tuckerová, Veronika, "The Remains of the Triple Ghetto in the Praha Underground", in *Brucken. Germanistisches Jahrbuch TSCHECHIEN-SLOWAKEI 2015 / Germanic Yearbook CZECH REPUBLIC-SLOVAKIA 2015*, 23/1–2 (2015), Praha: DAAD, Nakladatelství Lidové noviny 2016, pp. 193–210.

Typlt, Jaromír Filip, "Absolutní realismus a Totální hrobař" [Absolute Realism and the Totalitarian Gravedigger], *Host* 22, no. 1 (2006), pp. 38-41.

Typlt, Jaromír Filip, "Dvě svědectví o Židovských jménech" [Two Testimonies of Jewish Names], *Host* 13, no. 3 (1997), pp. 36-37.

Uhl, Petr – Pavelka, Zdenko, *Dělal jsem, co jsem považoval za správné* [I Did What I Thought Was Right], Praha: Torst, 2013.

Vaněk, Miroslav – Urbášek, Pavel (eds.), *Vítězové? Poražení? Životopisná interview / Disent v období tzv. normalizace* [Winners? Losers? Biographic Interviews / Dissidence in the Times of the So-Called Normalization], Praha: Prostor, 2005.

Vanicek, Anna Naninka, *Passion Play: Underground Rock Music in Czechoslovakia, 1968-1989*, Master's thesis, North York: York University, 1997.

Vašinka, Radim, "Vydolováno z nepaměti I-V" [Retrieved from Time out of Mind I-V], *Divadelní noviny* 10, no. 5-9 (2001), pp. 16.

Vašinka, Radim, "Bondy a Orfeus" [Bondy and Orpheus], in *Bouda Bondy, projekt Bouda IV*, Praha: National Theatre, 2007, pp. 70-86.

Vávra, Stanislav – Machovec, Martin (eds.), *Libeňští psychici. Sborník básnických a prozaických textů z let 1945-1959* [Libeň Psychics. Collected Poetic and Prose Works from 1945-1959], Praha: Concordia, 2009.

Vávra, Stanislav – Typlt, Jaromír F., "Ukázat pramen a podat pohár" [To Show a Spring and to Offer a Goblet], *Iniciály* 2, no. 17/18 (1991), pp. 21-24.

Vávra, Stanislav, "Ať to drásá" [Harrowing Business], *Haňťa Press* 2, no. 11 (1991), pp. 21-41.

Vávra, Stanislav, "Záběhlická skupina surrealistů – Libenští psychici" [The Záběhlice Surrealist Group – Libeň Psychics], *Jarmark umění*, no. 2 (April 1991), pp. [7-8].

Veselý, Luboš, "Underground (Charty 77)" [The Underground (of Charter 77)], in *Opozice a odpor proti komunistickému režimu v Československu 1968-1989* [The Opposition and Resistance to the Communist Regime in Czechoslovakia 1968-1989], Petr Blažek (ed.), Praha: Dokořán, 2005, pp. 111-118.

Vladislav, Jan (ed.), *Václav Havel, or, Living in Truth. Twenty-Two Essays Published on the Occasion of the Award of the Erasmus Prize to Václav Havel* (transl. by A. G. Brain [Gerald Turner]), Amsterdam – London: Meulenhoff – Faber and Faber, 1986.

Vodrážka, Mirek, *Filosofický sendvič. Jak chutná Bondyho dílo?* [A Philosophical Sandwich. What does Bondy's Work Taste like?], https://www.advojka.cz/archiv/2015/10/filosoficky-sendvic.

Vodseďálek, Ivo – Mazal, Tomáš, "S Ivo Vodseďálkem o letech radostného budování 49-53" [With Ivo Vodseďálek on the Years of Happy Building up Socialism 49-53], *Vokno*, no. 18 (1990).

Vodseďálek, Ivo, *Dílo Ivo Vodseďálka* I–V [Works of Ivo Vodseďálek], Praha: Pražská imaginace, 1992.

Vodseďálek, Ivo, *Felixír života* [Felixir of Life], Brno, Czech Republic: Host, 2000.

Vokatý, Zdeněk Londýn, "Sen o kole" [A Dream about a Wheel], in *O svobodě a moci*, Köln – Roma: Index – Listy, 1980, pp. 343–350.

Volková, Bronislava – Cloutier, Clarice (eds.), *Up the Devil's Back – Po hřbetě ďábla*, Bloomington, IN, USA: Slavica, 2008.

Vondruška, Josef, *Chlastej a modli se* [Booze and Pray], Praha: Torst, 2005.

Vondruška, Josef, *Rock'n'rollový sebevrah* [Rock'n'roll Suicide], Brno, Czech Republic: "Zvláštní vydání…", 1993.

Vrba, Tomáš, "Nezávislé písemnictví a svobodné myšlení v letech 1970–1989" [The Independent Literature and Free Thinking 1970–1989], in Alan 2001, pp. 265–305.

Wagner, Zdeněk, *Virgule* [A Divining Rod], Praha: Cherm, 2007.

Wilson, Paul, "Tower of Song: How The Plastic People of the Universe Helped Shape the Velvet Revolution", in Kamicheril, Rohan – Robinson, Sal (eds.), *The Wall in My Head. Words and Images from the Fall of the Iron Curtain. A Words without Borders Anthology*, Rochester, NY: Open Letter, 2009, pp. 89–98.

Wilson, Paul, "What's it Like Making Rock'n'Roll in a Police State?", *Musician magazine* (Gloucester, Mass.), February 1983; also in *Views from the Inside. Czech Underground Literature and Culture (1948–1989)*, Martin Machovec (ed.), 2nd, amended edition, Praha: Karolinum Press, 2018, pp. 37–54.

Wilson, Paul, *Bohemian Rhapsodies*, Praha: Torst, 2011 (an anthology of Wilson's essays on Czech dissidence and underground culture, translated into Czech).

Yanosik, Joseph, "The Plastic People of the Universe", March 1996, see: http://www.furious.com/perfect/pulnoc.html/.

Z[Zajíček], Pavel, *DG 307 (Texty z let 1973–1980)* [DG 307 (Texts from 1973–1980)], Praha: Vokno, 1990.

Žáček, Pavel, "Celostátní projekt 'Klín'" [Nation-wide Operation 'Wedge'], *Securitas imperii*, 1, Praha 1994, pp. 60–87.

Zajíček, Pavel, *DG 307 – Gift to the Shadows (fragment)*, Uppsala: Šafrán and Boží Mlýn, 1982 (the leaflet added to the record contains some of Zajíček's lyrics translated into English).

Zajíček, Pavel, *DG 307 – SVĚDEK SPÁLENÝHO ČASU 1979/1980* [DG 307 – The Witness of the Burnt Time 1979/1980] (5 CDs), Louny: Guerilla Records, 2013 (the booklets added to the CDs contain all of Zajíček's lyrics, both in Czech and in English translation by Marek Tomin).

Zajíček, Pavel, *Zápisky z podzemí (1973–1980)* [Notes from the Underground (1973–1980)], Praha: Torst, 2002.

Zand, Gertraude, *Totaler Realismus und Peinliche Poesie. Tschechische Untergrund-Literatur 1948–1953* [Total Realism and Poetry of Embarrassment: Czech Underground Literature 1948–1953], Wien: Peter Lang, 1998.

Zand, Gertraude, *Totální realismus a trapná poezie. Česká neoficiální literatura 1948–1953* [Total Realism and Poetry of Embarrassment: Czech Underground Literature 1948–1953], Brno, Czech Republic: Host, 2002.

AKTUAL - ATENTÁT NA KULTURU, Jaroslav Riedel (ed.), Prague: Anne Records, 2003.

AKTUAL - DĚTI BOLŠEVIZMU, Louny: Guerilla Records, 2005.

BÍLÉ SVĚTLO - DĚLNÍCI BÍLÉHO SVĚTLA, Vladimír Lábus Drápal (ed.), Louny: Guerilla Records, 2006.

CHARLIE SOUKUP - GENERACE, Globus Music, Praha, 2001.

CHARLIE SOUKUP - RADIO, Martin Machovec - Karel Kourek (eds.), Prague: Galén, 2012.

DG 307 - GIFT TO THE SHADOWS (FRAGMENT), Uppsala: Šafrán and Boží Mlýn, 1982.

DG 307 - 1973-1975 [LP], Prague: Globus International, 1991.

DG 307 - DAR STÍNŮM (JARO 1979), *PTÁK UTRŽENEJ ZE ŘETĚZU* (PODZIM 1979), *TORZO* (LÉTO 1980) [3 CDs], Prague: Globus International, 1993.

DG 307 - HISTORIE HYSTERIE. Archiv dochovaných nahrávek 1973-75 [2 CDs], Jaroslav Riedel (ed.), Louny: Guerilla Records, 2004.

DG 307 - SVĚDEK SPÁLENÝHO ČASU 1979/1980 [5 CDs], Louny: Guerilla Records, 2013.

JIM ČERT - SVĚTLU VSTŘÍC, Prague: Aske Globus International, 1990.

JIM ČERT - POUTNÍK Z TRANSPORTY, Prague: Puky Records, 1997.

SVATOPLUK KARÁSEK - SAY NO TO THE DEVIL, Uppsala: Šafrán 78 and Boží Mlýn, 1979.

SVATOPLUK KARÁSEK - ŘEKNI ĎÁBLOVI NE (1978), Jaroslav Riedel (ed.), Prague: Globus International, 1998.

SVATOPLUK KARÁSEK - RÁNY ZNÍ (BLUES, SPIRITUALS & ...), Prague: Globus Music, 2000.

SVATOPLUK KARÁSEK - ŘEKNI ĎÁBLOVI NE [2 CDs], Jaroslav Riedel - Karel Kourek (eds.), Prague: Galén, 2012.

THE PLASTIC PEOPLE OF THE UNIVERSE I. Muž bez uší (1969-1972), Jaroslav Riedel (ed.), Prague: Globus Music, 2002.

THE PLASTIC PEOPLE OF THE UNIVERSE II. Vožralej jak slíva (koncerty 1973-75), Jaroslav Riedel (ed.), Prague: Globus Music, 1997.

THE PLASTIC PEOPLE OF THE UNIVERSE III. Egon Bondy's Happy Hearts Club Banned (1974-75), Jaroslav Riedel (ed.), Prague: Globus Music, 2001.

THE PLASTIC PEOPLE OF THE UNIVERSE IV. Ach to státu hanobení (koncerty 1976-77), Jaroslav Riedel (ed.), Prague: Globus Music, 2000.

THE PLASTIC PEOPLE OF THE UNIVERSE V. Pašijové hry velikonoční (1978), Jaroslav Riedel (ed.), Prague: Globus Music, 1998.

THE PLASTIC PEOPLE OF THE UNIVERSE VI. Jak bude po smrti (1979), Jaroslav Riedel (ed.), Prague: Globus Music, 1998.

THE PLASTIC PEOPLE OF THE UNIVERSE VII. *Co znamená vésti koně* (1981), Jaroslav Riedel (ed.), Prague: Globus Music, 2002.

THE PLASTIC PEOPLE OF THE UNIVERSE VIII. *Kolejnice duní* (1977–82), Jaroslav Riedel (ed.), Prague: Globus Music, 2000.

THE PLASTIC PEOPLE OF THE UNIVERSE IX. *Hovězí porážka* (1983–84), Jaroslav Riedel (ed.), Prague: Globus Music, 1997.

THE PLASTIC PEOPLE OF THE UNIVERSE X. *Půlnoční myš* (1985–86), Jaroslav Riedel (ed.), Prague: Globus Music, 2001.

THE PLASTIC PEOPLE OF THE UNIVERSE XI. *Trouble Every Day*, Jaroslav Riedel (ed.), Prague: Globus Music, 2002. [including bonus: the PPU discography, lyrics in Czech and English, photos]

THE PLASTIC PEOPLE OF THE UNIVERSE & AGON ORCHESTRA – *Pašijové hry / Passion Play*, Prague: Knihy Hana, 2004.

THE PLASTIC PEOPLE OF THE UNIVERSE: *Do lesíčka na čekanou 1. 12. 1973* [2 CDs], Guerilla Records, Louny, 2006.

THE PLASTIC PEOPLE OF THE UNIVERSE & AGON ORCHESTRA – *Obešel já polí pět. Koncert na počest Ladislava Klímy* (2003), [2 CDs], Jaroslav Riedel (ed.), Louny: Guerilla Records, 2009.

THE PLASTIC PEOPLE OF THE UNIVERSE. *Komplet nahrávek 1969-2004*, Jaroslav Riedel (ed.) [2 DVD comprising the music on CDs I.–XI. + PPU: Bez ohňů je underground (concert 1992) + PPU concert 1997 + PPU Líně s tebou spím / Lazy Love (2001) + PPU & Agon Orchestra – Pašijové hry (2004)], Prague: Levné knihy 2008.

THE PRIMITIVES GROUP – COMEBACK 2017, LIVE & THE PRIMITIVES GROUP 1968 [2 CDs], ed. Vladimír Lábus Drápal, Louny: Guerilla Records, 2017.

UMĚLÁ HMOTA: BARBARA [LP], Prague: Globus International, 1991.

UMĚLÁ HMOTA II. VE SKLEPĚ – 1976/77 [2 CDs], Vladimír Lábus Drápal (ed.), Louny: Guerilla Records, 2003.

VONDRUŠKA JOSEF: THE DOM & UMĚLÁ HMOTA III – ROCK'N'ROLLOVÝ MILÁČEK [2 CDs], Vladimír Drápal, Martin Machovec, Štěpán Smetáček (eds.), Louny: Guerilla Records, 2010.

20 minut z Říše [a TV documentary about I. M. Jirous]; dir. Václav Kučera; Czech Television (ČT), 1994.

Alternativní kultura I. [a 13-part TV documentary; on underground poetry: parts 4, 5, 6: *Od avantgardy do podzemí, Od undergroundu k šedé zóně, Ke konci věčných časů*], dir. Petr Slavík; Czech Television (ČT), 1998.

Alternativní kultura II. [an 11-part TV documentary; on underground poetry: parts 4 and 5; - *Poezie v podzemí I., Poezie v podzemí II.*]; dir. Petr Slavík; Czech Television (ČT), 2003.

Atentát na kulturu [a TV propaganda documentary, condemning and vilifying Czech underground culture], dir. not mentioned, probably Ladislav Chocholoušek; Czechoslovak Television (ČST), 1977.

Bigbít [a 25-part TV documentary; on underground music: parts 24, 25], dir. Václav Křístek; Czech Television (ČT), 1998.

ČARODĚJ OZ / PIGI-FILMY [4 DVD with 22 featured and documentary films, 1980–1987; directors: Lubomír "Čaroděj" Drožď and Irena "Pigi" Gosmanová; with a booklet], ed. Martin Blažíček; Prague: FAMU/PAF Edition, 2012.

CONCERT, (Premiéra) [a documentary TV film (FATE): presenting the underground festival in Postupice, September 1974; accompanied by statements from participants (1990)], dir. Josef Dlouhý; Czechoslovak Television (ČST), 1990.

Fenomén underground [a 40-part TV documentary on underground culture, especially music and life style], directors: Břetislav Rychlík, Jana Chytilová, Jiří Fiedor, Václav Křístek; Czech Television (ČT), 2012.

Fišer alias Bondy [a TV documentary], dir. Jordi Niubo; Czech Television (ČT), 2000.

My žijeme v Praze [a documentary featuring Egon Bondy, 1984–85], directors Tomáš Mazal and Pavel "Pablo" Veselý; released on a DVD + CD: Egon Bondy: My žijeme v Praze..., Louny: Guerilla Records, 2007.

O kočkách, beatnicích a všeličems jiném [a TV documentary: M. Dohnal's interview with Bohumil Hrabal talking about Vladimír Boudník and Egon Bondy, 1966]; dir. Rudolf Růžička, FTF AMU, Prague, 1966.

Revolver Revue - 5 let pod zemí, 5 let na zemi, dir. Eva Koutná; Czech Television (ČT), 1996.

Samizdat [a 15-part TV documentary; on underground/samizdat literature, part 1 - *Padesátá léta*, part 6 - *Další samizdatové edice 70. a 80. let*, part 11 - *Undergroundový samizdat*]; dir. Andrej Krob; Czech Television (ČT), 2002.

Sie sass im Glashaus und warf mit Steinen. Ein Film von Nadja Seelich und Bernd Neuburger [an Austrian TV documentary about the life of Jana

Krejcarová, featuring Egon Bondy, Ivo Vodseďálek, Johanna Kohnová, and others]; dir. Nadja Seelich; EXTRAFILM, 1992.

The Plastic People of the Universe [a documentary film, with English subtitles]; dir. Jana Chytilová; Czech Television (ČT) and Video 57, 2001.

The Plastic People of the Universe 1969–1985. Více než 2 hodiny autentických dokumentů [DVD with 12 documentaries; directors: César de Ferrari, Jan Špáta, Petr Prokeš, Jan Ságl, Josef Dlouhý, František Stárek "Čuňas", Tomáš Liška, Aleš Havlíček, Lubomír Drožď, Jan Kašpar etc.], Prague: Levné knihy, 2011.

Vlasatý svět uprostřed holohlavé republiky [a TV documentary about the hippie youth in Czechoslovakia in the late 1960s]; dir. Tomáš Škrdlant, Angelika Haunerová; Czech Television (ČT), 1994.

Zblízka: Vis Magor [a TV documentary on I. M. Jirous], dir. Andrej Krob; Czech Television (ČT), 1999.

Z Ruzyně do New Yorku [a documentary on the conference on Czech literature held at New York University, 1990], dir. Jitka Pistoriusová, Czechoslovak Television [ČST], 1990.

The texts found in this volume were written over eighteen years (2001–2018) on different occasions and for different purposes, the main and unifying topic of them being Czech (or Czechoslovak) underground culture, especially literature of the years 1948–1989, i.e. the times of a totalitarian, pro-Soviet political system in the country with all its peculiarities, one of them being the fact it generated "unofficial", "illegal", "banned", "alternative", "samizdat", "dissident", and "underground" culture which had some features similar to "counter-culture" in the West.

The contemporary Czech literary scene is small, especially when compared with literary scenes of the English-speaking world, and had it not been for Václav Havel, Bohumil Hrabal, and Milan Kundera (the latter one, however, belonging rather to French than Czech literature now), it would be probably mostly unknown in the UK, US and other English-speaking countries.

Luckily, in certain periods of their lives, both Havel and Hrabal played an important role in the development of Czech unofficial, samizdat literature, thus readers will find their names in this volume also.

Moreover, a number of publications of essential importance have come out recently, both in English and in Czech, that help elucidate the position and role of Czech (Czechoslovak) dissent and the cultural underground of 1948–1989 which fact diminishes the relevance of my own modest contributions; nevertheless, as far as the texts written earlier are concerned, I tried to confront them with the most recent research in the given area, to update them especially with the help of footnotes and bibliographical references.

It is first of all Jonathan Bolton's book *Worlds of Dissent. Charter 77, The Plastic People of the Universe, and Czech Culture under Communism* (2012) which radically re-interpreted the significance of Czech underground culture within the East European dissent of the past.

I also have to mention a recent anthology edited by Tomáš Glanc: *Samizdat Past & Present* (2018) in which it is especially Tomáš Glanc's treatise "Samizdat as a Medium": its author elaborated and re-thought the phenomenon of samizdat in a much more sophisticated way than anybody else ever before.

Rich photographic commented documentation of the life and activities of Czech underground community of artists, musicians, poets, and their friends is found in one older and two recent bilingual volumes: 1/ Abbé J. Libánský: *My Underground. Rodinné album - Family album - Familienfotoalbum 1972/82*, Vienna, Austria: Institut für Culturresistente Güter, 2002; 2/ Jan Ságl: *Tanec na dvojitém ledě - Dancing on the Double Ice*, Praha: KANT, 2013; 3/ Zuzana Brikcius (ed.): *Charta Story. Příběh Charty 77 / The Story of Charter 77*, Praha: Národní galerie, 2017.

And there are two Czech volumes that must be mentioned here: 1/ Jaroslav Riedel: *Plastic People a český underground* [The PP and Czech Underground], Praha: Galén, 2016; 2/ Michal Přibáň et alii: Český literární samizdat 1949-1989. Edice - časopisy - sborníky [Czech Literary Samizdat 1949-1989. Series of Editions - Periodicals - Anthologies], Praha: Academia - ÚČL AV ČR, 2018.

Of the ten texts found in this book only four (1, 3, 7, 10) were meant as serious contributions to literary history and/or textual studies, though texts 3 and 7 were first delivered as lectures at respective conferences and only later augmented for the purpose of publication. Others (2, 4, 5, 6, 8) were written as lectures which required a conciseness and no extensive footnotes. Text 9 was written as an epilogue to the edition of Ivan M. Jirous' selection of poems translated into English. This, together with a relatively wide time range within which the individual texts were written, causes a certain degree of heterogeneity: some themes are treated repeatedly, some quotations occur again and again, in one or two cases reasoning and arguments overlap texts in succession. I tried to get the whole set of texts rid of such textual redundance, replacing some quotations with other, similar ones, but I soon gave in. I believe the redundance is not too excessive, and besides, with it readers can realize better that repeated arguments witness of what the author had believed to be of crucial importance, that he felt it necessary to remind them more than once.

1. "The Group of Writers Around the Půlnoc Series (1949–1955)" was originally published as a sub-chapter entitled "Skupina literátů kolem edice Půlnoc (1949–1955)" within the chapter entitled "Od avantgardy přes podzemí do undergroundu, skupina edice Půlnoc 1949–1955 a undergroundový okruh Plastic People 1969–1989" [From the avant-garde to the underground, the Půlnoc Series Group, 1949–1955, and the Underground Circle around The Plastic People, 1969–1989], in *Alternativní kultura. Příběh české společnosti 1945–1989* [Alternative Culture. The Story of Czech Society, 1945–1989], Praha: NLN, 2001, pp. 156–167. Its translation is based on the reworked and supplemented edition in Machovec, M. (ed.), *Pohledy zevnitř. Česká undergroundová kultura ve svědectvích, dokumentech a interpretacích* [Views from the Inside: Czech Underground Culture in Testimonies, Documents and Interpretations], Praha: Pistorius & Olšanská, 2008, where the text came out with the same title as the sub-chapter (on pp. 101–114) of the chapter entitled the same as in its first publication. The English translation by Melwyn Clarke was first published in Glanc, T. (ed.), *Samizdat Past & Present*, Praha: Karolinum Press, 2018, pp. 141–159. Parts of the chapter, including the translated sub-chapter, were translated into Russian and published under the title "Через подполье к андерграуну" in Блестящая история. Чехословацкая культура в подплье (1968–1989), ed. Machonin, Jan, Moscow: Czech Centre, 2011, pp. 7–9, 14–17, 23–25, 32–36 (translated from Czech by Inna Bezrukova).

2. **"Underground and 'Under-the-ground'"** was originally written in English and the author read it in April 2006 as a lecture at the Center for Russian, East European and Eurasian Studies (CREEES), College of Liberal Arts, the University of Texas in Austin, under the title "Radical Standpoints of Czech Underground Community (1969–1989) and Variety of Czech Underground Literature as Specific Values". Part of it was published in Polish under the name "Czeska społeczność undergroundowa (1969–1989) i jej literatura" as an introduction to the anthology *Czeski underground*, Wroclaw: Atut, 2008. Then came its Czech publication under the title "Podzemí a underground. Postavení undergroundové komunity v české společnosti 70. a 80. let a specifické hodnoty undergroundové kultury" in the journal *Paměť a dějiny* 9, no. 1 (2015); for this purpose the author translated the text into Czech and rewrote it in many places, mainly abridging it. This Czech translation was subsequently translated back into English by Markéta Pokorná and

published in the journal *Behind the Iron Curtain* [*BIC*], vol. 4, 2016. In 2015, the Czech version was also translated into German by Raija Hauck (Ernst-Moritz-Arndt Universität, Greifswald) and read by the author at a workshop in Staatsgalerie Prenzlauer Berg, Berlin, on 20th May 2015; however, this German translation with the title "Die Stellung der Underground Community in der tschechischen Gesellschaft der 1970er und 1980er Jahre und spezifische Werte der Underground-Kultur" was never published.

3. "**Charter 77 and the Underground**" was written in Czech in 2007 and read at a conference on Charter 77 at the Philosophical Faculty, Charles University, Prague, on 21st – 23rd March 2007. It was published in Devátá, Markéta – Suk, Jiří – Tůma, Oldřich (eds.), *Charta 77. Od obhajoby lidských práv k demokratické revoluci 1977–1989. Sborník z konference k 30. výročí Charty 77. Praha, 21.-23. března 2007 / Charter 77: From the Assertion of Human Rights to a Democratic Revolution, 1977–89. The proceedings of the conference to mark the 30th anniversary of Charter 77. Prague, 21–23 March 2007*, Praha: ÚSD AV ČR, 2007, pp. 195–215, under the Czech title "Charta 77 a underground". The text was translated into English only for this volume by Gerald Turner. Ten years later, the author published an article "Předchůdce, součást i oponent" [A Predecessor, a Part, also an Opponent], in *Lidové noviny*, 14th January 2017, p. 30, in which he tried not only to sum up the previous text, but also to suggest some more conclusions.

4. "**Ideological Orientation and Political Views and Standpoints...**" was written in English in 2010 and first delivered at a seminar "Berauschte Zeit. Ästhetisierung der veränderten Bewusstseinszustände" on 26th January 2010 at Forschungsstelle Osteuropa an der Universität Bremen; next it was read on 4th February 2010 at a seminar "Approaches to Counter-Cultural Movements in East-Central Europe 1960–1990" at Central European University (CEU) in Budapest; for the third time then in April 2011 at a workshop held by the Center for Russian, East European and Eurasian Studies (CREEES) of the College of Liberal Arts at the University of Texas at Austin; it was published in English under the unchanged title in *IL SAMIZDAT TRA MEMORIA E UTOPIA. L'editoria clandestina*

in Cecoslovacchia e Unione sovietica nella seconda metà del XX secolo. *eSamizdat*, 2010-2011(VIII), eds. Catalano, Alessandro - Guagnelli, Simone, Roma: eSamizdat, Rivista di culture dei paesi slavi registrata presso la Sezione per la Stampa e l'Informazione del Tribunale civile di Roma, 2011, pp. 177-188.

5. **"The Theme of 'Apocalypse'..."** was written in 2009 in Czech in which it had the title "Motivy 'apokalypsy' jakožto významný stavební prvek undergroundové literatury doby 'normalizace'", and it was read on 22nd May 2009 at a round table held by Università degli Studi di Padova, Dipartimento di lingue e letterature anglo-germaniche e slave, Udine, Italy, where it was simultaneously interpreted into Italian; it was published in its Italian translation by Alessandro Catalano under the title "Letteratura senza primavera. Il motivo dell''apocalisse' come importante elemento strutturale nella letteratura underground del periodo della 'normalizzazione'", in *MALEDETTA PRIMAVER A: IL 1968 A PRAGA. eSamizdat*, 2009 (VII) 2-3, eds. Catalano, Alessandro - Guagnelli, Simone, Roma: eSamizdat, Rivista di culture dei paesi slavi registrata presso la Sezione per la Stampa e l'Informazione del Tribunale civile di Roma, 2010, pp. 61-71. The text was never published in Czech and was translated into English only for this volume by Gerald Turner.

6. **"Exploring Modern Art: Czech Underground Rock Musicians"** was originally called "Czech Underground Musicians in Search of Art Innovation" and was also written in English in 2009.

First it was read on 28th January 2009 at Central European University (CEU) in Budapest; for the second time at a seminar "Berauschte Zeit. Ästhetisierung der veränderten Bewusstseinszustände" under the title "Czech Underground Writers of the 1970s and 1980s and the Dope Inspiration" at Forschungsstelle Osteuropa an der Universität Bremen on 27th January 2010; under the original title it was published in *Mapping the Merry Ghetto: Musical Countercultures in East Central Europe, 1960-1989. East Central Europe*, 38, 2011, eds. Klaniczay, Gábor - Trencsényi, Balázs, Leiden, the Netherlands: Brill, 2011, pp. 221-237. For the purpose of the current publication the text was revised, augmented and was given a new title.

7. **"The Types and Functions of Samizdat Publications in Czechoslovakia"** was written in English in 2006 to be read at a conference "Samizdat and Underground Culture in the Soviet Bloc Countries" held at the Department of Slavic Languages and Literature of the University of Pennsylvania, Philadelphia, on 6th – 7th April 2006; in 2009 it was published in its reworked, edited version (namely with the help of the editor Meir Sternberg) in *Poetics Today. Publish and Perish: Samizdat and Underground Cultural Practices in the Soviet Bloc* (II) 30, no. 1 (spring 2009), ed. Vladislav Todorov, Durham, NC, Duke University Press, 2009. This text was never published in Czech.

8. **"Three Examples of a Variety of Relations Between Czech Samizdat and 'Tamizdat' Book Production of 1970s and 1980s"** was written in English in 2011 and delivered at a symposium "CZECHOSLOVAK SAMIZDAT AND ITS LEGACY" held in the Czech Center (Bohemian National Hall), New York City, on 10th – 11th November 2011 (the symposium took place on the occasion of the exhibition "SAMIZDAT: THE CZECH ART OF RESISTANCE, 1968–1989"). The paper has never got to print, but in 2014, in its abridged, slightly altered version, it was published in the Internet journal *Fair Observer* under the title "On Czech Samizdat and Tamizdat: Banned Books of 1970s and 1980s"; see https://www.fairobserver.com/region/europe/czech-samizdat-tamizdat-banned-books-1970s-1980s/

9. **"My Itinerary Has Been Monotonous for Quite a While: Magor's Swan Songs"** is an afterword to a collection of poems by Ivan M. Jirous in the English translation by Marek Tomin, chosen mostly from Jirous's *chef d'oeuvre* collection *Magorovy labutí písně* [Magor's Swan Songs]; the afterword has no name in the book; it was translated from Czech by Vanda Krutsky, Marek Tomin, and Kip Bauersfeld; see Jirous, Ivan Martin, *My itinerary has been monotonous for quite a while*, London: Divus, 2017, pp. 107–123.

10. **"Report on the Third Czech Musical Revival by Ivan Martin Jirous – Its Origins, Structure and Function"** was written in 2018 in Czech with the title "Jirousova *Zpráva o třetím českém hudebním obrození* – vznik, struktura a funkce" just for this current publication and was translated into English by Gerald Turner. Some parts

of it were read in its Czech original at a workshop "OD MÁNIČEK K UNDERGROUNDU. Československo 1970–1975" organized by ÚSTR and held in Václav Havel Library, Prague, on 16th October 2018.

The cover photo was taken on 4th or 5th November 1974 in the pub Na Zavadilce in Klukovice, a village in the southwest of Prague. The underground community gathered here for two evenings to listen to Egon Bondy's first reading from the manuscript of his novel *The Disabled Siblings*. Ivan M. Jirous stands in the foreground with a spotlight in his hand. Photo by Ivo Pospíšil.

Photographs except those mentioned here are from the author's personal archive. The photo by Alan Pajer on p. 40 is published by courtesy of the photographer. Photos by Jan Ságl on pp. 106 and 113 are published by courtesy of the photographer. The photo on p. 110 was reprinted from Knížák, Milan, *Unvollständige Dokumentation / Some Documentary. 1961–1979,* Berlin [West]: Edition Ars Viva!, 1980. Olaf Hanel's photo on p. 115 was reprinted from in Jirousová, Věra (ed.), *K.Š. - Křižovnická škola čistého humoru bez vtipu* (Art Catalogue), Hradec Králové - Praha: Galerie moderního umění Hradec Králové - Středočeská galerie Praha, 1991. Other photos are covers or parts of booklets mentioned individually in the list of Undeground Music on pp. 233–234.

June – November 2019

MODERN CZECH CLASSICS

The modern history of Central Europe is notable for its political and cultural discontinuities and often violent changes, as well as its attempts to preserve and (re) invent traditional cultural identities. This series cultivates contemporary translations of influential literary works that have been unavailable to a global readership due to censorship, the effects of the Cold War and the frequent political disruptions in Czech publishing and its international ties. Readers of English, in today's cosmopolitan Prague and anywhere in the physical and electronic world, can now become acquainted with works that capture the Central European historical experience – works that have helped express and form Czech and Central European identity, humour and imagination. Believing that any literary canon can be defined only in dialogue with other cultures, the series publishes classics, often used in Western university courses, as well as (re)discoveries aiming to provide new perspectives in the study of literature, history and culture. All titles are accompanied by an afterword. Translations are reviewed and circulated in the global scholarly community before publication – this is reflected by our nominations for literary awards.

Modern Czech Classics series edited by Karolinum Press

Published Titles

Zdeněk Jirotka: Saturnin (2003, 2005, 2009, 2013; pb 2016)
Vladislav Vančura: Summer of Caprice (2006; pb 2016)
Karel Poláček: We Were a Handful (2007; pb 2016)
Bohumil Hrabal: Pirouettes on a Postage Stamp (2008)
Karel Michal: Everyday Spooks (2008)
Eduard Bass: The Chattertooth Eleven (2009)
Jaroslav Hašek: Behind the Lines: Bugulma and Other Stories (2012; pb 2016)
Bohumil Hrabal: Rambling On (2014; pb 2016)
Ladislav Fuks: Of Mice and Mooshaber (2014)
Josef Jedlička: Midway upon the Journey of Our Life (2016)
Jaroslav Durych: God's Rainbow (2016)
Ladislav Fuks: The Cremator (2016)
Bohuslav Reynek: The Well at Morning (2017)
Viktor Dyk: The Pied Piper (2017)
Jiří R. Pick: Society for the Prevention of Cruelty to Animals (2018)
Views from the Inside: Czech Underground Literature and Culture
(1948-1989), ed. M. Machovec (2018)
Ladislav Grosman: The Shop on Main Street (2019)
Bohumil Hrabal: Why I Write? The Early Prose from 1945 to 1952 (2019)
Jiří Pelán: Bohumil Hrabal: A Full-length Portrait (2019)
Ludvík Vaculík: A Czech Dreambook (2019)

Forthcoming

Jaroslav Kvapil: Rusalka
Jan Procházka: The Ear
Ivan Jirous: Collected Works
Jan Čep: Common Rue
Jiří Weil: Lamentation for 77,297 Victims